:e

Of The Mosquito

by

Mary Curtis

M.L.C. (Hom) Dip Hyp ISCH

Acclaimed Author of

'The Goldfish That Jumped'

'The Kingfisher That Rocked'

'The Heart And Soul Of Success'

'Reflections of a Hummingbird'

much love & fondest ds. Hoping the book inspires & teaches you.

xxx
xxx
xxx

First published in the United Kingdom by
Mary Curtis September 2020

ISBN 978-0-9933734-8-0

Published by Mary Curtis

marycurtishealer.com

Front cover & logo designed by Daniel Calabrese

Travel is rebellion in its purest form.

We follow our heart.

We free ourselves of labels.

We lose control willingly.

We trade a role for reality.

We love the unfamiliar.

We trust strangers.

We own only what we can carry.

We search for better questions, not answers.

We truly graduate.

We, sometimes, choose never to come back.

(Author Unknown)

Dedication

This book is dedicated to the late Diane Mather and my dearest grandmother. Thank you for leaving me with precious memories, your profound love and deep wisdom.

It is also dedicated to my beloved family and friends, who inspire me daily.

To Jay for his support, advice, wisdom and so much more. To India, Nepal, Bali and New Zealand. This pilgrimage has changed my life, especially meeting Bape Mangku; my dear, ever patient teacher and my precious soul family in Bali, Indonesia.

Sincerest thanks to you all.

Mary

PART ONE

Chapter One

Sitting on my favourite well-worn wooden bench by the fountain, I watched the water as it sprayed up into the crisp, cool morning air. Here I knew I would at last begin to restore my inner peace. It was so desperately needed. My mind had been in overdrive for many months. The sleepless nights were beginning to take their toll and my whole body was desperate to feel calm again. Here, by the fountain I knew, I had at least a chance to embrace the beginnings of some sort of clarity. My whole being yearned for peace.

The sound of the water from the fountain seemed to soothe something deep within my core. I loved it here and I knew I had come to the right place. Something that had been broken, or disconnected seemed to begin to re-join. My body finally began to relax and it seemed the things that had been knotted up so tightly, deep within my whole being, could finally be softened and potentially unravelled. I breathed deeply and welcomed feeling the coolness of the sharp, crisp morning air against my skin. It reminded me that I was still alive.

I had always loved these cold, frosty early mornings when most people were still tucked up snugly in their beds. Today, of all days I needed to breathe in this freshness and this tangible peace. The hustle and bustle of my day would begin soon enough. All I had was this present moment.

I needed to make a decision and it had to be made today. The fountain was the perfect place to be and I knew there was no other place where I could feel more connected to all things; both within and outside of myself. It was a decision that would have huge implications and I was aware I needed to have immense clarity and stillness in order to ensure that I made the right choice. If I had learnt anything these last few years it was that harmony and balance were absolutely essential to my being, my soul and my very existence.

Mornings had always been special to me. They were certainly my favourite part of the day. There was something special about its very beginning. It was like a new canvas, or a new slate, a re-birth and certainly an opportunity to press the 'begin-again' button. 'God knows,' I thought to myself, 'I need to press that re-set button.'

I always felt each morning welcomed me. It was as though the day was a gift potentially of something more; should I choose to embrace it. There was no point denying that some mornings were certainly easier to embrace than others.

If I was up early enough, I would often watch the sunrise. It was truly such a blessed gift. I enjoyed looking and feeling the warmth of the colours: the reds, pinks, oranges and yellows against the morning sky. They were always such a joy to witness and a privilege. If I had the gift of being a painter, I would capture this magical moment provided by Mother Nature and paint a most magnificent canvas.

Today, however, feeling the pressure and the weight of knowing I had to make this decision, I wasn't sure at all what colours I would need. A tear rolled from my left eye and as I reached to wipe it with my glove, I felt another and yet another, replacing the first. I knew the full implications that were at stake here and I knew that suppressing my emotions was no longer an option. Years of working as a therapist and a life-coach had taught me that. I had seen hundreds of people with the 'stiff upper lip syndrome' drowning in their emotional pain and at the very point of despair; rather than admitting their presence and listening to the messages and the lessons that they were teaching. Now my time to listen had come. It felt like judgement day on some level. There would be no going back once that decision was finalized.

Sitting by the fountain I recalled the words of my close friend Jennifer;

"You're not an 'Arthur' girl are you? You've never been an 'alf of anything, have you? You're a woman of substance and integrity. Whatever you have done, you have always done with utmost commitment. You will know when the right time comes for you to make your decision, though my suspicion is that it will be sooner, rather than later."

The tears continued. I was blessed to have such close friends who knew what I was going through and how difficult it was to find the courage, not only to make the decision but also the grit, determination, faith, hope and trust to complete the journey once that decision was made.

To me the mornings represented exactly that, a new dawn, a new beginning, a new way of being and new opportunities for change. I knew my life was about to change and I knew embracing that change would be the key to whether I sank, or swam. Floating was not a choice. Change was now inevitable. It was inconceivable that I could, or indeed would, carry on with life in this manner. Carrying on, carrying on, was not an option. I knew it would suffocate me on every level; crushing my heart and soul.

To an outsider everything looked wonderful. I had my own home, a beautiful car and a supportive family. My business was successful with endless opportunities. I had earned my stripes as a therapist and was well-respected in my field. I had encouraged thousands of clients to make positive changes to enhance their lives. And yet, something within me was unsettled.

Something deep within me was discontented. Something within my whole being needed more. I felt broken and I knew there was no quick fix here that wouldn't require my maximum effort, on all levels, to allow this much needed transition. I thought of my close friend Paul and his wise advice.

"No-one likes it when you out grow your pot. There are hundreds of crabs in any one bucket, at any one time. Some will never get out and some will struggle to get higher, and higher, until eventually they reach the brim of the bucket and finally manage to make their escape. They will inevitably find a new home, a new life, a new relationship perhaps.

But they will certainly find a new and brighter bucket. It takes courage, absolute commitment and determination to make positive changes. The crab doesn't know what's on the outside of the bucket. It can't be seen and it's the great unknown. To most people the unknown represents absolute fear and terror.

You know fear will prevent most people from even beginning their journey out of the bucket and breaking the mould. Many are happy at the bottom. Some never consider peering over the rim, or even that there might be other alternatives, options and opportunities.

You've been at this precipice for a long time. Going backwards is not an option. You have to jump. There simply is no other way for you now. You have to trust in yourself, listen to your soul and in The Universe. You will indeed be supported. Trust is your key now." His words echoed in my mind. He was being honest and quite direct with me and I knew it was both his truth and indeed mine. I had known Paul for almost a decade and we both respected one another totally.

Remember that the crabs you'll leave behind will be frightened. They'll feel that because you've changed, they don't know who you are anymore. You've broken the status quo. You've outgrown the bucket." I knew he was right. I knew there had to be a change. Could I really find the courage to make that final jump? Was it a leap of faith or was it going to be the mistake of my life?"

The one thing I knew for sure was that my life needed to change. Remaining stagnant had now become exhausting to my whole being; body, mind and soul. The mere thought of it was far more suffocating than the thought of facing the unknown alone. It was indeed 'crunch time' and the decision that had overhung me now for well over a year was finally screaming to be made. Being here by the fountain was the perfect place to surrender myself into making this resolve.

Chapter Two

The tears I had cried whilst chatting to Paul on so many different occasions over the previous twelve months seemed endless. It felt as if they came from the very depth of my being, my one-ness, my is-ness. 'Maybe even my root' I thought, as I continued to watch the water from the fountain make beautiful arches against the skyline of the winter's morning.

As I considered the shapes of the arches, I thought about what they represented and I knew I needed to walk through a new doorway of my own desired creation. Was it already waiting for me, or was I simply creating it? There was always the duality with the principles of the law of attraction. Was it simply that your soul was aware of what was to come? Or was it that you were creating it on a daily, moment by moment basis? It was rather like the chicken and the egg scenario. Which came first, the chicken? Or the egg? Did it even matter?

I was so exhausted as these repetitive thoughts ran around inside my weary head. I breathed out a deep sigh and felt grateful for all I had, especially the support and wisdom of good friends.

Feeling grateful for the warmth of my coat, thick boots and socks, my favourite patterned scarf and patent black leather gloves, my thoughts drifted to distant memories. I had been in this place before and recognised the signs. It was a place of deep discontent, deep pain of a huge longing; a calling from both the heart and soul. I had heard these calls from my soul before. I was wise enough to know that ignoring them was not even worth contemplating. It never would be, because once that cry, or call was heard and acknowledged, action had to be taken. Now it was my call to action and making that decision was imperative.

Thinking back to when I had first experienced this deeply unsettling feeling, I realised it was now almost twenty years ago. I had found myself in a very similar life situation then. Reflecting on that challenging time, my whole life felt stagnant and heavy, without movement and it was incredibly oppressive. It felt as though my wings had been clipped and my whole being felt anxious, restless, unbalanced and unsettled.

I had worked in the Civil Service for over a decade then and I knew I could no longer continue, enough was definitely enough. Each and every day I felt sick and weary as I dragged myself into work to sit at my desk and continue the seemingly endless cycle of pointless policies and procedures in administration of benefits. The cliques, 'brown-nosing' and so many other things made me feel as though, little by little, they were killing my soul. It was as though a part of me was dying on a daily basis. This cycle could not continue, it was not an option. But just what options did I have? Truly I didn't know. At that time resigning was not a viable choice with four children to feed, clothe and care for. I also needed to consider the mortgage and the bills.

How often at that time, I cried and sobbed, even at the mere thought of having to continue with the daily monotony. It felt like insanity. Each and every day I painted on a new brave face for both my children and my work colleagues. I had learnt to master the art of wearing THE mask. I was well practised in changing the subject when someone got too close to my weaknesses. Being vulnerable was not an option. If I failed to remain strong and in control of my whole life then surely it would fall apart?

As I remembered those feelings as a single mother to four growing children with the pressure of being the only bread-winner, I had to be strong in order to make the everyday necessary decisions. I alone had to decide what choices were right for my children and I alone had to play the role of both the father and the mother. I always needed to remain strong, decisive, and firm with my children, consistent and yet loving and nurturing. It was certainly not always such an easy task. Inevitably, when the weight of the bills, the mortgage, the house renovations, the car maintenance and not forgetting the shitty job, all added more stress to my already heavily laden shoulders. I did indeed feel the weight of the 'life' I was living.

That was now almost twenty years ago when I had been so absolutely desperate for change. At that time though I had no idea how I could escape the nightmare existence? Was it really possible? All I knew then was that I had come to the end of that particular slippery road.

It was imperative at that time to relieve myself of the pointless, soul- sucking, heart-numbing, seemingly empty life. In complete desperation, I approached the local 'Connections' for careers advice and hoped for an answer to my many prayers. I had to find an escape route, before my life-force and sanity were completely crushed out of me.

Over the coming weeks, after lengthy discussions, IQ and other multiple ability tests, having looked at so many different options, it seemed my most sensible choice was to return to college. It was agreed that to further enhance my educational qualifications, a Foundation Degree Course was the most suitable option. It felt right as I followed my intuition, allowing it to guide me through the current maze of life.

Coming back to the present, I listened to the sound of the water as I sat by the fountain. I smiled to myself. I still remembered clearly, the feeling of intense relief that the fun of learning and studying again at night school brought to me. It eased my despair. At that time it gave me a much needed sense of hope. Despite working full-time, managing a family, renovating and restoring my home, I completed the course within an academic year. Achieving a very respectable grade had been no easy task; though incredibly worthwhile.

I loved getting to know the other mature students. I found myself smiling again as I remembered fondly that one of my fellow colleagues suggested that Reiki healing might help restore my faith and provide me with the much needed courage to move forward. He explained that it had brought huge positive changes to his life, in so many, many ways. I knew I had nothing to lose and again was led by my intuition.

Thinking back with deep gratitude to the first time I experienced Reiki and met Trish; the Reiki healer, life soon began to change for the better. From that very first simple welcome as we got to know one another through the Reiki healings, Trish suggested I attend T'ai Chi classes too. Once again, allowing her intuition to show me the way forward, I agreed.

As the months progressed I had noticed that I was certainly feeling much better about life generally. Many of the traumas that I had experienced previously were certainly beginning to heal. I began to find a new kind of peace and a new, even deeper connection to my beloved children.

Most importantly, for the very first time in my life, I was beginning to connect to myself. I had no previous self-awareness. Life had been consumed with 'doing-ness' and seemingly endless tasks. I finally began to consider who I was, that I might even have a place in this world. I finally acknowledged the young woman in her early thirties who had been hiding behind so many masks. At the time, as I reminisced, I didn't even know the masks were there.

Little did I know that they were nothing more than out-dated patterns of behaviours and coping mechanisms, to help me to get through the 'everyday stuff.'

I remembered thinking 'who was this woman who could actually begin to honour herself and give herself permission to attend a T'ai Chi class for one hour per week? Was it okay for her to make time for herself? Was it okay to pay for Reiki treatments, when the children needed things like shoes, schoolbags, sportswear and so much more?

Was I allowed to break the mould? Was I allowed to welcome happiness and to follow this path? Could I trust that I deserved it?'

The combination of attending T'ai Chi weekly and becoming involved with the spiritual group of people changed so many things. Little did I know how much, at that pivotal time. In fact it was changing me on every single level. I was evolving. I was awakening to my spiritual intelligence; finally feeding my once-starved soul at last. Besides the obvious benefits of the physical fitness, toned muscles and core strength, my mental awareness was sharpening. My mind had now been trained to slow down through regular meditation.

Making so many new friends fulfilled my need for connection, joy and fulfilment. I was completely immersed as I enjoyed learning about the philosophy of living life through the heart and soul. I benefitted hugely and life was definitely improving. My children delighted and loved to see the 'new mum' who was immerging at last from the pungent, murky, stagnant waters.

Each and every day I made time for myself to meditate and exercise using the T'ai Chi exercise forms I had been shown. Determined to bring positive change, I took time to pray to The Universe daily to assist me in escaping this life of working full-time in the Civil Service. I knew I wanted more quality time, a sense of gratitude, appreciation and fulfilment, not to mention abundance. I simply had no idea how to jump from point A (my current life), to point B (my new fulfilling and happy life).

Within the coming months, I was very ill with Chronic Fatigue Syndrome. It started with an everyday common infection and I never recovered my strength. The days turned into weeks and the weeks into hopeless, endless, pointless months. The frustration of being so weak and weary left me feeling completely useless. For someone whose life had been so incredibly busy, when it suddenly came to a full stop, with no end in sight it was such a shock and had been completely unexpected. Yes, I wanted desperately to escape the Government office, but this certainly hadn't been the way in which I wanted it to happen.

Now unable to work, although I was grateful to be out of that particular sickening cycle, I now faced another cycle. This one was the absolute terror that I might never work again. As the weeks turned into months and no improvements in my health were materializing, I was becoming desperate.

I smiled and wished I had the wisdom at that time to embrace the 'dark night of the soul.' If I had only known then the changes it would bring. Some days it seemed that my very sanity was threatened. Fears seemed to loom up in every direction, threatening to engulf my very being. The questions about my future were never ending. How would I cope if my health never improved?

What if my ex-husband found out I was ill and requested custody of the children? What if I could never work again and could no longer pay the mortgage? What if I lost my home and everything else? The 'What Ifs' seemed endless and were crippling me daily.

Re-remembering back to the 'dark night of the soul' I was grateful for all it had taught me. It created the space to induce change. I had always loved nature and hiking. At that time, during the illness, walking approximately one hundred metres exhausted me. What if I never hiked again in my beloved places such as The English Lake District? Day in and day out, these thoughts were all consuming and incredibly destructive. I often felt as though I were hanging on to my sanity by a very, very thin thread.

I remembered the power that my 'Monkey Mind' had previously enjoyed daily as I thought back to the many 'What Ifs' that were draining me of my much needed energy. Each day I had so little energy to begin with and there seemed no end in sight. At least repeating the mantra; 'I am slim, fit and healthy, I am slim, fit and healthy, I am slim, fit and healthy...' allowed me to return to a still place sooner than if I allowed them to run riot with my exhausted mind. I felt as though I had at least a hundred and one monkeys chattering away in my brain!

I dearly missed the T'ai Chi group and was far too tired to even go shopping. Managing to stay awake for more than three or four hours at any one time, without then needing to sleep again was a challenge. I felt angry and betrayed, cheated out of my life. Why was it happening to me? What had I done to deserve this? Had I not been a good daughter? Wife? Mother? Guilt and shame fuelled many of my thoughts as I questioned everything about my life.

I feared losing my children the most. It had always been my deepest fear. Now, being ill with seemingly endless days alone in the house whilst my children were at school, the 'Monkey Mind' played its tricks. It was hard enough coping with the fact that I was barely able to care for their needs. If only I had known and understood self-love and compassion back then. Things could have been so much easier.

I shivered in the cold morning breeze and breathed out a huge sigh that seemed to come from the very bottom of my lungs. Watching the breath touch the outside air, it seemed to make its own cloud as I continued to let go of each of those once very painful memories.

I remembered how much power they held at that time and how desperate I was. If only I could have held my previous self with a hug providing loving kindness and the wisdom of life experience at that time. The whole of that part of life's journey could have been so much easier. Or would it? No-one would ever know. All I had was now. Thinking back to those memories and taking the learnings they gave were touching my soul once again. The sun was beginning to warm the morning as my thoughts continued.

The household chores which I had found so easy prior to being ill, now exhausted me to my very core. Choices had to be made on a frequent basis, dependent upon my low energy levels. If I did the washing, then I had no more energy to do the cleaning. If I did the ironing, then there was no more energy to make a meal. Decisions. Decisions. The whole illness exhausted me; mentally, physically, emotionally and yet day by day, unbeknown to me, my soul was gathering its strength. It was as though I was being reborn. If only I had known at the time. I sighed another deep sigh, turning the air from my breath white, from its once invisible state. It made the things that were invisible, visible. I thought of all the things that were invisible then.

A close second on the all-engulfing Chronic Fatigue Syndrome induced fear list, was then losing my beloved home. The third was the thought of never being well again which was utterly consuming and heart-breaking. The intensity of the three combined was like a tsunami: threatening to engulf my every single, seemingly pointless, never-ending, lengthy day.

Throughout this time, with the help of Diane, my very dear friend from the T'ai Chi class, somehow I was finding a previously hidden depth to my inner strength that previously I had no idea I possessed. I remained determined that I would eventually come through this battle. Diane provided me with compassion, patience and constant reassurance in each and every daily phone call. Despite the fact that throughout most of our daily conversations I was in tears, sobbing and distraught, Diane would inevitably lift my battered spirits....albeit eventually. Often she used 'tough love' wherever needed, to keep me focused on the end goal, which was of course to make a full recovery.

I smiled with gratitude and deep appreciation that is only shared with such deep friendship as I recalled that with Diane's much needed support and encouragement. I took this time; when I could actually stay awake, to read and to learn all I could about the esoteric world. Quantum physics, the law of attraction, dharma and karma, the wheel of life, Buddhism, and anything related to self-healing and the incredible, vast power of the super and sub-conscious mind were all part of that journey to self-healing. I repeated my daily mantra; 'I am slim, fit and healthy' and whenever the fear, which was like a creeping dark shadow threatened to engulf me yet again, I would keep repeating it until the fear eventually eased. Little did I realise at the time the power of sound, chanting and using daily mantras.

Unable to care for myself properly without the help of my precious family I was certainly receiving a life lesson in vulnerability and humility. I had so much time to reflect on my life and realized now how much stress I had endured over these past years.

Raising four youngsters, working full time, renovating my home and coping with a tumultuous divorce, which I had never healed from, had all finally taken their toll. I had been running on empty for so long. My whole being had been screaming exhaustion to me and I had simply carried on, carrying on. Running on nothing more than adrenaline daily had been so normal to me. Now I had well and truly crashed. My body was telling me loud and clear to 'sod the hell off.'

I often thought back to that day, now well over twelve months earlier, when I had screamed at God. In an angry rage, engulfed in frustration and deep emotional pain, I remembered standing at the top of the stairs and shouting loudly that I could no longer continue with this crappy existence and I desperately wanted more. So much more: more time, more abundance and a much more positive lifestyle.

I wanted a life which held meaning, deep satisfaction and fulfilment. Not this emptiness and dissatisfaction. Surely there had to be more to life and living? Surely? I screamed, cried, punched the air and then sobbed, until my whole body shook right to its very core. Consumed with rage I curled up into the foetal position and slept with the overwhelming magnitude of complete emotional exhaustion.

Chapter Three

Some things in life are never forgotten. Sitting by the fountain reflecting on all the events that had brought me to this point in my life, I was now grateful for those exhausting, endless and seemingly meaningless days whilst I was ill. Humility, patience, trust and courage were just some of the many lessons I learnt.

Almost a year after starting to be ill, a very dear friend suggested I try Homeopathy. Together with qualifying as a Reiki Master towards the end of 2003, my health improved greatly. Returning to physical health was such a welcome relief and it was so wonderful to experience well-being once again. I had finally learnt to listen when I was tired and now respected my physical body. No longer could I allow myself to run on adrenaline and put myself last. I was finally beginning to find my place in the world. Through extensive research into quantum physics, the law of attraction, understanding the importance of synchronicity, listening to my heart's own wisdom and not that of my head, my life had certainly changed for the better. As I continued to follow my soul and nurture it daily, my intuition deepened.

By now I knew all too well that there were no coincidences. Almost a year later, when I was offered the opportunity to run my own clinic locally, my simple answer was a resounding 'Yes'. After experiencing what had been one of the hardest years of my life, I had finally learnt to listen to the whispers of The Universe and simply trust that it would surely take care of the rest. I no longer needed to control everything, in fact I now knew that I had never had control anyway, it had all been part of the illusion.

Within two years my business was thriving. My reputation gathered pace and went before me. My old life seemed to be a million miles away. In subsequent years I trained as a homeopath, hypnotherapist, psychotherapist and life-coach.

By simply following the trail of most obvious breadcrumbs, The Universe had offered, my life had improved dramatically. The illness had created the much needed space to allow these changes and I now welcomed them in to my everyday life. Had I invited these changes into my life? Or had my soul been destined to bring them to me? It seemed so at that time. Now I was thriving. I was earning more than double my previous salary; working less than half the number of hours. I finally had time to rest, to work and most importantly to play. Appreciation and gratitude for life and everything it held were now paramount in everything I did each and every day.

At that time I was happier than I had ever been. I had more time for my beloved children, and perhaps more importantly, finally for myself. I realised that I mattered. When I took care of me I was far more capable of taking care of everyone else. After almost a year of being too weak to hike, once again I could reconnect with nature and the great outdoors. Gratitude and appreciation filled my whole being as I was able to enjoy hiking in the mountains, walking in the local parks and on the beaches. Knowing I would never take my body for granted again, appreciation radiated out throughout my whole being. Life was definitely on the up. For the first time I was experiencing and embracing freedom. For the very first time I felt really, vibrant and alive. I was embracing the simplicity of simply be-ing. I was finally living.

Just be-ing was such a new feeling and was so welcomed. I was now beginning to understand what it really meant. The experience was so much more powerful than what I had read in the many books over these last two years. Now it was tangible and I was grateful to experience connection, contentment, peace and a deep profound inner stillness. My mind was at last silent as the 'monkeys' lay dormant.

Now as I reflected on the memories and the valuable lessons that the Chronic Fatigue Syndrome had brought me over a decade ago, I finally understood the essential learnings that it had provided. I had changed so much and this had in turn resulted in profound life changes.

Sitting by the fountain I recognized that I felt rather like a caterpillar about to crawl into a completely new cocoon; of course I had done it before but now the stakes were so much higher. What the resulting butterfly would be like and whether it would ever be ready to spread its wings once more, depended on my ability to make this current decision. Now the only way forward was to leave behind the comfort and the safety of my existing cocoon. There was to be no going back. It was all; or nothing.

At the time of my first initiation into such a massive life change in 2003, I knew nothing of the law of attraction, the heart's own intelligence and its infinite wisdom, the huge vast world of quantum physics and so much more than I had ever imagined. I breathed heavily, as I sighed with an ever deepening appreciation, re-remembering all I had learnt and subsequently now taught successfully. I recalled how I had used it with deep wisdom and respect to improve my life and how, by teaching it to my beloved children, it had changed theirs too.

As the fountain continued its gentle song on this perfect winter morning, I watched in awe as the water made the most beautiful arches against the clear, blue morning sky. Pondering and reflecting over all the experiences my spiritual awakening had brought me in these years since 2003, I felt the incredible depth of gratitude exude from my very being. I had met some amazing, inspiring people along this particular soul's journey. I had already been inspired to write four highly acclaimed books, assisted thousands of clients to live more fully and I had held numerous inspiring workshops. I had been invited to speak at many spiritual groups throughout the North West and Yorkshire. I had even worked internationally and inspired others through my own television show 'Living A Dynamic Life.' The gratitude for having experienced all these was tangible.

And yet despite all this, my soul was now ready to grow once more. The cry had been heard and this time I would honour it, rather than allowing fear to steer the rudder of life's ship. I knew I had to expand even further. I was wise enough to know that this time there would be so much more courage needed to make this particular leap. This time it would mean selling my beloved home, letting go of all my treasured belongings, closing my business and travelling abroad. It had to be a completely clean break. It had to be a letting go of everything, in order that the new, emerging me could reach completion. This time I had the wisdom to know that the soul's cry came directly from The Universe and if I could allow myself to trust that I would be guided along the path, then this next life change would indeed be so much easier that the first. Or would it?

Chapter Four

India was calling to my very being and had done for well over three years. My heart and soul had been screaming at me for such a long time, and each and every time I listened, it returned to this momentous, life-changing decision. No other option carried any meaning, substance, nor weight.

The tears began to fall as I sobbed remembering all the people who had touched my life; all those I would be leaving behind especially my beloved family and most precious granddaughters.

Despite the fact that I treasured my home and the beautiful, mature gardens that were my sanctuary, I knew this had to be a complete break. As the many salty tears poured, I thought of my clients, many of whom had become close friends. I truly hoped that I had empowered them enough to continue using the simple effective techniques I had taught them: allowing them to further embrace more positive changes in their lives. I thought of the knock-on effect that these changes had with clients and their loved ones, the other improvements they brought in to their lives and relationships. The pure joy of watching someone transform from just existing, to living fully, gave me such a deep sense of satisfaction and gratitude.

I wondered if all those I had worked with actually knew just how much joy they had brought to me over these many years. I had watched couples be reunited, families find peace, clients set up their own businesses and many change careers. I had watched people let go of old fears and hurts that had once engulfed them and prevented them from travelling, or embracing life in some way. Others had finally honoured their anger and disappointments. I had watched so many open their hearts to finding their niche, finally listening to their souls, allowing themselves to flower as natural artists, singers and dancers. I watched so many resolve disputes with their parents and re-unite with long lost relatives.

I had lost count of how many times clients had walked down the garden path after a professional session and looked at least ten years younger. The power of true peace, unconditional love, respect, gratitude, forgiveness and ultimately connection were all essential to the journey of becoming more whole-hearted. That was the key to bringing about the transformational change from existing to living.

By learning for myself, the journey from the head to the heart, I had assisted so many. As the heart centre opened, I felt the physical pain as the petals of a most beautiful flower, reaching up for the sun each and every day opened ever wider. I now lived a life of commitment and dedication to my own souls' journey. I learnt to take quiet time daily to meditate, to connect to nature and to find balance; mentally, spiritually, physically and emotionally.

I had learnt the hard way of the magnitude and consequences of not listening to my needs. The fact that the law of cause and effect was always at play. I had finally learnt the power of self-love and self-forgiveness. I had learnt respect: ultimately respect for myself and an ever deepening acceptance and respect for others. This had by no means always been an easy journey.

I thought back to those dark, painful times when I had judged myself the harshest and was truly my own worst enemy. I no longer berated myself. I finally learnt to value my time and my energy. Every day I now focused that energy on self-improvement, self-realization and personal growth; everything was a choice and making conscious choices had been a huge part of this journey into the soul and positive living.

I appreciated everything I had and all those I had met along the journey; following the doom and gloom of my previous existence. My children had seen such huge changes in my well-being. They had seen the changes I brought to others, encouraging them to flower, to re-connect to their souls and to blossom.

The difference now, almost twenty years later, was that I needed to do this solely for myself. The journey was now changing once more and I knew this would inevitably bring about the biggest change of my life. There was to be no going back. It was all or nothing. My future well-being depended on making that one decision.

Chapter Five

I remembered the many conversations I had had with her life-coach Paul, as we talked at length about how much I loved my life, about how I loved my work, my family and so much more. The children had all grown up and moved on to new pastures. I worked mainly from home. It meant the world to me. It represented many aspects of me and it really was my haven. My home was so full of love. It oozed through each and every brick, through each window and even the doors. All the rooms and the different parts of the house were loved equally. No one room was more important than another. It was a stunning four bedroomed detached dormer-bungalow in its own beautiful, corner plot.

I bought the house well over a decade earlier and it was indeed my sanctuary. The fact that I had moved in to my new home on my eldest granddaughter's first birthday, was testimony in itself that this was to be a very special home. I knew I had been destined to live there from the very first time I viewed it. I remembered walking down the path feeling my whole being acknowledge to me that this was, without doubt, to be the perfect home.

Reflecting back I recalled that on the exterior of the house there was so much to do. It been neglected for many years. The garden was in desperate need of tender loving care and a complete overhaul. To the rear of the property were three well-established fruit trees; apple, pear and plum. The garage provided ample storage room and there was plenty of outdoor space here to park my car and my sons' vehicles. The decision was made. This would be my new home. My three sons and I would move in at the earliest opportunity.

Grateful that I had restored it with the help of my father and my sons; we all knew the design of the bungalow was perfect for me to work from home. A huge hallway with two rooms off to the left and the main living and dining room to the right, with a kitchen extension to the rear of the property. At the end of the hallway was a bathroom; always essential with clients. Upstairs there were a further two double bedrooms running the full length of the house and a second bathroom. The views looked out over the local countryside and I loved it all.

Having converted and restored previous properties, I was under no illusion as to how much work needed to be done. Just as the exterior had been neglected, so indeed had the interior. The fact that I now worked mainly from home, meant that until it was much improved, no clients could be treated here. Renovation work started straight away and it was a priority to get the new flooring down, as the bare floorboards were unsafe. Aware how costly the repairs and essentials would be, I was incredibly grateful for the help of my family as wallpaper was stripped, flooring was laid and new paint brightened the walls.

A new stylish bathroom suite was ordered and fitted downstairs, along with new tiles. My father assisted me in designing and ordering the new kitchen units and a new built-in cooker. I thought it interesting that despite the fact that the bungalow was built in the 1930s and all the plaster was of the same age, the only room where it all needed replacing was in my own bedroom. Each time the wallpaper was stripped off, the plaster followed too, even on the ceiling. The dust, wood, lathe and plaster filled so many heavy duty rubbish bags. The whole room needed to be rebuilt: nowhere else in the house, just my own private bedroom. I was wise enough to know that it was significant of my particular need to be personally rebuilt. Life had changed after a relationship breakdown and now I had a perfect place to start over. Out with the old and in with the new.

Everyone loved their home. Working from home now added love and joy to the mix. The design of the house was perfect for me to teach and run inspiring workshops.

Each and every flower, tree, bush and shrub in the gardens held the love that I gave them so freely. It represented all of me. I knew what I would be leaving behind should I follow the call of my soul.

I loved each of my beloved family members, especially my granddaughters. I cried as I remembered laying the paving stones at the side of the house, so that the girls could play stepping stones, or pretend they were in a river with crocodiles ready to eat them if they missed a step. I cried as I recalled the girls colouring with chalks on the paving flags and writing 'Grandma's House'. I cried as I remembered the sound of the wind chimes through the trees. I cried as I thought of those precious years when the apple, pear and plum trees produced such an abundance of delicious fruit. I had so much fruit and delighted to share it with family, neighbours and friends. I cried again at the thought of passing pears, plums and apples to my neighbours over the fences.

Inevitably, my sons got older and one by one they left the nest. Nicholas was the first to leave to attend university and Matthew left to live with friends before emigrating. Interesting I thought as following his leaving the snowdrops never again raised their beautiful heads from the dark garden soil. Now it was just me and my youngest son Phil. In his own time, he too moved to New Zealand.

How lucky I was, I thought to have such joy in one single abundant life. I was grateful for such an extensive support network of dear family and friends.

Coming back to the present moment; watching through tear-filled eyes, as the water splashed in to the pools below it sometimes seemed as though the sprinkles were actually trying to touch the morning sun hanging in the clear blue sky. I loved the sound of the water, as the individual molecules kissed and re-joined the water below. It was forever remoulding itself, reshaping, reforming and effortlessly adjusting to the environment.

Ever constantly, the water sprayed, moving silently, gracefully and peacefully, moment by moment. No whingeing, no moaning – just pure and simple readjustment and acceptance of the differences and the possibilities of its rather inevitable fate.

Watching the water, I pondered if I would have the grace to trust that once this decision was made, I would naturally become absorbed into my new life: which was as yet completely unknown. Was it possible? Was I completely crazy to let go of all this? What if I was wrong? Should I carry on? Was I even capable of carrying on, carrying on? The endless questions continued. My brain felt foggy, heavy, tired and square.

I wondered if the water molecules allowed themselves to be moved, or were they simply trusting that they would be guided to their onward journey. Was the decision for them already made? Was the decision for me already made? What came first? The chicken or the egg? Had this decision about my fate already been made? Or was I creating it?

The law of attraction always fascinated me: was it my destiny or was I the creator? I knew all too well the power of fear and I knew fear had blocked me so often in the past. Finding the courage to break through had allowed such powerful inspiration and the momentum to move forward. Was fear holding me back now? What did I want for my future? Over the last two years I had requested freedom, love, abundance and the fulfilment of my soul purpose from God. I wanted completion in all aspects of my life. I wanted to embrace the joy of life and become the true limitless being that I am.

I thought back to the time almost two years ago, when I was asked what it was I really wanted when I visited a clairvoyant for a personal reading. Annie had no idea who I was, though she *knew* through the reading that I 'wore many different hats' and that I was an incredibly, gifted and capable lady. The Universe expressed its gratitude to me for all I had done and for all the people I had inspired.

"You are going to have to decide what it is you want to do. You must choose what you enjoy doing the most", said Annie who was point blank clear.

I thought back to that particular day when I sat with Annie on the sofa and knowing she was right to ask that all important question. What was it I loved doing the most? Writing? Teaching? Homeopathy? Healing?

Hypnotherapy? Psychotherapy? Life-coaching? Psychic readings? Earth Healing? Running workshops?

The truth was that at that moment in time I didn't know the answer. However, I knew that through meditation and listening, the answer would indeed come to the surface to be heard. It most certainly would become clear in its own time. This was not to be forced. Patience and trust were the only keys needed here.

Several months later the lightbulb moment came and I knew in my soul that I wanted to write and travel to do earth healing. Earth healing was something I had always loved doing and my passion made it completely effortless. I felt this decision was absolutely right throughout my whole being. I knew the potential power that one book had to change so many lives. I knew how much I loved writing and had received wonderful, touching testimonials from many clients and friends when they had read my written work. Delighted that I had finally joined the dots, I felt a deep contentment knowing that this would indeed be my path. The soul's journey is so important and listening was no longer the challenge. The relief I felt was tangible as my body began to relax.

The passion in my whole soul was growing and my heart yearned for this new beginning. I re-remembered the time recently when I had screamed once again to The Universe. This time requesting assistance in my wishes to fulfil a writing career and a deep longing to travel. I desired to live with financial freedom close to nature, overlooking a beautiful lake; or possibly the ocean, and with a home large enough to house beloved friends and family when they came to visit. I also requested an infinity pool, where I could relax and be inspired. Water and travel were so key to my being-ness. I again requested the abundance of finances that would allow me time and provide financial freedom. Abundance was paramount; abundance in all aspects of my life; love, grace, health, wealth, inspiration, friendships, motivation, success and inner peace.

Time to enjoy being with loved ones; time to think, time to write, maybe to research and time to simply be in my own space. Writing gave me the biggest sense of joy and connection. Writing fulfilled my heart and soul. Could I truly believe that this was possible? Was there anything that might block me from fulfilling this dream? Had I any remaining fears? Did I really deserve it? Was my writing of a good enough calibre? Was it all too much to ask for? Was I being greedy? Did dreams really come true? The real question was could I really trust, allow and accept? Did I trust in myself?

As I monitored my thoughts and listened to my body's reaction to them, I found that my body had remained calm, quiet and still. Maybe I had indeed cleared the path? I had long since learnt to listen to the body's whispers, as they held the key to my internal truth. There were no reactions, no ripples, no coughs and no shudders. My body was indeed at peace.

Chapter Six

Continuing to reflect on my life, as I watched the water in the fountain, I could see that if the breeze blew to the west the water molecules were guaranteed the safety of the fountain's catchment pool below; joining with the other water molecules to become one. 'United we stand, divided we fall,' I thought.

If the wind blew the water spray to the east, then that's how it was. Simple really – the water would then rarely end up in the fountain's pool below. Its fate was rather less fortunate and it would inevitably end up in a dirty, dejected muddy puddle.

'Wasn't life like that?' I wondered. I considered the constant movement, constant change, constant breathing, and yet, at the same time, it was the same fountain that had been here for so many years. It had been here as far back as I could remember and my grandparents often said they loved to come here when they were children.

Remembering them brought back that wonderful, familiar warm glow I always felt when I thought of them. It continued to grow inside my chest as I breathed out into the fresh morning air. I held that radiating warmth with gratitude and became immersed in the power of love, which knew no boundaries.

Smiling to myself, I thought fondly of my sons Matthew and Philip who had emigrated several years earlier. Both had said that they felt my love each and every day; despite being in New Zealand. Matthew had even said to me that he felt the love surrounding him daily. My beloved grandparents had been dead for some time, but that warm glow still remained whenever I remembered them. It was tangible, unconditional love. It was in the very air that I breathed. I made the choice to breathe it in. Love was a choice after all.

It was January in the north-west of England; still cold and very chilly. Although I was dressed in warm, sensible clothes, I knew the garments I wore were not the reason why I was so warm on this particular frosty, winter's morning. The New Year had recently come and gone and I knew it was time to implement change. My whole future depended on it.

My thoughts deepened. 'Was love like the water? Could it be carried and transported anywhere? Could it transform things and breathe life into things? Water could be transformed into so many different forms: water droplets, clouds, steam, snow, fog, hailstones, ice, frost and it produced the most stunning water crystal formations when it froze. It could be blended and mixed with things too like cordial, paints, or batter for pancakes.

I smiled fondly as I remembered making 'perfume' as a little girl with my cousin. She loved mixing the various petals with water and whatsoever else caught their attention in the garden that day.

My thoughts continued, as the sun began to shine more brightly and was finally beginning to warm the morning air. 'Yes, water was like love, it was an essential ingredient in a concrete mix used to cement things. Yes, love was like water, it could join and connect things. Salt and sugar were easily dissolved to become one.

The birdsong caught my attention and I smiled as I sat listening to the water. I embraced the feeling that its love gave me. I sat and enjoyed its warmth. It was as though love was flowing through each of my veins and could be carried anywhere within my being.

On that particular cold, frosty morning, I fully embraced my deep appreciation and gratitude for this feeling of pure connection. The connection seemed to spread to everything; the trees in the park, the shrubs, the birds and the squirrels, the river a few metres away and the beautiful stone staircase and its statues.

Surely gratitude and appreciation were forms of love? Feeling that emotion of love and connection in the quiet stillness, watching moment by moment, as the sun lifted the colours of the morning sky, my thoughts moved to human emotions. I had come to the fountain to think about my decision after all, to think about the philosophy of life and living. I had come here to decide whether or not I could embrace more life and living a fuller life – or at least take the chance. What would be on the other side? Just what was it that connected people? Why was it that some people had the natural ability to embrace and enjoy life, when others seemed empty and hollow? Could some people allow colour to light up their lives? Were some people afraid to allow light into their dark spaces? Was there anything to be afraid of?

I had certainly seen the power of light transformation when I worked with clients who were in 'the dark night of the soul.' 'Interesting that they should call it dark,' I thought, as I pondered what it was that put people's lights out, as it were?

My thoughts continued, emotions were like colours. Some were light, bright and colourful, often appearing from nowhere; like a rainbow lighting up the sky after a thunderstorm, or a heavy downpour of rain. I loved rainbows. Other emotions were dark, grey, brown and red, sometimes a really dirty, reddy-brown colour, or even black at times and seemed to weigh the whole person down.

I shivered, almost as though I were shaking off those thoughts. I had been in that particular darkness and I never wanted to go there again. Ever. And yet, I had now accepted the wisdom of the learnings I had been able to take from the dark times. Everything had brought learnings: my divorce, subsequent relationship breakdowns, upsets and misunderstandings with my family and other people, the challenges that motherhood brought and the everyday choices I made to become a better version of myself, for me and those around me.

The journey to this present point in my life had been long and had certainly taken a determined and committed effort, though I knew I wouldn't change it. All my many life experiences had brought me to this point right now in this one present moment. I shivered once more, making sure I was letting go of the last of those unwanted, surrendered thoughts.

Thinking back to the times when I had worked with clients and seen the colours in the aura lift incredibly quickly as the emotions, or shock, stress and trauma were released. 'How simple' I thought and yet how truly amazing. Light would *always replace the darkness.* Maybe that's what enlightenment was? Simply allowing light into every part of our lives and our being-ness?

Some people naturally glowed. Some people had a pure radiance about them. I had always seen energy fields around people and this provided me with such an awareness; knowing how my clients were feeling; mentally, physically, spiritually and emotionally: not to mention the volume of the emotional baggage I would be helping them to clear in my professional capacity; should they be willing to let go and move on. I had seen the destructiveness of victimhood or playing the rescuer and how it took away people's power and often led to poor physical health.

I knew through working with, rather than against, my own traumas and upsets that I had raised my vibration. My ability to hold even more light had increased significantly. It was so clear and evident in my recent aura photographs. I felt connected to myself now and was so grateful. That connected feeling led to deeper thoughts. What was it that connected people? What was it that kept them connected? What was it that separated people?

What was I going to learn in India? How would I connect? I would have to face the language barrier, deal with a completely different culture, extreme poverty, different religions, be extremely careful to drink only bottled water, get used to different foodstuffs, I knew I would also have to cope with the heat and potentially snakes, spiders and various insects. Could I cope with this new dance? Was I ready?

Most of all my thoughts were taken up by the mosquito. All too often I had been bitten or 'eaten alive' as I often remarked. I knew they loved me! I had certainly tried everything that had been suggested as a preventative: vitamin B supplements, aromatherapy oils, not wearing perfume, not eating meat....the list was endless. Over these years some bites had become infected and looked like red golf balls...and itched, and itched. Some were less big, though incredibly painful at times.

Would I cope with the dance of the mosquitoes? Could I cope with this huge unknown step?

Chapter Seven

The dance of the mosquito indeed. After considering this pending dance of the unknown, I knew that I was finally ready. The decision could now be made. Listening to my body, mind and soul I knew now was the right time. I was ready to do this dance.

The steps of the dance could be fast, or slow. Some might sting as mosquitoes do. Some might be very painful and others simply the steps of the dance of life itself. Sometimes the dance had to be played out and enjoyed. Taking part was the only essential thing. My dancing shoes were comfortably on and my feet were ready and more than willing to carry me where ever I needed to go. My heart assured me that now it was my time.

I had no idea where it would take me, but I knew that eventually the windows of opportunity would open up to me. I would need to pay very close attention. Looking and listening for all the synchronicities and coincidences. In fact, I realised that I had probably been ready for quite some time. Maybe it had been nothing more than a question of timing? Perhaps other things had needed to be lined up for the journey?

I breathed a huge sigh of relief now that my life-changing decision was finally made. I would phone the estate agents as soon as I arrived home and set the necessary wheels in motion.

Moving to reach for my handbag on the bench, I realised how stiff I was. I yawned and stretched, welcoming the movement in my exhausted body. I was aware that I could stretch and move more easily now this final decision had been made. Rolling my shoulders, I thought I should perhaps start a new journal, to share my thoughts as I began to embrace this new chapter in my life and this one particular dance.

As I walked home through the park enjoying the tree-lined avenue, I was grateful it provided a stunning canopy above me. I knew today would be a day that I would remember forever. I had several travel brochures at home and planned to look through them again when I arrived.

The photos in the holiday brochures looked stunning as I sat curled up on the leather sofa pondering my future over a most welcome, piping hot cup of Lady Grey. My toes were still tingling as they thawed. Flicking through the many pages, the holiday which appealed to me the most was a twenty-eight-day package tour around India. It would include the Golden Triangle. It was priced at almost three thousand pounds and although it seemed expensive, I certainly didn't feel I could travel alone through India as a single lady. I decided that once the house was sold, I would book the tour and looked at the available dates; knowing that from there, I would at last be visiting my two youngest sons in New Zealand.

The phone call to the estate agents to arrange a viewing and valuation was relatively simple. Two days later, the manager arrived on time to view the property. He was clearly impressed by the size and the beauty of the house as he walked around taking photographs of the house and the beautiful, mature gardens. Tears flowed as the magnitude of my decision rippled through my body. There was to be no going back and knowing this company had much success and experience in sales within the local area, I knew it wouldn't take long before I was embracing the changes which were now inevitable.

Looking at the colourful 'For Sale' sign in the garden each and every day, which was particularly poignant when I drew the living-room curtains first thing every morning, reminded me daily of what I was leaving behind. My neighbours were deeply saddened, as were many of my clients. So many had literally been in tears at the announcement that I was leaving the country once the house was sold. My family too had expressed their concerns and thoughts, questioning me about my intentions.

Little did any of them know: apart from my closest friends that fear still threatened to rob me of my courage on rare occasions. I knew in my soul I had to make this journey and although so many people said I was so brave and so courageous, in truth, my decision was simple. I knew I had to do this. The thought of not fulfilling this journey and the thought of not listening to the pull of my soul was far more destructive and uncomfortable than the thought of staying in my current status quo. This journey and the dance of the soul had to be done: regardless of the outcome.

In July, the house finally sold and the relief I felt was huge. I had long forgotten the stress involved in selling a home, it all came tumbling back as I decluttered, cleaned, tidied and felt ready to leave for distant shores.

Out of the blue, my dear friend Caroline had asked me to house-sit for her and her family in France. The house was very close to the border with Switzerland. I had stayed there in previous years and loved it. Knowing that if I accepted, I would have two weeks away to enjoy some rest and recuperation, before everything was finally packed and my very precious belongings shared between friends and family, was a most welcome thought. It would give me a much needed break.

The stunning house was situated directly across from Mont Blanc and overlooked Lake Geneva. It was indeed a perfect and most welcome haven for a lady who had been stressed and exhausted from having emptied a four bedroomed house, tidied two large gardens, de-cluttered a huge log store, a double garage and endless piles of paperwork.

The necessary official documents had all been signed at the solicitor's office the day before I left England and now I was looking forward to getting on the plane, embracing the mountain air and looking over my beloved lake. This place had always soothed my whole being. My soul longed once again for that connection.

Situated in a sleepy village in the French mountains, I could enjoy a daily walk to the view point where Mont Blanc and the Jet D'eau could be seen clearly. I loved it here. Few places held such a deep, tangible and abiding peace. The house was beautifully decorated and it really was home from home. Here I could recharge my soul and meditate daily; seeking the peace, courage and strength I would need for the final stages of the house move, when I returned to England.

Chapter Eight

Arriving on time in Geneva airport, I was so grateful that my old, trusty suitcase was rattling along on the conveyor belt within minutes of me exiting passport control. Now I needed to find that huge mop of blonde, curly hair which was Caroline's signature. Hugs, smiles and more hugs followed.

The power of friendship was so evident and clear. Within the hour, we arrived at my much treasured haven. I was so excited to see the beloved Mont Blanc and the lake. Tears fell, as they usually did whenever I arrived here.

I was quickly settled into my favourite bedroom and was sat on the veranda overlooking the whole valley, drinking tea and breathing in the most welcome clear, mountain air within minutes.

The family were leaving very early the following morning. As they all packed and prepared themselves for the journey, Caroline introduced me to the neighbours. Dale had just finished reading my first book: 'The Goldfish That Jumped'. As Caroline introduced us, Dale hadn't realised initially that I was the author. As she began to join the dots, she was in peals of laughter as she explained that she had loved reading about the numerous interwoven spiritual lessons I had learnt through my life which I shared in the book's pages. She had certainly enjoyed the read and clearly loved it. She said she found she could easily relate to it directly from her own life experiences.

Dale explained that she had set up and managed a women's shelter for many years and was highly respected within the local community and across the wider counties too. Our connection was instant and I have fond memories of sharing our early morning walks in the surrounding mountains and countryside. We shared so much in our many conversations about what we had both learnt from life. What we had learnt as mothers from each of our beloved children, what we had learnt from our personal relationships besides what we had learnt in a professional capacity working with our clients. We both agreed that perhaps most of all, what we had learnt about ourselves was the inevitable key to the evolution of our souls. The philosophy of life, of caring, sharing and being of service to others: whilst at the same time losing the dis-ease to please and finally learning and fully understanding the importance of the basic essential need to take care of ourselves first.

We both felt that we had known one another forever. We agreed it was probably over many lifetimes. Dale was from Canada, she had recently retired and was visiting France to spend time with her daughter. She had instantly fallen in love with the Swiss mountains, the lake and seemed to love the whole area as much as I did. I have so many precious memories of sharing our deep, spiritual conversations, of sharing our hurts, sadness and regrets. And yet the joy of realising that actually they were simply learnings: each one providing us with more life experience, so that we could in turn, share these with others. But perhaps most importantly allowing us to honour our natural humanity and our vulnerabilities with each other. Some people you simply connect with so easily, some people you'll never forget and some people touch your very being. Dale was guilty on all of these counts. Blissfully guilty.

My usual daily jaunt took me right into the heart of the mountains which were directly across from Mont Blanc. How many millions of years had it taken to produce such a thing of extreme beauty, strength and endurance. How many lifetimes of constant pressure and force? How many endless cycles before it could be here now. Right in this very moment. Just present. Simply being. Simply shining. Simply just....unbelievably magnificent. My love for Mont Blanc grew daily.

As I looked over the lake and the Jet D'eau, I pondered my future. I was fifty-one years old, single, fit and healthy, a mother of four treasured children, a grandmother of seven granddaughters and about to embark on a journey of deepening my own soul – or at least that was the plan. I felt the remaining fear that morning throughout my whole body and allowed the many tears to flow. It had been such a tumultuous time these last few months and being here brought much needed respite to my whole being. I knew all too soon enough I had to embark on the final leg of this particular life journey. Just what would lay ahead of me in the coming weeks? Would I ever visit here again?

I had fallen in love with Switzerland many years earlier, when I had received my first invitation from my dear friend Tracey. Since that time I had hoped to live here...now all that had seemed to change. A few days later whilst having lunch with my dear friend Peter in the local restaurant at the golf club we discussed my future.

"You belong in the mountains Mary, you loved this place since the first time you set foot in Geneva". I could not disagree and knew that I had visualised living in a stunning villa overlooking the lake for many years. The thoughts of living close to dear friends, the stunning surroundings, the local cuisine and the French\Swiss way of life certainly appealed. My thoughts were simply 'what will be, will be.' I had to trust that I would be guided to where I was meant to be.

Within these last six years, I had made many friends and had many clients in the area around the lake; both on the French and the Swiss side.

As the tears continued, I was happy to cry in Peter's presence. I looked over the lake towards Mont Blanc and said a quiet prayer to her for her help and assistance in the next chapter of my life's journey, as the dance deepened. There is a very special magic in these mountains surrounding the lake and I felt something move within me, within my very core. It was a new strength, an even deeper courage and sense of renewal.

Walking up the old familiar mountain path on the final day of my stay, I knew that wherever my destiny lay, I would forever be connected to The White Mountain and this most precious lake. I knew my dear friends were in my heart and I knew that they would support my decision and keep in touch, respecting and continuing with our friendship.

Some people call it 'The Golden Thread.' Some people say we are all connected in some way. I had to trust that these connections would remain. I said another silent prayer of immense gratitude to the mountain, for all I had experienced here in this magical place. Then I expressed my very personal 'Goodbye,' as I returned to the worn mountain path. How many connections would I make in India? Would I make connections? Would I connect with the right people? Just what was it that connected people? Would those connections be as powerful and enduring as these here in Switzerland? Only time would tell.

Chapter Nine

The flight home from Geneva was smooth and easy. I always felt sad when I was leaving and knowing it would be the last time I saw the mountains for a while, I said another prayer of deep thanks. I felt a part of me belonged there. This place has a magic all of its own and touches the essence of my being, each and every time, I have visited. Perhaps unlike some places that lose their magic the more you become accustomed to them, Switzerland; Geneva particularly and the French border towns hold an incredible power and restorative energy; at least for me. It has never lost its ability to allow me to connect so deeply to a place. I hold it so dear; in both my heart and my whole soul.

Looking down over the beautiful lake through the tiny window of the plane, brought yet another tear to my eye. I was feeling a mixture of grief at my leaving, but joy at her splendour. So many of my friends had said they would love to visit here. I feel honoured to have had that privilege.

As I sat on the plane I knew now that I needed to concentrate on those essential things that awaited my return to the United Kingdom. I always felt the same once I have flown over the lake. It's as though I need to reassemble myself.

The sight of the Thames meandering through London as we headed for Liverpool brought feelings of my present reality to another climax. I was really looking forward to seeing my dear son Nicholas as he had arranged to collect me from Liverpool airport. He usually had my granddaughters with him and in many ways it softened the feelings of loss after leaving my beloved Switzerland.

I was surprised he wasn't waiting for me in the arrivals lounge at the airport. I checked my phone. He texted me to say I needed to meet him in the carpark. Nicholas is usually most helpful, especially with a heavy suitcase in hand, though he said he felt sick and had vomited the night before. He apologised and asked me to put the suitcase in the boot myself. As I opened it, I gasped when my youngest son Phil appeared. It really took my breath away! I was shaking and crying with delight. I hadn't seen him for almost two years when he had originally moved to New Zealand.

Although we were in touch frequently, seeing him in the flesh was incredible. We hugged, we both cried and then we hugged some more. I kept pinching him to prove to myself that he was really there. I was thrilled at see him again. It was such a magical surprise.

Spending precious quality time together despite his jet-lag and knowing I would now finally meet my daughter-in-law Rachel was such a pleasure. I treasured every moment. He had travelled half-way across the globe, settled in Queenstown and within a few months he met his beloved. Ironically she had previously lived only minutes away from us in Lancashire. Life was like that sometimes...I had missed my son dearly since his departure. Now I had also gained another daughter.

They were looking forward to seeing me again in New Zealand once everything was finalized with the sale of the house. Knowing I would see them again very soon, made their eventual parting; a fortnight later more bearable. Little did I know what lay ahead.

Within two weeks of them leaving, the house sale fell through as the people buying my property had lost the buyer for their property. After all the soul-searching, the tears, the packing, the cleaning and the expectations, I felt broken. Shattered into a million pieces. I had told most of my clients I would be leaving the country imminently. I had even suggested they seek other therapists, whom I had highly recommended. Now I was in despair.

I had trusted, up until recently, that everything was in Divine order and yet, before I got the news from my solicitor, I had already intuited that something was amiss two days earlier. This 'knowing' saved me from falling into, what could have been, an even worse downward spiral of chaos, mistrust and fear. Nonetheless, I began to panic. I still had the mortgage and the bills to pay. As a professional woman, I felt as though I now looked like a complete fool.

All my plans seemed to turn to dust in my hands and I was really concerned that selling the house was beginning to feel like 'Mission Bloody Fucking Impossible.' The disappointment, upset, hurt, anger, frustration and general 'pissed off' feelings I felt, poured out, as I decided I needed to go to my 'go to' place immediately. I set off in the car to my local haven to be near the water and the trees.

In times of stress and discord, I always turn to Mother Nature for relief. Today called for a particularly magical haven. My favourite local walk was by the canal at Rufford, which allowed me the space to breathe and to simply be. Standing on the swing bridge overlooking the reeds where I often saw the kingfishers, I said yet another quiet prayer for peace and Divine assistance.

Believing that The Universe always has your back and having hope, faith and trust in your daily life, doesn't mean that you feel that way every day. This particular day I felt like screaming, punching someone's lights out and kicking something hard, not to mention ripping out my own hair. Was I being tested to see how much I wanted a new future? Was I being tested to see if I could remain in trust? Was I ready for my new dance with the mosquito? Was it to prove to The Universe, or maybe myself, that I had the necessary courage? What the FUCK! I felt as though my head would explode at any moment.

I stood by the canal in tears, feeling adrift and confused. I knew I needed to focus. Deciding on my plan of action, I knew my only sensible option was to return to trusting that for whatever reason, I was being given more time. Despite having packed and de-cluttered so much, the house was still a home, my home where I still lived and had a roof over my head. The encompassing atmosphere of love still remained there so I decided I would continue to enjoy it as the space that I had created; at least for now.

Breathing deeply and ensuring my voice didn't croak or break through the conversation, I phoned the estate agents. They assured me that the buyers were still desperate to purchase the house. In fact, he said that they were very upset and had asked him to pass on their most sincere regards. It seemed that they were even more upset than I was at the time. So, I had no other choice other than to trust that all would be well. I knew that friends, family and clients would all be pleased when the 'Sold' sign was removed.

"Bloody Hell", I exclaimed as I put the phone down and remembered to breathe once more.

Chapter Ten

Trusting is never an easy option. Patience is not a life lesson that any of us relish. However, despite everything, I tried to practise both daily. I was still asking friends and family who would like to receive my last remaining pictures, ornaments, pieces of furniture, flower pots, garden furniture, spare beds, curtains, bedding and kitchenware.

This was going to be a complete break. A complete letting go. As everything was labelled and noted, as to who was having which items, they all assured me that should I come back to the United Kingdom, then my belongings would also be returned.

I had no knowing, nor intentions whatsoever of any future plans at that time. My focus was purely to ensure my belongings went where they would be appreciated and loved. I certainly didn't know if I would ever return. I knew I had to get to India, however long the journey would take; whether three months, six months, or longer. After India, maybe I would visit Nepal and Bali. Then at last I would finally be heading for New Zealand, to see my dear sons and my daughter-in-law.

I had wanted to visit New Zealand since I was a teenager. I remembered the pictures I had of both the North and South Islands as a young girl. I'm guessing I must have obtained them from a magazine? Maybe they were mentioned in a geography lesson? I certainly knew that for me, there was always a magnetism to the place and I knew that one day I would indeed set foot on the islands. Knowing the importance and the power of the law of attraction, it was essential that I remain in trust. Even though at this moment, it was through tightly gritted teeth.

Finally in October, three months later, the house sold to the original buyers. I was so relieved when I finally received the phone call. The family only ever viewed the house once. As previously, they offered me just short of the full asking price. I hoped that as things had already been signed with the solicitor; rather than taking the usual six to twelve weeks, things might move more quickly. This time I had decided to keep in touch regularly with both the estate agents and my solicitor, to ensure that progress was indeed being made. After all this time I wanted the completion date sooner, rather than later. A part of me felt like my whole life depended on it.

The seasons in New Zealand are opposite to those in the United Kingdom. Our winter is their summer, and vice-versa. The thoughts of being on a beach on Christmas Day with my sons, in the bright sunshine standing over a barbeque brought a huge smile to my face. Could this finally be happening? Could I really trust that all would indeed be finalised? I had seen my son

Phil and Rachel his partner only a few months earlier. My son Matthew and I, hadn't seen each other for almost two years. Matthew is six foot seven inches tall and stands head and shoulders above everyone else – usually. The thought of seeing them at Queenstown airport brought several tears to my eyes; as did the thought of their upset should this sale fall through again.

Chapter Eleven

A month later, in November, I received an email from a new client requesting he learn Reiki Two with me at the earliest opportunity. I was out walking in the local country park in Cuerden Valley at the time and, as I hadn't replied to his enquiry, he decided to phone me directly. As we spoke on the phone he explained that he was only in the country for a few weeks, as he would soon be leaving for Australia, or New Zealand. He explained that although he was English, he had lived in both countries for many years. He was here to spend time with his family over the festive season and would be returning early in the New Year. I explained my situation regarding the imminent house sale and that I too would be travelling soon. We agreed that the coming Friday would be a mutually convenient day for us both.

Teaching Reiki Two was one of my very favourite things. He understood many of the esoteric principles, though I did find that as he had learnt Reiki One with someone else, many of the vital learnings and subjects were missing. As I filled in the gaps, we discussed so much and he was delighted with the extra tuition.

After lunch we discussed healing this current lifetime and why we attract certain situations and people into our lives; even if it is incredibly challenging at times, and maybe even painful. Things may not always seem to be what they first appear, although we get what we need so that the soul can grow; rather than what we want and desire. By developing personal responsibility and self-awareness; becoming aware of our behavioural patterns and separating those which serve us from those that don't, then we allow ourselves to go with the flow in life, rather than remaining stuck, or falling into the trap of playing 'The Blame Game.'

In the teaching, I mentioned the importance of listening to the soul's guidance through our intuition and explained my desire to visit India and then New Zealand, as my soul was pulling me there. He immediately asked if I wanted to travel with him - simply as a travel companion to India. I was stunned. He explained that he had visited India several years earlier and now felt that as he was more soulfully aware, he would get more benefit from the second visit. I agreed without any hesitation.

Over the coming weeks we each applied for our six month Indian visas. It was certainly not quite as simple as I thought. Navigating through the on-line system was certainly a challenge when answering questions that seem completely and utterly irrelevant. Four attempts later, after much frustration we had finally arranged to visit the visa office in Manchester to be interviewed. This would certainly be the litmus test. Time was running out and without them, travelling was not an option.

Whilst in the waiting area we chatted to a man from Ireland who said he had returned four times to the visa office. He was hoping this would be his final interview, as he was travelling a week before we were hoping to fly. I stayed positive and focused that our visa applications would be accepted and that we would obtain them that day, rather than having to return to Manchester numerous times.

Taking a deep breath as we left and smiling with relief, I was thrilled. Although I still didn't have a completion date for the house sale, we had the visas and now we could finally book the flights.

The 28th January was to be 'D' day. The final countdown had begun.

Chapter Twelve

My dear friend Frank and I met when he photographed my aura in June 2018. I knew immediately that we knew one another from other lives. He's a wonderful inspiration to many and, at eighty two years of age, he is still going strong and working at Body, Mind and Soul exhibitions across the United Kingdom.

We both laughed when he saw my aura come up on the screen and he realised how soulfully aware I am. The aura holds so much information about a person and he could see that I was a spiritual teacher, psychic, healer and so much more. Chatting easily and knowing there was so much information that we both needed to share, we agreed to keep in touch and arranged to go for a pub lunch a few days later.

He mentioned his friend Phill so often in the months that followed and I knew that Phill and I we were destined to meet. As my leaving date loomed ever closer, time was becoming short. On Boxing Day with little over a month to go, Frank arranged a special meal for the three of us and finally we all met in Chester.

Phill is a natural psychic and healer like myself. He has always seen and heard spirits and he works similarly to me. Within a few minutes he intuited quite a lot of information about my life. Frank had not breathed a word about me to him. He had merely stated that we needed to meet. (Frank was well aware of Phill's gifts, and he knows it's unprofessional to share information beforehand).

Sitting at the table together, the three of us chatted easily and within minutes Phill was asking when I was travelling. He said I would met the love of my life, whilst I was away. After being single for many years; I accepted what he was saying. Having many friends in this field of work, I had been given the exact same information in three other readings, which I had received in the previous two years. I knew within myself that my journey would be life-changing and had felt that I would indeed meet someone. Meeting the love of my life would be amazing. There was a part of me that wondered if it could be true. The upper limits of happiness indeed. What if?

I had chosen to be single these last few years. I felt there was no room for compromise. What if I did meet someone who fulfilled me?

I knew I had cleared so much 'emotional baggage' which had previously prevented me from experiencing such a fulfilling relationship. I decided that I would accept the information. It was simply time to allow whatever was about to unfold to manifest into the physical world.

Time was short and in the coming days and weeks, Phill and I wanted to get to know one another. We shared so many conversations about what it's like to be a natural healer, medium and gifted psychic. We shared how isolating we have both felt throughout our lives finding it difficult to share our esoteric personal experiences; simply because most people do not 'see' and feel what we do.

Together with the weight of the huge responsibility as healers we frequently experience, having the gift can sometimes feel like a double-edged sword. There was so much to share about our personal stories and clearing unbalanced, toxic energies. We laughed often and I knew this man 'had my back' in many ways. He is a warrior and a spiritual protector. Over the coming weeks many people felt we had such a strong connection that we were in fact in a relationship. His answer would always be:

"No, she's going to meet her man when she is away." I just smiled, laughed or both.

As the New Year approached, he explained he had booked a meal in a Welsh castle for the celebrations and asked if I would like to join him. The thought of being in a splendid castle overlooking the coast was wonderful and I gladly accepted the invitation. Towards midnight as we watched the New Year fireworks over the bay, I sent my private prayers to The Universe for myself and my loved ones. I had so much to be grateful for and yet I still had occasional moments of nagging doubt. Phill always reassured me that I was definitely doing the right thing.

Phill and I hugged as we brought the New Year in together. What lay ahead for me? Would I really meet the man I had desired for so long? Dare I hope? There was one thing I knew, and that was, that I had the endearing support of a man with a huge heart and I was glad he was here to get me through these coming days. I was under no illusion that my journey between here; the very first day of January and up until the 28th were simply going to be a walk in the park. I said a quiet prayer of gratitude that I had been sent an earth angel to help.

Chapter Thirteen

The final leg of the journey now loomed. I had only weeks to go before I was due to get on *that* plane. Most of my furniture and belongings had been allocated to friends and family, many items had already gone. There were still the bulk of the kitchen items and other essentials that could only be packed nearer the time.

I spoke to the estate agents more frequently now to ensure smooth passage to the completion date. The buyers' mortgage offer ended on the 8th of January so my solicitor had assured me that the completion date would be earlier than that. I was pleased as it would give me precious time to spend with my family and friends. A few days later, I was told that my buyers had requested an extension of their mortgage offer. When I heard the news, I truly thought my nerves would finally crack. It felt like a thousand pieces of glass shattered in that one single, shitty, heart-breaking moment.

I could hardly speak on the phone as a million and one thoughts crammed their way into my already frazzled brain. I surely thought my head and my heavily-burdened heart would burst. The stress had been more than enough over these last few months. The flights were booked, visa's were en-route and I felt incredibly desperate. As the tears fell, I looked out from my bedroom window across to Pendle Hill. My nerves were shredded.

In a state of shock, stressed and upset, the tears continued to fall as I telephoned my dear friend Judy. She too is a gifted psychic and I pleaded with her to 'tune in' and check what the hold-up was now. She calmed me down and simply advised me to stand firm, tell the estate agents to put the house back on the market and remain positive. She intuited that all would be well and the sale would still go through, although now was the time to get tough.

Minutes later I phoned Phill who gave me the same advice and despite the tears, I somehow managed to have the necessary conversation with the estate agents and expressed my huge disappointment and the crappy stress this seemingly-no-end-in-sight-situation was causing me. Despair, hopelessness, fear and panic threatened to engulf my very being.

Finally after a few more days of feeling that my whole life and my whole future were hanging on a very precarious precipice, the completion date was arranged for 16th January. Now I knew I would only have eleven days to spend with my loved ones.

Chapter Fourteen

My dear son Nic and friend Phill were so helpful once the moving date finally arrived. The relief when everything was packed and the house was finally emptied, was a feeling that I cannot describe. I was exhausted and had been for the previous two days. I had been running purely on adrenaline. I couldn't sleep properly and could barely eat. Nic had no problem letting me know that I looked terrible:

"You look like shit Mum." He was right. My stress levels at having to ensure people came to collect various items on time, cleaning a huge four bedroomed house and the pure intensity of emotions were clearly taking their toll. I knew this was to be the final time I would ever walk around what had once been my haven and my sanctuary. It challenged me to my very core.

Saying my 'Goodbyes' and also my 'Thank You'd to this house which was soon to be a home for a new family, was both a relief and yet a most sorrowful moment. The tears flowed as I clipped all the house keys together on the keyring ready to hand in to the local estate agent. There was definitely no going back now. Any final doubts I had about making my decision was tossed to the Gods.

Chapter Fifteen

It was a welcome relief to stay with my parents in those final days. I was exhausted and glad to be nurtured by them both. The love that passed between me and my mother each morning, whilst we sat in our dressing gowns drinking tea, was something I will truly never forget. Once we heard dad descending the stairs and he plonked himself in his favourite armchair, the cheek and the laughter started. His usual remark when I asked him if he wanted a cup of tea was:

"No good having a dog and barking yourself."

The simplicity of the connection between the three of us and just being in the moment was truly wonderful. They had no expectations of me. I was not allowed to do any cooking, ironing, or cleaning at all. I couldn't even put the washing machine on to wash my own clothes. Mum took care of everything and I would find them washed, dried and ironed on my bed at the end of the day. After years of living alone and doing everything myself, I had truly forgotten what it was like to be nurtured in such a beautiful, easy manner. I am forever grateful for those final days we spent together.

Chapter Sixteen

I was under no illusion that leaving my beloved family was going to be easy. Each Wednesday for several years I had cared for my dear granddaughter Eve. We had a good relationship and she had a very sharp sense of humour, combined with a wicked grin that melted my heart every time. Blond, cute and even more so when she smiled making the two dimples in her cheeks appear she was, as are my other girls, completely adorable.

She calls me 'Silly Grandma' because I often act silly with her and she has grown very used to my sharp sense of humour and my magical tickles. Her baby sister Rose is equally as adorable. I knew leaving them would be heart-breaking and painful, as would leaving my eldest son and his wife. It was a combination that would certainly challenge my heartstrings.

My other four granddaughters had lived in Kent for three years and had recently moved back up north to Lancashire. The thought of leaving my daughter, her husband and my other very precious girls was certainly not going to be easy either.

I'm a very 'hands-on' Grandma and loved taking them to the park, out for a picnic, to the beach, watching Disney films and much, much more. I knew I had to prepare myself for that forthcoming separation.

After the New Year, in the local village, my son Nicholas was to take one of the main roles in the pantomime, 'Jack and The Beanstalk.' We both knew that if I sold the house and completed before Christmas, then there was a chance that I would miss his performance. Eve was also cast in the pantomime.

It's funny how sometimes things take care of themselves when we simply allow, rather than force. As the end of the year approached, the estate agents said that the buyers now requested a completion date in the New Year; so they wouldn't have the stress of moving around the festive season. Whilst I was upset, I also felt great relief as I knew I could enjoy Christmas with my family in England. Now my leaving was imminent and I truly had no idea what my return date would be, or even if I would in fact return, it made the celebrations even more poignant.

The Friday that I was due to attend the pantomime I collected Eve from school as her parents were working. A very sulky, quiet and unhappy Eve awaited me in the schoolyard. I had very rarely seen her like this and wondered what to do, as I knew she had her star performance later. She neither looked at me, nor her baby sister in the pushchair. As I moved to cuddle her she was obviously angry. Nothing could have prepared me for the answer she gave when I asked her what had upset her.

“It’s you Grandma. I don’t want you to come to the pantomime tonight because you’ll make me laugh when I’m on the stage in front of everyone.” I was so close to tears. I know her well enough to know that when five year old Eve sets her mind to something, there’s only a very small hope that it can be changed. I was really upset as she means the world to me and the thought of missing this particular event left me feeling particularly sad. She had obviously been upset and worried for quite some time. Her needs had to come before mine and I promised that I would not go if she really didn’t want me there. I also promised that if she allowed me to attend the pantomime, I would behave and certainly not make her laugh. She took some convincing though eventually agreed. I remember crying with relief and hiding my tears from her.

The other pantomime dates were booked and my other granddaughters, nephews, nieces and my mother all wanted to attend. It was wonderful because we were all gathered together. I was appreciating the extra precious moments with each of them before my pending departure.

Seeing my son on stage as the king was a very proud moment. The Longton village pantomimes are full of fun, humour and inevitably bring fits of laughter. Mum and I knew we were in for a real treat. The previous year they had managed to include a Freddie Mercury look-a-like to sing 'I Want To Break Free'. I remembered having tears of laughter rolling down my cheeks. The scene fitted perfectly into the story of the genie in Snow White's wicked step-mother's mirror who wanted to break free of her tyranny. What this particular pantomime would bring was anybody's guess. Nic and Eve were sworn to secrecy.

As mum was handed a 'BOO' sign to hold up at the 'right' moments when the village villain appeared on stage, we sat happily together knowing the value of this special, quality time. In true Longton style, the pantomime was hilarious; full of wit and ridiculous humour. Both Nic and Eve performed extremely well, as did the other cast members. These are often the moments we recall with sheer delight. With tears in my eyes, I felt humbled and privileged to be a part of their lives. Many more memories were bottled that evening.

A few nights later as the 28th January loomed, I was babysitting Rose, while all the other family members attended the final performance of the pantomime. She was usually in bed before 7pm. I knew it was only days before I was leaving and wanted to bottle even more of those precious minutes with her.

After having had four children of my own and seven granddaughters, I watch in complete amazement at what they seem to know, without knowing. Whether Rose intuited that potentially, this would be our last evening together for some time, I shall never know. She was full of energy and played, laughed and smiled throughout the night. As I finally put her in her cot about 9.30pm, I smiled to myself as I kissed her 'Goodnight.'

A few minutes later the rest of the family, my mum, my other granddaughters, my son, his wife and my dear daughter-in-law's family appeared. They had loved the performance. Another moment captured in that ever-expanding priceless memory bottle.

As I kissed and hugged them, wishing them a wonderful 'Goodnight.' I hoped that with only two days left, I would have time to see them again before my early morning flight on Monday. Thinking that I would have more time over the weekend, I never actually said 'Goodbye' to Eve. Something for which I have been grateful. She was too young to understand what it meant that I would be away for many months. Driving back to my parent's house the tears flowed with thoughts of duality. The simple joy of celebrating and sharing time with loved ones and also knowing exactly what I was leaving behind, as my venture into the unknown was now fast approaching.

My dad had recently had a hip replacement and his health had caused me concern. He is in his late eighties, so leaving him and my mum; also with general health problems, would be a challenge. Phill had promised to keep in touch with them and keep a watchful eye on them when I left. I will be forever grateful of his generous support.

Chapter Seventeen

Phill continued to support me through those final days. Sunday the 27th January would be my last full day, as I was leaving very early Monday morning for Manchester Airport. We had arranged to take my granddaughters out for the day. Each and every cuddle, hug and smile was yet another bottled in that magic, very precious, bottle of memories.

Hebden Bridge is a wonderful local village and we decided to take them there for the day. As my granddaughters played happily on the swings and the slides, the tears came randomly as I knew what I was leaving behind. Phill kept a watchful eye on me and would distract the girls if I needed a moment to calm myself.

Raphena was only two years old and I wondered if she would forget me. Lavender aged five, had been heartbroken so many times when we had been parted previously when I left Kent. My daughter said sometimes she cried for several hours. Gracie aged nine, seemed to be okay 'though still waters run deep' I thought, and Esmae, my eldest granddaughter kept smiling the most radiant smiles across to me.

Phill was so hands on with them and had kindly offered to do all the driving. Once again I was so grateful for his help. I had learnt over the years the power of accepting help; not an easy task when you really believe that you have to be strong all the time. However, I knew and readily admitted that currently I was so, so vulnerable. We all thoroughly loved that magical day. The whole experience is safely bottled.

Sharing a lovely meal when we arrived back with my daughter and her husband, together with Phill and the girls, great conversation and laughter: if not the occasion tear, was all treasured.

Kissing each of the girls 'Goodnight' as I put them to bed, one by one, and fighting back the tears was one of my toughest moments. My daughter held me close, as I continued to cry when I arrived downstairs again. She and her husband understood that I had to do this journey for myself, though none of us knew when we would see each other again. They knew I had a six month visa for touring India and then Duncan and I planned to visit Nepal, maybe Tibet, Bali, Australia and then eventually New Zealand. It would be several months at least.

Phill insisted that his intuition was showing him that it would be approximately two years before I would once again set foot on English soil. I could neither agree, nor disagree; as I truly had no idea of my pending future.

Midnight was fast approaching as hugs and more hugs, and even more tears were exchanged between my daughter and my son-in-law. I was exhausted physically, emotionally, spiritually and mentally. Leaving that evening was very emotional and particularly overwhelming.

I was relieved that Phill was driving back to Lancashire, as my thoughts now shifted to last minute essential packing. I had to be up at 5am to catch the train to the airport. I also had to say 'Goodbye' to Phill and my beloved parents. 'Just how much can one heart take' I thought, as I could feel it expanding rapidly in my chest as we neared the house.

Packing and checking the weight in my suitcase, passport, tickets and the usual planning took at least another hour. By now it was early morning. As Phill wished me well and we hugged promising to keep in touch, the volume of what I was doing hit me like a tsunami. Within a few hours I was beginning my journey to the other side of the world; without a return ticket, or a date, as to when I would see them again.

Watching his towering figure walk through the gate, the tears fell as I took a final look around the family lounge. Thinking of all the memories, all the Christmas's we had spent here, all the other family gatherings and a million and one other things, I eventually crawled in to bed.

Chapter Eighteen

Nicholas, my son had agreed to collect both me and my travel companion, Duncan to take us Preston railway station. I was delighted we made good time. As we stood on the railway station waiting for the train to Manchester airport, I had no knowing of when I would see him again. I made that hug last. At over six feet tall and extremely muscular due to all his physical training, I felt so safe in his arms. As we both eventually let go of the hug, we looked deeply into one another's eyes. He asked Duncan to take good care of me and, as men do, they shook hands. As I watched him climb the railway stairs, then walk across the bridge until he was out of sight, I truly felt the measure of the love and appreciation a mother has for her children.

All four of my children mean the world to me and leaving behind two in England to visit my youngest two sons in New Zealand; felt very peculiar. I had no idea what my life would bring and where I would choose to live. It really was to be an unknown adventure. I trusted doorways and opportunities would present themselves should I be open enough to welcome them. I needed to trust the process and allow it to unfold, watching for the Universal clues when they were presented.

My mind, body and soul were feeling very much at ease and deeply contented as the train arrived at

Manchester airport. The process of checking in and security were smooth. I was glad that after all the organising, the stress, the prayers, and the emotion roller-coaster of the past few months, this day had finally arrived.

As Duncan, my travel companion and I sat waiting for the announcement of the departure gate I looked across at him. I had only met him in November and I barely knew him. When I had agreed to travel with him, I had no doubt that I was making the right choice. We had met a handful of times for lunch, or just a coffee, to arrange the practical things like accommodation, sight-seeing and of course to sort out the travel visas. Here I was sat in an airport lounge with a guy who was almost a complete stranger, setting off over four thousand miles away to a strange country, foreign lands, foreign tongue and a completely different culture. I had placed so much trust and faith in him. We had agreed to share a room to keep costs down and I felt that there was certainly a deep enough respect between us to ensure that barriers and boundaries were firmly rooted and established.

After boarding, as I sat on the plane knowing I would not be returning to England for quite some time, I allowed the tears to fall. Aware that Duncan was to my left and other passengers to my right, I discreetly reached for a tissue. 'Just breathe, just breathe, just breathe. You know you're doing the right thing. You know you are. Just breathe, just allow yourself to feel it. You're going to be fine. It's all going to be okay. Duncan will take care of you and you're looked after.' My thoughts raced and my heart felt like it was torn into at least two pieces – some had already landed in India.

The longest flight I had ever experienced up to that point, was approximately four hours when I had flown to Egypt. This would be a long-haul of nine hours. I love flying and the feeling of joy it brings. I allowed myself the opportunity to simply embrace each and every moment; like a child who had never flown previously.

I had no expectations and we had no real set agenda. I knew I had to do this spiritual pilgrimage for my souls' growth. I trusted I would know intuitively which towns, cities and holy places that I wanted to visit. We were certainly not travelling with 'Thomas Cook' and our experiences would not be cossetted in any way. We would be living in the real India, exposed to local people and their way of life, rather than being shown around the nicest tourist places with the best hotels and luxury transport.

We were due to arrive in Goa within the next few hours and I trusted Duncan's judgement and his experience that would allow me to get used to India, the heat and the culture. I was aware that I would experience first-hand the extreme poverty, the continuous need to barter, the fact that I would be stared at, the need to drink only bottled water and to remain vigilant when assessing any eating establishment for cleanliness every single mealtime. Western travellers are advised to check how the salad, fruit and vegetables are washed, as the tap water is full of potentially dangerous microbes. 'Delhi Belly' was not an option! The rest was completely unknown. I resolved that I would learn quickly.

In our discussions, we had many options for visiting the main spiritual sights. We agreed it was after all to be a spiritual pilgrimage, rather than a holiday. The travel brochures I had read and the research I had done were very informative, as were my spiritual friends who had already travelled around India.

There were two places I definitely wanted to visit. The city of Varanasi and the shrine of a Grand Sufi Master in Ajmer. Duncan and I had agreed that we could accommodate these into our schedule. The rest was completely unknown. Trusting was paramount as this journey unfolded; like the petals of the lotus flower.

PART TWO

Chapter Nineteen

Finally arriving in Goa the heat hit us immediately as we descended the stairs from the plane. There was certainly no going back now and once again I felt the sadness. I already missed all of my loved ones, who were now thousands of miles away.

Landing at one am, we had several hours before we could get into our accommodation in Northern Goa. We decided to organise a taxi to the nearby town where the bars would still be open. We hoped to get something to eat and drink before we made our onward journey north to Kiranpani Bridge: over two hours' drive away.

Walking out towards the taxi, I was aware this place was certainly unlike anything I had experienced previously. With only artificial light from what little I could see, I knew I had much to learn and that many new experiences awaited me. The constant noise of the honking, the heat, the smells and the volume of general traffic felt as though my senses were on overload and this was only the very early hours of the morning. What would it be like through the daytime?

The taxi drive was certainly a rickety one as we neared the beach resorts. The very poor state of the roads and the standards of driving were drawn to my attention immediately. People were driving on the wrong side of the road, no-one paid attention to the traffic lanes and two lanes usually became four. Traffic overtook on the inside lane and people drove so closely to one another it was a huge shock. In the United Kingdom I loved to drive and thought myself to be a good driver. I had already decided that I would not be driving here.

The relief I felt when we finally found a clean looking bar and ordered food was almost immeasurable. We still had several hours until sunrise. This has always been one of the most precious times of the day for me. There was still a part of me that wanted to pinch myself and, despite months of planning, I wondered if it was all real. Feeling the heat on my face, even at this ungodly hour, I had no doubt that indeed, here I was finally on Indian soil. Mother India had called to my soul and I had listened.

The simple meal of curry and chapatti was most welcome. From my vantage point I took a look around to see the quality of the houses, other hotels, the roads and listened to all the sounds around me. In the dark I could see very little detail. Every one of my senses seemed to be on high alert. Everything was so different here, the heat, the sounds, the language, the smells. It was most definitely already a very steep learning curve.

We sat drinking fruit juice, grateful for somewhere to sit whilst we waited in those early morning hours. As all the other guests left, it was just the two of us and the remaining staff. A couple of hours later, nearing sunrise, there were people on pushbikes carrying their wares to sell. They were loaded up in such a way that I was amazed how it was even possible to gather so many items on one bicycle. Various different buses came and went. The age and the physical state of the buses amazed me. These would never even be allowed on roads in Britain. They were battered, dinted and damaged so much. It was a miracle they were actually running at all. Clearly I had so much more to experience. There was nothing else I could do and I simply allowed myself to be. I needed to sit and absorb it all.

What would this journey through India bring? What would it look like once the sun came out? Was I really prepared to handle all these different experiences? Had I truly made the right decision? Only time would tell.

Another couple of hours later, we were finally beginning to feel tired. Watching Duncan barter with numerous taxi drivers, I was shocked as I realised that this is their 'normal' way of everyday life. I had to watch and learn quickly, as I knew I would have to barter once I was out and about alone. Eventually several taxi drivers later, after finally agreeing on a reasonable price, we set off.

Watching the sunrise as we journeyed through the towns, villages and countryside was truly amazing.

Seeing a scarecrow dressed in a beautiful red saree made me smile. The sight of the huge bright red sun on that particular morning was something I will remember forever. It was huge and glowed so much more than it ever seemed to do when I had seen the sunrise in France, Switzerland, Egypt and the many other places I had visited. I felt connected to it somehow and was simply pleased that at last we could reach our destination and I could sleep.

Chapter Twenty

Arriving at the eco-farm was a welcome relief after experiencing the most scary taxi ride of my life. The driver overtook on blind corners, drove almost bumper to bumper with the driver in front and ignored all red traffic lights.

The accommodation was basic and clean. I relaxed more when I saw that the bathroom had a toilet, rather than a 'squat and drop.' The owner seemed pleasant. We were glad that we could finally crash at last. The bed was as hard as nails, the mattress clearly old and well past its sell-by-date, as were the pillows. I was too tired to care and within moments I was fast asleep.

A few hours later when I awoke, I was grateful that it was still daylight. I felt refreshed and was surprised that I seemed to feel reasonably 'normal' considering the lengthy journey. I had expected to experience jet-lag by now. Duncan was still asleep and I decided to go for a wander to the nearby bridge down the hill, which was about 500 metres away. The heat of the afternoon sun was intense and I was sweating within a few minutes. I knew I would have to walk back up the hill later, in this heat it would be a challenge. Luckily I had a bottle of water with me, as I had no idea where the nearest shop or market stall was located.

The sound of the nothing-ness, unless traffic drove past was most welcome. The view was spectacular across the lake. Looking at the variety of huge palm trees and the banana trees, I was stunned by their magnificent beauty. I had never seen anything like this. It was truly spectacular.

There were no pavements here on the road and I was extremely careful as the local traffic drove past me. I had certainly experienced enough crazy driving for one day. When I approached the bridge, I was saddened to see the poor state of the pavements there. Walking only in flip-flops, I watched every precarious step I took over open and broken manholes. Many of the paving flags were cracked and potentially dangerous too. The people who passed me looked at me in a very peculiar manner, as though it was rare that anyone would walk here. Was it because I was white? I certainly wasn't sure.

I felt overwhelmed by the beauty of it all. I could see lush jungles in the distance and was aware of the vast expanse of this beautiful river from my vantage point. The surroundings were magnificent, the greenery and the pure joy of seeing the abundance in this open, untouched countryside. After being in sub-zero temperatures in the United Kingdom, I was grateful for the warmth of the sun on my skin and as I stood there suddenly the reality of the magnitude of this journey hit me. Many tears flowed and were swiftly wiped away, only to be replaced by many more. I was alone, in a strange country without any awareness of how to speak the language, little awareness of the culture and I was already missing my loved ones.

Walking towards the far end of the bridge, I said a silent prayer to the Universe, asking for a sign to show me that I had indeed made the right choice in travelling here. As I looked below at the river, I could see a bird sat on top of a piece of wood by the shoreline. As I looked more carefully, I noticed it had a red breast and turquoise wings. It simply sat there as I watched in pure wonder. I hadn't thought to check the wildlife here in India. There was no doubt in my mind that it was a kingfisher.

If there could have been a more welcome sign at that particular moment, I honesty failed to think of one. I allowed more tears to fall as I welcomed this confirmation. For many years now the kingfisher had been very dear to me. It had appeared in many meditations and dreams. I had even called my second book 'The Kingfisher That Rocked'. I stayed on the bridge for quite some time simply watching this beautiful bird. It was at least twenty minutes before it opened its beautiful wings and disappeared within moments. Saying a quiet and very personal 'Thank you' to the bird, I recognised its departure as a sign that I should head back to my accommodation.

Chapter Twenty One

The following morning I was up early and once again had the honour of watching the sunrise. The colours were truly magnificent. I loved to capture them on my iPhone and was grateful that my son had added iCloud so that they would be saved easily. I was looking forward to my first full day here in India and despite experiencing numerous emotions; on both ends of the spectrum, I decided to fully embrace the new experiences that awaited.

Duncan made it clear that he was not a 'morning person' so I made a cup of Lady Grey and sat quietly absorbing the birdsong and watching the chipmunks dash up and down the trees. The accommodation comprised of five units in total. No-one else was awake yet and I was glad of this precious time to simply gather my thoughts. I could see the traffic a few yards away and was already adapting to the heat. I wondered what Duncan had planned for the day. I was acutely aware that there were certainly no nice looking shops, or inviting, clean looking restaurants within walking distance. I had no idea where the nearest beach was located and was grateful that I had brought some cereal bars to eat.

When Duncan awoke and the owner arrived later that morning, Duncan enquired about hiring a moped so we could get to know the area. I'd only ever been on the back of a motorbike as a passenger a handful of times in my life. This time I knew I would have to embrace the experience much more fully.

It wasn't long before we headed to the nearest beach and I was looking forward to seeing the Arabian Sea. Just as the previous days taxi drive had been quite an experience, so too was the journey to Arambol beach.

In the daylight I could now see the many temples and the variety of houses along the roadside. Passing the shanty town was really quite a shock. The shanties were made up of nothing more than simple wooden posts and tarpaulin. They were so tiny and I could see laundry hanging from a number of random washing lines dotted around the site. Many people; men, women and children alike, were washing themselves with soap and nothing more than a bucket of water. Small open fires burnt as they cooked various foodstuffs. I watched as children sat quietly watching the day go by. Rubbish seemed to be everywhere and as an onlooker there was a feeling of despair, rejection and misery about the whole camp. I was quietly reflective as I allowed humility to wash over my entire being. It saddened me greatly to witness this scenario and I truly wondered how in this modern day world this could actually be possible. I was also wise enough to know that I would no doubt visit many other shanty towns while on this pilgrimage. I sent a private prayer of love and compassion to the camp as we rounded yet another bend and Duncan narrowly avoided the potholes.

Turning right towards Arambol Beach, I was astonished once again to see the rules of the road being ignored. I knew for sure that I would never be able to drive here. The constant honking and sheer volume of people was once again overwhelming to each of my senses. There were no shops here along the roadside; simple stalls selling food and a huge selection of restaurants. The various outlets were selling clothing, scarves and jewellery. As we continued to drive towards the beach, the variety of aromas; different oils, incense, foods and spices amazed me. There were many offering a wide variety of teas and it really was quite an experience to witness this first hand. The number of people along the roadside and the way everything was so crammed together was certainly different from what I had known. It wasn't quiet and I was aware that as Duncan drove he seemed to need eyes everywhere as other motorcycles approached from all angles.

I was trying to absorb it all, the way the Indian people were dressed; so many were without shoes, very few wore any jewellery and even fewer had a genuine smile. The whole place felt odd; as though it could never experience peace.

The relief when we finally arrived at the beach and parked the bike was intense. The vastness of the beach itself and the clean, beautiful water was a sight to behold. Feeling the sand between my toes, I really appreciated the quiet here. There were many nationalities; Russian, English, Spanish and very few Indian people. I had expected to see Indian children playing on the beach with their families and enjoying themselves. My assumptions were so wrong.

We were both hungry and needed to find somewhere for breakfast. We saw some multi-coloured buildings in the distance and decided to head towards them. Trying to discern which were clean and would provide us with a healthy breakfast was not as easy as I had first thought. Some had staff wearing clean matching T-shirts and the tables too were clean and tidy. Some were clearly not as clean, plates and dishes were left on the tables and their clothes were dirty. Settling down and looking through the menu there was a wide variety of international cuisine. I was relieved that I didn't need to have curry for breakfast. I was amazed to find that most of the staff spoke good English and we managed easily to order what we requested. The food was delicious and the service was excellent.

Over the coming days I learnt quickly how to discern an acceptable food establishment from one that was border-line, or definitely un-acceptable. I learnt how to barter; the key was to halve their original price and work it out from there. I knew I always had to be prepared to walk away; or at least act as though I was.

My dear friend Angela had suggested I get some grapefruit seed extract from the local health food shop in England to add to the bottled water in India. It was known that often the bottled water had come from the tap or an equally unreliable source and the grapefruit extract would reduce the risk of parasites. I was vigilant as eight drops of magic were placed carefully into each bottle of water.

A few days later Duncan felt quite ill. It was not 'Delhi Belly' though he was weary, achy and had a sore throat. I needed to let him rest. I definitely didn't have the confidence to drive the motorbike and I desperately wanted to explore the area. Our accommodation was in a rural location and there were no local taxis here, the nearest beach was several miles away and with the heat, walking was not an option. When the owner of the property advised me that the buses ran every thirty minutes to Arambol, I was thrilled. I was also quite nervous. The price was fifteen rupees, equivalent to a few pence in pounds sterling. I was already amazed at the prices of food and most things here, but only pennies for a bus ride was astonishing.

The bus was packed with local people who looked at me as though they had never seen a white woman before, or was it that they had never seen a white woman on a local bus? I was amazed as the driver had people sat up in the front cab with him, the 'conductor' had the main door open continuously and actually hung out of it for much of the journey. The bus was filthy, the seats were so damaged I was astounded that the ride was reasonably comfortable, until we hit the potholes. Ouch! In England this bus would only be fit for the scrapheap. It was covered in dints, bumps, sharp edges and some of the windows were missing. Corners were a real experience and I had no choice but to lean into whoever I was sat alongside of. And yet here I was embracing it all. To be honest I loved it and was hoping to get used to it in the coming days; depending upon Duncan's recovery.

Being alone in Arambol was a real experience. I was still getting used to being stared at and randomly approached for a selfie. I was aware that the area had a reputation for pick-pockets and knew that I needed to be vigilant. Finding the café where we had eaten in a few days earlier, I sat happily watching the waves. It was a very busy place and people constantly walked alongside the restaurant towards Fresh Lake beach. I was learning to find my own inner quiet amongst all the busyness; it was quite a challenge. There were market stalls all the way along the passage and the bartering and chatter were constant. I decided after breakfast that I would walk to the next beach and find a quiet spot to meditate.

Walking past the many stalls with merchants desperate to sell their wares was yet another hurdle. It took me some time to assert myself and say a firm 'No thank you.'

As I neared the beach around the peninsula, several child beggars approached me with open hands and I was caught off guard. It was clear that one older girl; aged about ten years old was responsible for her younger sister. The whole scene saddened me greatly. These children were filthy, their hair so dirty and their clothes were little more than rags. They had no shoes and it was clear that they had a very tough life.

Some people have said in the past that I have a 'glass-face'. Whether my expression gave away my shock I will never know, but one of the restauranteurs quickly shooed the little ones away. I was stunned as I walked to the other end of the beach. How sad this scene was, a stunning beach, beautiful lake and children who were begging. I said a silent prayer for them and for their parents. Inevitably it made me think of my dear granddaughters back in England. I was grateful that they were not here to witness this scene. I allowed the tears to flow and breathed deeply, as I neared the other end of the beach. I was grateful that this beach was much quieter than the main one and sat on a rock whilst I gathered my thoughts.

As the waves washed ashore I allowed them to take away my sadness. How could it be that there was such a huge difference between those that have in this world and those that don't? Was it right? Was it down to politics? Religion? Education? Would there ever be a resolution in such an over populated country? I was wise enough to know that even if I had given them a handful of rupees the problem would remain.

Listening to the waves and the welcome quiet this beach offered, I decided to simply send healing to the whole situation and to my loved ones. Who choose to experience this extreme poverty? Where was their mother? Their father? Surely they had a carer?

Gratitude and humility began to fill my whole being and I was grateful that I had the means to pay for food, drink and accommodation. I knew there would be other occasions where I would come across beggars too. For now all I could do was accept my experience. I vowed to myself that I would allow myself time to cope with the future instances one by one.

Chapter Twenty Two

Water became a huge part of everyday life. Occasionally we would run out of water and when something so vital is taken away from you, you learn very quickly to value it even more. Having to carry huge water bottles back to the accommodation was most humbling. I was quickly learning about how much I had taken for granted in England. I appreciated a daily shower and I certainly appreciated a clean toilet too. I appreciated being able to boil water in the morning to make a cup of my favourite Lady Grey tea and I appreciated each and every meal I ate.

I realised now that I had to wash my clothes in the shower. It too was a most humbling experience. In this climate it was easy to get clothes dry and I was grateful to be able to hang the items on the veranda railing. One particular day I hung my knickers out to dry, only to notice that one of the neighbours in the first room had also done the same. She was a size zero and my 'Bridget Jones' were swiftly removed to dry inside the accommodation.

Washing my own laundry by hand touched me deeply. It brought a connection. I became more grateful for the water, soap and for my clothes too. I was ever grateful for the sun which allowed them to dry. I eventually found a washing line to hang them on which was high up in the garden. I was most grateful for pegs too and over the coming days life became very simple.

I felt connected here. Connected to nature and all things. I had become quite used to the monkeys by now and I loved to watch them climb and jump between the exotic trees. The speed and agility of the chipmunks amazed me and the various songs of the many different birds that sang happily throughout the day. I loved this location. It was perfect for me; the trees, the river, the lake and Mother Nature shining in all her glory. The beautiful blue sky added the last touch of icing to this sacred cake. Sunsets were truly spectacular and it was well worth the walk down to the bridge in the late afternoon. I gave a prayer of thanks daily for all that I was experiencing and for my loved ones. I was beginning to feel at ease with the bartering, the local bus rides and my confidence was growing daily. I had learnt quickly to expect the unexpected and this became my daily mantra, allowing me to ease into the many adjustments that I needed to make daily from my previously cossetted western life.

I had agreed to write blogs daily for my friends and clients back in the United Kingdom and was always grateful for their comments saying they had enjoyed a good read. I found a great solace here with the simplicity of life. There was no rush, no pressure, no diary to fill and no real plan for the day. Life was easy and the day was allowed to unfold of its own natural accord.

I was incredibly grateful for social media and WhatsApp, allowing me to contact my loved ones. I missed them daily though found that by sending love to them on a regular basis; just as I had done when my son Matthew first left the United Kingdom, life was much easier and missing them became more bearable. Some people say that we are all connected by a golden thread despite being thousands of miles away, I felt those many connections and I embraced each of them with gratitude and unconditional love.

I have always treasured being outdoors in nature and here I had the added bonus of the sun on my back. It was so welcome. Being able to sit outside comfortably in the warmth each and every day was blissful. I did miss the rain occasionally, although this climate certainly suited me very much.

Simply having the time to be here was peaceful and restful. My soul had called me to this place and I knew things would unfold in their own time. I listened daily for any synchronicities and coincidences too. In those many moments of stillness, I reconnected back to myself. There were no bills to pay here, no post to sort through daily and although I did receive the occasional request for my services; such as a healing, reading, or life-coaching session, I referred the clients back to the website where I had listed several other therapists who would take over from me.

In quiet moments, I loved to sit on the veranda overlooking the river, or in the bamboo hut in the garden of the eco-farm. In those first few days I reflected on all that I had left behind. My home, all my furniture, most of my clothing, my shoes, boots, coats, jewellery, books and treasured journals too. Here I was with a bright pink suitcase and a small bag. Sitting there smiling to myself I thought of the hundreds of books I had given away and remembered the initial pile of thirty two pieces of treasured literature, which I had intended to bring along. Inevitably they too had been given away.

Here in nature, life was so simple. I realised that I had already become used to this basic way of life. I actually felt at ease with myself and whatever the coming months would bring.

Chapter Twenty Three

There were other beaches in the surrounding area and now that Duncan had recovered, I loved riding with him on the motorbike to the many different locations. Feeling the wind against my skin brought such a wonderful feeling of freedom. We ventured to several different places and one day came across an old disused Portuguese fort. I felt the energies there were incredibly spiritual and as we walked around it seemed we were in the sacred temple of Angkor Wat in Cambodia. It felt as though every inch of the place was built on holy ground. I took time to meditate quietly. This place was touching my soul and this was one of the first spiritual experiences I had in India.

Later in the day we travelled further into the rural areas. There were so many small huts; humble houses and as we passed by many of the locals smiled at us. It seemed the further away from the main towns and places we were, the happier the local people were.

Paradise Beach was breath taking. Walking along the beach with the stunning turquoise water and the most perfect waves. I loved it and really felt the earth's beauty. It felt like heaven and earth kissed one another here. The banana and coconut trees behind us gave the whole scene the most perfect background. As I looked up, there was a make-shift wooden stand on the beach and there, once again was a kingfisher. It seemed to be waiting for me to acknowledge its presence. Gratitude and peace swept through my whole being and I will always treasure those memories.

I loved walking by the local river, maybe because it reminded me of the river near my home in England. Maybe it was simply because I love to be near water.

One afternoon as I wandered down to the bridge, I watched as the local men shovelled powdered cement from the wooden boats to the shore, where they made concrete blocks used as sea defences. Most things were done by hand here and this was no exception. After renovating several properties and happily getting my hands dirty, I know the weight of concrete. These men were working hard for their days' pay with sweat and toil in each and every loaded shovel. I was humbled to watch such simple manual labour which would have been automated in the United Kingdom. These men worked together quietly and with a tangible dignity.

Late one afternoon as we returned from the beach, I caught sight of many men washing themselves by the river. They wore only their undergarments and I could see their makeshift homes underneath the huge bridge. As I watched them they happily laughed and joked between themselves. I love to people watch. These men were clearly in the moment and thoroughly enjoying themselves. I honestly couldn't think of a time when I had seen such natural, genuine camaraderie amongst adults in England. I was saddened and learning that although to the outside world these people seemed so poor, perhaps in many ways they were so much richer.

India was already providing me with so much to think about. I was learning new things daily about their way of life and deepening my own sense of gratitude for everything I had. It wasn't simply about material things, it was about love and connection. I noticed that the children here rarely cried. I wondered whether it was because they were with their parents, or grandparents? Often they would assist on a market stall or watch their parents at work. I rarely saw or heard a child ask for anything and they seemed contented and connected to their families. I never heard a parent raise their voice to their children and wondered about comparisons with the western family system where the parents often seemed to be so stressed and tired. Had we really lost this natural connection and regard for simple family values? The elderly here all seemed to have a place in the community, even if they simply sat with the stall holder or watched over the children while the parents were busy working.

Along the streets men sat sewing on the old Singer sewing machines and again I saw only contentment on their faces whilst they worked. Despite the busyness and the noise all around me, I was learning to detach from the unnecessary distractions. India was beginning to grow on me and I surprised myself how quickly I was coping with so much change.

Duncan and I were still getting used to one another and I knew I needed time alone on occasions. I had become used to travelling on the bus now and loved to venture out alone. I felt it gave me courage while also challenging my confidence to further my experiences in new situations.

One day as I walked towards Sweet Lake, I noticed a really beautiful Tree Of Life pendant and as it was reasonably priced, I purchased it from a man with a lovely, clear aura. I asked him if he knew what its spiritual significance was and soon we were chatting about religion, philosophy and Sufism. He said he had a friend a few stalls lower down who was a very spiritual and knowledgeable man. He explained that he spoke better English too. Moments later the three of us shared tea and I was grateful for stimulating conversation and all the soulful wisdom we shared.

One man normally lived in Pushkar and the other Kashmir; they worked here for the holiday season. As he mentioned Pushkar, the Holi Day festival and the camel markets which took place there, I felt a powerful shiver of energy run down my spine. Duncan and I had already agreed to visit Ajmer.

When I researched the surrounding area I was drawn to Pushkar. It had a sacred lake so I would be near water. As I looked at the photographs of the town with the surrounding mountains, I experienced powerful déjà vu. I suggested to Duncan that I would love to stay in the town.

It was probably three hours later when I finally left and said 'Goodbye' to my two new friends. We had all shared so much and I will treasure my pendant forever. The story would unfold, although at that time I had no idea how.

As my confidence grew Duncan felt that it was time for us to make our way inland to Rajasthan. One Saturday morning we sat together at my favourite café and planned our next destination. We agreed it would be Ajmer and as we sat drinking chia tea we looked at the available public transport. There was no direct route and we would need to change trains at some point. Over ninety minutes later, we were still no further forward and although I had no interest whatsoever in visiting Mumbai, it seemed that unless we travelled from there by train initially to make the connection to Ajmer, then Ajmer would not be possible. Maybe we were meant to visit Mumbai after all? Was the Universe showing us a sign? We agreed that we would only book a hotel in the city for three nights.

Duncan had made it clear that once we moved more easterly we would be moving away from the popular tourist areas and therefore the language barrier would probably be more evident. He also stated that we might not always find such clean restaurants, only local street food would be available. It could mean that we might miss an occasional meal. My decision was already made, I would simply 'go with the flow.'

Chapter Twenty Four

The train journey was an overnight sleeper to Mumbai. Duncan was concerned that we might not get adjoining bunk beds and as we waited for confirmation that our seats had been booked, he was getting increasingly nervous for my safety; especially if we were in separate carriages. I was simply in a state of complete trust, despite knowing that the Indian trains were often overcrowded.

The availability of the seats was confirmed only hours before we were due to leave Goa. Taking the local bus to the nearest town in order that we could catch the train was quite an experience. The scenery was stunning, as most of the journey ran alongside the local river. One of the local Indian women fell asleep on my shoulder and I felt most humbled to be able to allow her some much needed rest. She looked exhausted and I wondered about her life. I knew many of the people here worked long hours doing hard, manual labour and I felt a deep and genuine compassion for her while I listened to her gentle snores.

Arriving at the railway station I was surprised at how modern and clean it was. When the train eventually arrived, two hours later than expected, I was amazed at its length. There were at least twenty carriages. It was packed and knowing it was an overnight sleeper, I knew that no matter how strong my pelvic floor muscles were, I would have to use the toilet facilities at some point.

The journey would be approximately twenty-six hours. It would also mean that I would have to eat and drink whilst on board too. I loved it. Although our seats were in a separate compartment, a kindly Indian man agreed to swap his bunk so that I could take the top bunk whilst Duncan slept in the bottom bunk. I used my rucksack as a pillow. The most important things I needed were stored safely in there; it was the only way to ensure its' safe-keeping. The bunk was comfortable enough and I felt both safe and somewhat contented to be sleeping amongst the locals. Sleeping proved to be no easy task with so many other passengers snoring loudly and many train personnel passing through the carriage throughout the night.

In the morning various vendors moved through the train with a most welcome chia tea and a variety of Indian foodstuffs. I loved watching the morning sun rise through the windows of the train. As we passed through various towns it was interesting to see how the locals were starting their day. Seeing the wildlife in their natural surroundings was almost surreal; seeing these vast open spaces and the antelopes, gazelles and giraffes enjoying their freedom. I could never imagine ever wanting to visit a zoo again in my whole life.

Finally arriving in Mumbai we walked to our hotel from the railway station. There were so many people milling about and I really did not feel safe, nor was I at all comfortable. There was a most strange and decidedly peculiar atmosphere here and it was certainly nothing like the restful place where we had recently stayed. The streets were filthy, not to mention the smell. The people here stared at us; or rather at me in particular. It made me feel unnerved. I was deeply saddened that this place seemed to have no soul; or was it simply this particular area? It was something which I have certainly never experienced before and I hoped that I would never experience it ever again.

My back was aching and was becoming more and more painful, as I pulled my suitcase and carried the hand-luggage. I was close to tears due to the pain, not to mention this desperately uncomfortable feeling. Tuning in more deeply to what I was experiencing, I felt there was something else which deeply unsettled me, though at the time I wasn't able to put my finger on it.

As we rounded the next corner, people were washing themselves on the streets with nothing more than a bucket of water and some soap, while dressed only in their underwear. Some were still sleeping on make-shift beds and others slept under nothing more than a small piece of tarpaulin. Although I had to agree that I was tired from the train journey, there was something deeply disturbing to each of my senses in relation to everything here.

When we finally arrived at the hotel, I was so relieved. It looked lovely on the on-line photographs. However, when we arrived we found that it was right in the middle of the busy, main street. I was amazed at how over-crowded and noisy it was. The volume of constant traffic amazed me and the noise of the honking was almost unbearable. It had already become somewhere I would never forget and certainly not for the right reasons.

Once settled in the room, I was grateful that the noise from the air-conditioning unit almost drowned out the sounds from the city streets below. Looking out of the tiny window in the room, although I could see for miles, I couldn't see any trees at all. It was a sprawling mass of concrete and it seemed there was very little feel or vibe to this place; apart from the craziness and its disturbing resonance.

I will always make the most of whatever situation I am faced with though this was proving to be quite a challenge. After resting we decided to look for a restaurant. As we walked the narrow streets, there were market stalls everywhere. The noise and the general busyness was really quite an exhausting experience to me. There were fruits and vegetables, chickens and to my absolute dismay, goats. Some were headless. Their heads were in a metal box underneath the stall. It was all becoming a bridge too far for me. I had already become aware that there would be little, if any respite here.

Our trip was a spiritual pilgrimage; I certainly wasn't feeling anything remotely spiritual or peaceful here. It was a noisy, smelly, dirty hell-hole. I was glad we had only booked three days here. I was already counting down the hours to our departure; especially as I knew Pushkar would be much quieter and I was looking forward to seeing the mountains that surrounded the outskirts of the village.

That evening, over a meal, we discussed visiting Elephanta Island the following day. I was relieved to be getting away from the city and hoped that the hour-long sail to the island would restore of my inner peace. The following morning we walked through the streets to the harbour. The whole place was busy as people were getting ready to sell their wares at the markets. Seeing the chickens being removed from their cages so that they could be transported to the markets was heart breaking, so few had actually made the journey. The stench was unbelievably disgusting and it was all I could do not to vomit at the sight and smell of these poor wretches.

Arriving at the harbour was both a relief and a surprise. The boat to Elephanta was quite clean and I was grateful there was a toilet on board. The harbour was full of so many boats, layer upon layer of them going further out from the coastline. It was several minutes before we were freely out at sea. The water was filthy and I was deeply saddened that an ocean here could actually be so heavily polluted. How incredibly foolish and naive I had been to expect to see dolphins swimming here in beautiful turquoise blue waters.

Arriving at the island I was looking forward to be visiting a spiritual site. Indeed, after the steep hike up to the caves I was not disappointed, they were lovely and filled with huge statues and intricate carvings. There was definitely an air of a profound spiritual presence here. When we visited the last few caves which were to the far left of the main caves and clearly lesser known, there was a tour guide chanting the 'Om'. As the sound echoed inside and outside the caves, even the least spiritually aware person would definitely have to agree that something could be felt. We meditated, together and then separately. I allowed the whole place to bring me much needed peace. I was delighted that we had been guided to come here and it certainly was a lovely experience. We both wondered what it would be like if a group of monks chanted together. The original power of the place must have been truly awesome.

Whilst here in Mumbai, I really wanted to visit the beach. I knew we would be heading inland and it would be the final opportunity I would get to paddle and feel the sand beneath my feet. The next morning, bright and early we visited a Sufi shrine along the coast, which I had intuitively felt was part of this pilgrimage. It was lovely and a remarkably peaceful place despite the many other tourists. Prayer is a meditation to me and allows me to go inwards and simply be still in my own space. I sat quietly for several minutes with the other women before I went to join Duncan. Before I had reached the exit of the shrine, I was asked for selfies. I had no idea whether it was because I am white; or whether it was because my hair is dyed blonde. It was several minutes before I escaped. I couldn't see him anywhere and as I stood waiting on the steps more selfies were requested. I was becoming concerned as to his whereabouts when I intuited that I should return inside the sacred area. He was sat drinking coffee waiting for me. Within minutes the two of us received more requests for selfies. Eventually we managed to escape. We were both hungry and certainly ready for some lunch.

Mumbai is such a huge city and we were content to walk and explore the area by foot. Duncan and I had laughed often as he said that eventually I would become fed up eating so much curry and other Indian foods. I denied this as curry was my favourite food. My son-in-law Russ is a wonderful chef and often made me the most delicious curries whenever I visited. However, less than three weeks into this pilgrimage I had to admit that I never wanted to see, taste, or even smell another curry ever again. When I telephoned Russ to inform him of my demise he was in hysterics of laughter.

Duncan and I noticed a Domino's pizza outlet and agreed to have lunch there. It was ridiculously expensive and although I genuinely thought I would enjoy the whole aroma, taste and experience that only pizza, or Italian food can bring, I honestly did not. Did I have marsala-ruined-taste-buds? I will truly never know. After this experience the restaurants we found had such a wide variety of international foods that I could enjoy a wonderful selection of healthy meals; and the occasional curry.

Eventually we arrived at The Hanging Gardens and I was pleased to see greenery once more. My naivety had once again got the better of me. I had expected to see such a massive explosion of colour with all the exotic plants, trees and flowers that this hot climate could sustain. Perhaps it was also a combination of having visited many of the botanical gardens in the United Kingdom. However, here there were only a few simple trees and flowers. Nonetheless I was pleased that I could enjoy the greenery and the quiet of the park gardens.

We could see the beach below in the distance and as the day was getting even hotter, I was looking forward to paddling; if not swimming. It was quite a long walk down to the beach and we found a local café for some welcome refreshment in the shade.

Arriving at the beach I thought that I was seeing things as the sand seemed to be black. As we got nearer it was clearly a mass of litter, plastic bottles and wrappings. I was so close to tears. How could it be that this piece of coastline was so neglected and absolutely disgusting? Walking further towards the main business area it seemed to get even worse and the stench was unbelievable. As desperate as I was to paddle, there was simply no way I was happy to walk on the beach here. Pushing my personal feelings aside, I sent a quiet healing prayer to this place where nature seemed to have been forgotten. As we turned the corner of the beach, there were children playing and laughing by the shoreline. I thought I had already learned to expect the unexpected here. I clearly had so much more to learn. The whole scene left me with an intense awareness of cause and effect; how we as a population share the same planet and we really do impact each other. There are no excuses for this insanity.

Ever grateful that we would soon be leaving, on our final evening after a meal, I asked Duncan if he would mind if we simply walked. I wanted the exercise, despite the fact that we were in a concrete jungle. I dearly missed the trees, the river and the whole ambience of Goa. As we walked over the railway bridge, there were beggars in the street with nothing more than a piece of cardboard, a few blankets and a cooking pot. It was heart breaking and as a mother, I was deeply touched and troubled by the whole scene. When I saw the beggars daughter squat on the pavement as they had no toilet, I could feel my tears and my chest tightened. The little girl was roughly the same age and physical build as one of my youngest granddaughters. The thought of two-year-old Raphena living in these squalid conditions was unbearable. My feet couldn't carry me fast enough across the street and back to the hotel, though trying to get through the crowds was quite a challenge. I had certainly had enough of this God forsaken place and was so glad we were leaving the following afternoon.

In the morning we decided to walk around the local area. As it was a Sunday we thought it might be quieter. The streets were not quite as busy though they were still busy enough. The stench as we turned one corner almost made me retch. There was a man going through a huge pile of rubbish, which was about five feet high. He was looking carefully through everything to see if there was anything that he might be able to sell. The whole scene was so abhorrent in this modern age and quite surreal. Once again I was shocked and saddened.

Mumbai taught me many things; humility and gratitude certainly. Upon leaving I thought of my favourite restaurant; 'Mothers Kitchen' in Goa where I was always welcomed and made to feel so comfortable. There healthy conversation and laughter flowed in abundance. Sadly, I had never experienced anything like that in Mumbai.

Chapter Twenty Five

Arriving in Ajmer was such a relief, not just because I looked forward to a decent nights' sleep after travelling on the overnight sleeper, but I was desperate to see the countryside again. The sun was already setting at we stood in the car park of the railway station waiting for our taxi. Pushkar was approximately a thirty minute drive from here through the mountains. I knew it would be dark when we arrived and although I was excited to see the sacred lake, it would have to wait until morning. I was exhausted from the train journey, which had been delayed by more than two hours. And the experiences in Mumbai had certainly taken their toll. I was still digesting and reflecting on the many learnings that travelling had brought to my awareness thus far.

There was something else which I felt in both my heart and my soul. It felt like excitement, though it was on a scale that I had never experienced previously. It was very powerful and I felt it in my very core. We were due to visit the Grand Master Sufi shrine and I wondered if that was the sole reason. Perhaps I would meet someone really spiritual here? Pushkar was a spiritual place after all with over fifty ghats (steps), leading down to the sacred lake and hundreds of temples. I could do nothing more that trust my intuition; which was the whole reason I was here.

The guest house wasn't easy to locate and the relief when we finally arrived; much later than scheduled was intense. The owners had thought that we were a 'no show' and had given our room to another guest. The alternative room was not acceptable and I complained diplomatically. The next room was slightly better and the owners apologised profusely for the confusion. We were promised our original room would be ready the following morning.

India had already proved itself to be quite a challenge. We had learnt that sometimes we had no other choice than to accept and be patient. Duncan and I agreed to make the best out of a bad situation and hoped that tomorrow would be a better day.

The following morning we ventured out for breakfast. We had been given simple directions on how to find the lake. This was my priority; even if Duncan required more rest and needed to return to the guest house. It seemed the journey had really taken its toll on him. It was a welcome relief to find a nice, clean eating place here. After breakfast I was delighted as it was finally time to visit the sacred lake. I could feel its energy as I neared the steps situated on the corner by the market. I heard shouting as I walked towards the lake. As I turned around it was clear that the man was telling me to remove my flip-flops. Thinking it seemed a rather strange request, I initially ignored him. However, as I neared the lake he shouted even louder. I removed my simple footwear swiftly. He had by now walked over to me and advised me where to place my flip-flops; away from the lake on some of the upper steps. I was really taken aback; not only because I had been shouted at whilst in a semi-meditative, sacred place, but also because clearly it was inappropriate to walk around wearing, or even carrying my footwear.

It was hardly the start I wanted on my first visit to the much awaited lake. I had longed to meditate here and now felt quite discombobulated at both his tonality and his abruptness. I breathed deeply, acknowledged and released all the toxic emotions before I found a quiet spot.

Moving closer to the water, I was deeply saddened to see that it was green and evidently quite gloopy. Regardless, the huge black fish were abundant here and thousands of little fry were swimming about. My mantra, 'expect the unexpected' came to mind and softened the disappointment of not seeing a beautiful, clean and healthy looking lake.

As I meditated I knew that I had definitely been here before and as the déjà vu flooded in to my conscious mind, I simply sat with the many images and the emotions it brought. I already loved this place and I knew without question that we were certainly meant to stay here, rather than Ajmer.

Eventually I made my way back to the guest house and rested for a while. The owners had by now sorted out our room and I was grateful that it was clean and much larger too. It opened onto a courtyard with other rooms opposite, small gardens in the middle and a tiny temple at the bottom.

I felt quite settled here which was such a relief after Mumbai. We had booked to stay here for a week, although we had agreed that if we liked it we would stay for longer.

After we had settled in one of the staff asked if I would like to see the rooftop. I always love to view places from a vantage point and hoped that the view from here would be amazing. It was well worth walking up the three flights of stairs and this time my personal mantra lived up to its name in a great way. There were mountains almost all the way around. We were so close to the Thar Desert, the sparse greenery in the distance was reflective of the barren location. One mountain in particular drew my attention and I vowed to myself that I would visit in the coming days. It was away from the main town itself and would definitely be quite a walk from here. Energy seemed to radiate from it. It was a perfectly clear, extremely powerful white light. I had never seen anything quite like it before in my life and it felt as though it was calling me; although I knew there was no urgency to visit. Once again I was trusting that I would know when the time was right.

From here the other buildings could easily be seen, many with very impressive roof tops, although sadly I was unable to see the lake itself. I was already in love with Pushkar. The rooftop seemed the perfect place to meditate and journal, possibly even to write my next book. I wondered what the sunsets would look like from this beautiful vantage point. I made a vow to myself to come up here as often as opportunity allowed.

The streets of Pushkar were very narrow and there were vendors on either side. It seemed that every inch of space was used to sell or advertise their wares. It was certainly unlike Goa in many ways. It was quieter and yet still very busy. The restaurants and cafes seemed cleaner and the selection of food on the menus was much more varied; with a huge range of international foods included. The vendors didn't seem quite as pushy here to sell their goods which was a most welcome relief. The main road was quite away from the centre of town. I was relieved that the streets were so narrow; there would be no motorbikes, nor Tuk Tuks here. Some of the cows were huge and it was often quite an effort to manoeuvre around them. I was shocked when I almost got run over by a motorbike, I moved quickly aside only to watch as the driver narrowly avoided an oncoming Tuk Tuk. My illusions of peace and quiet disappeared in an instant.

I looked forward to seeing the lake every day as I found it sustaining in many ways. I felt a deep connection to Mother Earth here on a daily basis and perhaps more importantly a deepening of my connection to myself. Each day I sat and meditated by this sacred lake.

As a well-known pilgrim site, it could be incredibly busy with people travelling from far and wide. Luckily it was large enough for me to find another suitable spot away from the masses. No matter where I sat, either on the north, east, south or west-facing steps, I always felt it was an honour to be here and found such pleasure in the simplicity of simply being. I have always loved water, here the water had a magical quality about it. There was something else, something deeply touching and sacred.

I loved to watch the beautiful pelicans floating and diving majestically in and out of the water. They weren't here every day. Some days there were so many of them, others so few. I often wondered where they would go considering the location was so close to the desert. One morning I was thrilled when I noticed terrapins basking by the lakeside. I was always surprised to see the abundance of fish; despite the state of the water. I loved to watch them, especially when they jumped quite high out of the water. Tourism and deforestation in the surrounding areas had taken a heavy toll on the lake, reducing both the water levels and the water quality. I noticed that the lake was replenished daily with at least one hose pipe.

I would often sit and imagine it as it would have been in its original state with water that was almost thirty feet deep, clean and vibrant with life. Most days I experienced déjà vu and I knew I had been here before in many other lifetimes. It all seemed so familiar, comfortable and homely in its own way. Sitting quietly I wondered whether I was imagining it as it was in its original state or whether I was actually re-remembering it as it had once been?

The lake was surrounded by temples and I loved them. Each had its own unique design and I appreciated the Hindu architecture and the many statues of the different Gods, not to mention the many elaborate carvings. Combined with the smells of the incense and other fragrances, I was looking forward to more spiritual experiences here. I had visited several different temples in the United Kingdom. Here there were hundreds and I hoped I would find spiritual people; maybe yogis perhaps in the town.

Looking at the map of Pushkar, it seemed a simple lay out. The streets surrounded the lake and then the town expanded outwards from there. Over the coming days Duncan was quite unwell. He spent several days resting and sleeping which meant that I had much needed time alone. I had to keep reassuring him that I was very comfortable walking into the town alone and felt perfectly safe. The accommodation was located within a few minutes' walk of the centre and by now I was used to the poor state of the roads and the pavements in India. I soon learnt to negotiate my way around the streets, knowing the busier places and seeking out the quieter ones.

It was a lovely market town and it didn't take me long to get used to the many vendors. Duncan wanted to get well as quickly as possible and felt that by eating fruit it would speed up his recovery; allowing his body to detox. Too weary to venture out, I was happy to walk into the town to purchase whatever he needed. The stallholder who sold local fruit from his simple wooden cart spoke very little English. We always smiled as we somehow managed to communicate; through sign language and usually much laughter. With his missing teeth and tanned skin, he looked quite the part as he stood on the corner with so many different coloured fruits and vegetables to sell. I watched him most days as I had to pass by his stall to get to the main street of the town. He rarely exchanged so much as a smile with any of his other customers. He always looked so tired and weary; it was as though he'd had a hard life thus far. And yet, as soon as he spied me he seemed to light up like a beacon, with a huge, genuine smile that melted me. I was learning to deepen my compassion and connection towards these humble people.

The old man who I purchased bottled water from daily always had a most welcome smile for me too and I was grateful that he spoke excellent English. He reminded me of my beloved grandfather which was a massive additional bonus. We would chat about his family, the history of the town and so much more. I found that if I asked the various vendors where they had learnt to speak English it would often open the conversation to many interesting topics. I was always open to listening to their stories; even if I couldn't always be sure what it was that they were trying to communicate. It all came down to connection; the simplicity of human touch which Western society seems to have long forgotten.

Regardless of whether I was purchasing their products, I would always greet each of them with a 'Good Morning' and a smile, whenever I passed. Every day the same elderly lady sat in the same black dress with her many baskets of flowers making garlands of fresh marigolds and beautiful red roses. She sat by the steps which led directly to the lake from our accommodation. I loved to buy her flowers and she often gave me some extra rose petals too. The smell of the roses always reminded me of England and my dear mother and grandmother, who both loved to grow roses in their gardens. I found it very comforting to pray, or meditate with the flowers, and then sprinkle them into the water as an offering of appreciation.

Each and every day my focus; appreciation and gratitude deepened. I was grateful for my beloved family, my dear friends, my health and that I was able to do this pilgrimage. I was grateful for all the experiences that had brought me here, for each of the new experiences, challenges and opportunities which were allowing my soul even more expansion. The fact that I felt so incredibly comfortable and at home here accentuated each of these feelings.

Most of the other vendors in Pushkar spoke fluent English which certainly added to the mix of my continued contentment. I also felt safe and I now realised and appreciated the magnitude of its importance even more so after my experiences in Mumbai, which had left me feeling completely unsafe.

The feelings of appreciation seemed to reach a high peak daily as I watched the sun go down. It was a combination of bliss, peace, hope, connection, trust, faith and grace. Each and every day that initial feeling of powerful excitement in my soul, that I had experienced a few days before we had arrived, made its presence known to me. I still hadn't managed to establish exactly what it related to, I simply acknowledged its presence and enjoyed the feeling.

Over the coming days I spent several hours a day alone. I was by now comfortable deciding which restaurants were clean enough to eat in and where I felt settled. One particular day I ventured into town using a different route and ate at a 'new' restaurant. I was sitting alone when three Australian ladies started chatting to me. After we had all finished our meal one of the ladies approached me. She had a lovely light aura about her and I was grateful of the company. She explained that they were travelling here for her birthday. As the conversation progressed she explained that she was weary from her career as a nurse and knew she needed more from life. I could see clearly that she had many artistic and creative abilities in her aura. I asked her what she loved to do and she radiated such light when she told me that she loved to paint. She said she'd always been creative and thrived on her artwork. Her aura dipped as she went on to say that it was several years since she had produced any of her paintings. I gently suggested that possibly she might like to seek out a creative group once she returned home. She started to glow again and mentioned that her husband supported her in whatsoever she wanted to do lovingly. I was so pleased that the resolution to her dissatisfaction was such a simple one. As the conversation continued I asked about her husband. She radiated such a beautiful array of bright colours from her aura as she mentioned how they had first met and his marriage proposal. Love is such a powerful thing and

I felt honoured to share a beautiful afternoon with Claire. We promised to keep in touch.

My favourite café up to this point was called 'The Laughing Buddha'. It was situated at the other end of the main street and I was always grateful of the walk. It was only very small with some tables indoors and three tables on the balcony. The first time I visited I spotted rose lassi on the menu. It was absolutely delicious and I was soon quite addicted. The rear wall was full of pictures, photographs and quotes to encourage people to follow their heart and soul. I loved it here and was even more delighted when I read that they gave a percentage of their profits to a charity that provided education for young girls in India. The food was always beautifully presented and it stated clearly on the menu that all the salad was washed in bottled water. The ice too, was also produced from safe water; rather than tap water. I loved the view from the balcony overlooking the busy streets and enjoyed watching the monkeys jump from amazing heights between the many balconies and rooftops. I felt privileged to be here and always felt that every visit was such a treat.

Duncan and I had now spent almost a month together and we were both in need of our own space. One Sunday afternoon I ventured out alone; leaving Duncan to play his guitar and enjoy some time to listen to music. The last few weeks had been intense. He wasn't used to living with anyone and had felt particularly over responsible for my welfare. After living alone for many years whilst I was in the United Kingdom, I desperately needed time and space away from him too. I was really comfortable exploring the town alone now and felt safe whenever I ventured further than our usual haunts.

I was thrilled when I found a café which I hadn't even noticed in the previous week. It was situated towards what I now called the 'top of the town', as it was quite away from the accommodation. The lady who came to serve me seemed familiar and I could see from her aura that she was very spiritual. I also felt that I knew her, although we had definitely not met before. I was now quite partial to lemon, ginger and honey tea and once she had taken my order we chatted easily. She had only recently started the business and we discussed her many ideas and thoughts on how to encourage more customers. She wanted to install a water filter with reverse osmosis; to reduce the use of plastic bottles, get rid of the aluminium pans and would no longer be serving Coca-Cola or Pepsi. She had already spent several days cleaning the whole café and intended to have an art gallery with a quiet space for people to read spiritual books too. I was so impressed with her ideas. Her English was very clear and she explained that she had originally been a journalist and then decided to start a business of her own.

She was from a large Indian family and two of her many sisters lived in the United Kingdom. One was based in Glastonbury so I had a great opportunity to open up the conversation further in relation to spirituality. She smiled as she then realised that I too was very spiritual and we both agreed that we knew, we knew one another. I am always so grateful for stimulating conversation and we chatted at length about many diverse aspects of opening and living from the soul. She mentioned the Nakshatras and as I had never heard the term before, she kindly explained what they were. Taking my date of birth, she established which Nakshatra related to me and kindly leant me a much valued book on this vast subject. It's a most comprehensive and most interesting concept. I love to learn and expand my awareness. I was most delighted to find out more.

In between serving her other customers and making their food, I felt honoured when she asked me to sample items from her menu. She wanted a Westerners point of view; was it too spicy? Too rich? Not tasty enough? She clearly appreciated my opinion. I felt spoilt and I loved tasting the variety of foods; some of which I had never tasted before. The restaurant started to get many more customers than normal that afternoon and I smiled when she mentioned that I was a good omen for her business. I was welcome here anytime.

As I watched the monkeys jump from the branches of the nearby tree onto the balcony where I was sat, Anita swiftly gathered up her huge bamboo stick to warn them off. I assured her that they were not bothering me and when an adult monkey sat across from me at the table, the whole experience felt very humbling indeed. An English woman and her companion; the monkey, over a pot of tea; quite a surreal combination. The other guests were not quite so accommodating and were clearly scared of the monkeys. I offered my reassurance that they were merely being inquisitive and would soon return to the tree, or another rooftop.

I had thoroughly enjoyed my afternoon and as she was closing the restaurant for the day, she invited me to join her to take a look at the view from the rooftop. What a vantage point it was here. I felt truly honoured to share this beautiful landscape with her. It was at the opposite end of the town and so far away from the rooftop of our accommodation, it was such a different view. It was also much higher so I felt really privileged to embrace these moments to share a truly stunning landscape. I was surprised as the building was closer to the lake than I had realised. It all looked amazing, the lake, the temples, the mountains and so much more. We had time to chat further and I asked her the significance of many of the Hindu gods and enquired about which temples to visit, or attractions I should see locally. That precious afternoon will stay with me forever and was to prove its weight in gold in the coming days.

I have done earth healing as long as I can recall and often collect stones from most of the sacred places that I have visited. I had several with me and was guided to meditate with two of them the next day. Duncan joined me as we sat in silence meditating and placing our prayers of thanks and our dreams into the stones. It was Monday the 25th February. Almost a month since we had left England. The prayers felt incredibly powerful and as I threw my stone into the sacred waters, I prayed that my dreams and wishes would be heard and answered. We stayed by the lake for at least an hour after meditating. As the sun shone down and the cows, dogs and pigeons wandered nearby I felt a deep peace descend around me. I had accepted that whatever would come, would come. We had both decided that tomorrow would be a great day to travel to Ajmer and visit the Holy Shrine of the Sufi saint of all saints. Today felt as though it was a very auspicious day and I hoped that tomorrow would be too.

The following morning we were up early to catch the local bus to Ajmer. My inner child wanted to sit near the rear of the bus and I was looking forward to travelling through the mountains. The bus was packed with locals who stared at me in particular. Although I was used to being stared at, I still found it unsettling.

Like the buses in Goa this one was old and rickety; well past its sell by date. Sitting at the back proved to be a bad idea as the shock absorbers were broken. As my rear end endured shock after shock, feeling each and every pothole along the way, I made a mental note to sit towards the middle of the bus next time.

As we pulled into Ajmer bus station the smell of urine made me almost heave. Up to this point I hadn't seen outside urinals and I have to say it was quite a shock. The combination of the heat of India and the general lack of sanitation didn't quite provide the welcome I thought it would.

Our only view of the city of Ajmer had been from the railway station when we had first arrived here. Today we had decided to enjoy the other sights of Ajmer and visit the shrine after lunch. We stumbled upon a lovely local park that was well kept. It was bliss to actually see green, healthy grass. Walking barefoot on it brought a wonderful feeling of deep gratitude and connection. Up to this point I knew that I had missed the English countryside, though the simplicity of walking barefoot on the grass was very moving. I delighted to see the flowers, trees and the shrubs here. It was as though I was seeing them for the very first time in my life.

It all seemed surreal, as if it were in its own portal. And yet here it was within a city that was crazy busy with seemingly endless hordes of people, constant traffic lining the dirty streets and the rivers filled with every kind of rubbish; rather than fresh, clean water.

Once outside these walls there were horses and carts; some animals were clearly healthier than others. When I saw a horse with deep, open sores I was most saddened. These people had priorities to their family first, veterinary bills were probably last on the list. My experiences whilst travelling were bringing me so many examples of opportunities for learning acceptance, rather than judgement and criticisms. My compassion and empathy were deepening daily, as was my sense of appreciation and gratitude for so many things.

We would soon be visiting the Sufi shrine of a man who was described as the saint of all saints. This was truly humbling amongst such adversity. I felt myself move from my head-space to my heart as I had looked forward to this visit for many months. Stillness returned and I breathed deeply, focusing on how beautiful this city could be with some very simple changes.

My dear friend Saleem had arranged for us to meet his nephew, Noor at the shrine. I was certainly amazed by the size of the sight, located in the centre near the busy markets. It was huge. Upon entering I could see there were many people sitting with their feet in sacred water. Noor kindly showed us around and Duncan and I were amazed that there were two massive cooking pots used to cook rice for the many hundreds of pilgrims that visited daily. Although I felt an incredible peaceful energy as we neared the shrine, once we were inside I was most disappointed to discover that as it was so busy, I felt very little. We were jostled in and out of the shrine so quickly that there was no time for even a quiet prayer. I was so surprised, if not a little upset not to feel more than I did that afternoon. I had wanted to come here for so long and the feeling of excitement I had felt for almost two weeks now, didn't seem to be linked to the Grand Master at all.

Duncan and I sat by the water after thanking Noor. We said our good-byes as we explained that we would like to sit and meditate quietly around the shrine. There were some steps which led up to what seemed to be a quiet room which, amongst this chaos, seemed a perfect place to pray. Using sign language, I asked the guard if we could go inside to meditate. I was amazed that he allowed two Westerners to enter and finally, we were able to close the doors on the noise and the crowds below. I sat under a most stunning, glittering chandelier. As I closed my eyes to meditate, I felt my dear friend Saleem stood right next to me. I was amazed at the clarity, I could see his facial features so clearly. The bright, white light that then surrounded me was intense and brought a deep serenity to me on that Tuesday afternoon.

Returning to Pushkar as the sun was beginning to set, I was so grateful that we had agreed to stay here rather than in the city. We were pleased to find a lovely restaurant close to the bus station for our evening meal. Within minutes it began to rain very heavily and it actually became quite cold. The owners swiftly lit some logs and made small fires in old tin barrels. I was amazed how all the Westerners soon gathered around to keep warm. Conversation flowed easily between us fellow travellers that evening.

When I text Saleem later that night to share my experiences I described the room where we had meditated. He explained that it is used as a stage during performances. As a musician and famous Sufi singer, he loves to sing the sacred songs and chants that have been handed down through his generations in that very spot.

Chapter Twenty Six

The following day as Duncan and I shared breakfast, we agreed that we had enjoyed the previous two days. However, now we both needed our own space again. I was more than happy with this decision and respected that he was still very over-protective for my safety. I promised that I would return about six o'clock; around sunset.

It was Wednesday 27th February, we had been travelling for one day short of a month together. Early afternoon I set off with a spring in my step, smiling to myself as I walked towards Anita's café. I was really excited at the thought of sitting enjoying great food, great company and a wonderful, inspiring book to read. As usual it was hot and sunny with the temperature in the twenties.

I felt so contented as I walked to the 'upper part' of Pushkar. As I passed 'The Laughing Buddha Café,' my feet suddenly stopped. I really was surprised, as this hadn't been what I intended for my quiet, peaceful afternoon. I had already experienced several close shaves with a motor bike, a Tuk Tuk and a pushbike. Being rooted to the spot right in the middle of the main street in Pushkar was certainly not advisable. My concern was growing as my feet remained fully rooted. I was unable to move in any direction whatsoever.

I have been clairaudient all my life and I clearly heard a very loud voice;

"Go back, you need to go to 'The Laughing Buddha Café'. Go and enjoy a rose lassi." I really wanted to see Anita and was rather perturbed to be distracted from my plans. I questioned the decision;

"Can I not go later, I really want to spend time with Anita?"

"No...NOW" was the most abrupt, direct and truly unmistakeably commanding reply. Over these years I have learnt not to argue with my intuitive nudges and as my feet were well and truly rooted, I had no other choice. I was surprised to say the least as usually I would have a knowing or an intuition as to why I was being re-routed.

The café was a definite favourite of mine. I had a great fondness of the rose lassi here as it was certainly the very best in the town and I had become quite partial to it. It was situated on a main junction. A prime spot for people to watch from the balcony which I found to be an absolute joy. Unfortunately, there were only three small tables outside. Being one of the very best eating places in the town, it was usually very busy and I wondered whether or not I would be lucky enough to get a table; otherwise I had already decided that I would have to sit inside.

Arriving upstairs, the table to the left was occupied by a couple who were clearly enjoying their delicious lunch. The table in the middle was occupied by a gentleman and I breathed a welcome sigh of relief when I saw that the table to the right was free. The waitress came to take my order and profusely apologised as she explained that the electricity was off, therefore the menu was limited. This was quite normal in Pushkar and although it was an inconvenience, it had simply become a part of my everyday life in India.

She was clearly stressed and in order to keep things simple and to reassure her, I asked her what food and drinks were available, rather than asking which were unavailable due to the Indian heat. I decided I would make a choice from there.

I placed my order and sat happily watching the monkeys and the general hustle and bustle from the busy streets below.

"That was very English of you." The man on the middle table spoke very softly and gently with a distinct Southern English accent. There were many white people here in the town and so many different nationalities; French, German, Spanish, Russian; though very few English. I was very surprised to hear his voice, especially after rarely seeing any other English people: (besides Duncan), after almost a month. I hadn't conversed with any of them.

I had known there was something most captivating about his presence as soon as I had arrived on the balcony. I was somewhat surprised by the ease of the opening to our conversation. I decided to follow his lead in this discussion; being acutely aware that my spiritual guides had stopped me for a reason. I felt so at ease with him. I was truly amazed at how comfortable I felt in this man's presence. Being so sensitive and seeing auras, I am very protective of my own space. I am an incredibly private person when I need to be. The fact that I was happy to converse spoke volumes as to the level of trust that was instantly established between us. My reply was very simple;

"I certainly wasn't going to make her life any harder, she was clearly distressed and anxious."

"Yes you were incredibly diplomatic. Two German ladies came a few minutes earlier and left the moment she explained that the menu was limited. They never even said a word to her and they were quite rude."

I felt a connection when I first saw him. Now that we had actually spoken, within that very instant there was such a huge and most tangible relatedness. His voice seemed familiar to me in some way; we certainly hadn't met before.

Words cannot describe the ease of the flow of our conversation from that moment. Several minutes later, more customers arrived so the gentleman asked if I would mind if we sat together on 'my table' in order that the ladies could have 'his table.'

"So, what brings you to India then? Is it a spiritual pilgrimage? Are you studying The Vedas and The Upanishads?" I surprised myself as the words just seemed to flow freely from my mouth without any hesitation.

"Yes, in a way." He looked over at me with a depth of knowing in his eyes which spoke volumes. It is something that I have rarely seen.

"You certainly have done your research." There was something very deep to this man and his presence. I was rather taken aback as the feeling of comfortability was growing by the minute as we sat together. I had no inner knowing that we had had past lives together though I knew, I knew him. The conversation continued as I explained that I had read The Vedas and The Upanishads many years ago. I thoroughly enjoyed the wisdom on each and every page. The beautiful simplicity of their teachings regarding living a heart-centred, fulfilling spiritual life touched me. We both expressed our agreement and our love of these sacred texts. It was obvious he was intelligent, witty, and very knowledgeable. I loved each and every moment as we shared our thoughts about religion, philosophy and spirituality. Our views were incredible similar and heart-centred.

The conversation progressed as he could clearly tell that I had a northern accent. We exchanged the usual pleasantries about where we were from In the United Kingdom and general information relating to our backgrounds. When the waitress returned, we ordered another drink and agreed to share cake. As we looked into the streets below Jay made a very poignant statement;

"India challenges every one of your belief systems doesn't it? People living in poverty, the over-crowding, children begging in the street and yet such powerful religious beliefs and traditions. Not to mention the rubbish and the political nonsense." His passion for the Indian people was evident and I had to agree that this pilgrimage had already brought many learnings to me about their culture.

"Where does the resolution lie with all the overcrowded-ness and the huge contrast between the wealth of the western world and this absolute poverty? Where do we start to correct this disparity of wealth? Even the people of India have such differences between the wealthy and those less fortunate in their culture. Do you think there's an answer?" I had no answer to his question. Neither of us did. How could this duality of worlds exist on the same planet? It was crystal clear that we both held similar amounts of compassion for Mother India and its many peoples.

Witnessing the extreme poverty here had clearly touched him as much as it had touched me. We both agreed that travelling and being amongst the local people, was much more real and certainly eye-opening. He was clearly a passionate and ethical man, with a very simple belief system that was similar to mine. We discussed our experiences, as we had both been travelling for several weeks and had visited different places. Sharing our stories, intertwined with our philosophy was most interesting.

About an hour later the waitress came to say that they were closing for the afternoon siesta; she was very politely asking us to leave. Neither of us had realised how long we had actually been chatting, everyone else had already left. I had already mentioned Anita's café and he was happy to wander up there and share the rest of the afternoon with me.

Anita was delighted to see me again and pleased when I introduced her to Jay. We both ordered lemon, ginger and honey tea. As we sat watching the monkeys once more jumping across the rooftops, the simplicity of sharing easy conversation and the comfortability of being in each other's company was thoroughly enjoyable. Jay asked what plans I had for the following day. I explained that I didn't make plans and was happy to go with the flow. He asked if I would like to meet up late morning and spend the day with him. My heart leapt. The answer was a very resounding 'Yes'.

I was absolutely delighted that we would be spending more time together, rather than just this one incredibly special afternoon. Deciding where to meet was hilarious as there were temples everywhere and we couldn't really agree to meet at the steps as there were so many. Nor could we say we would meet near the fruit and vegetable cart, as there were numerous ones dotted around the town. I was much more familiar with the layout of Pushkar town and as we clearly couldn't decide exactly where we should meet after much laughter and even more sharing, we decided that we would meet up at the bridge on the other side of the lake.

Anita came to chat with us in between serving her customers and as the conversation flowed I mentioned how much I had enjoyed our time on the roof only a few days earlier. She promptly suggested that we all go up onto the roof together. I was amazed to find that there was an even higher vantage point than the one she had kindly shown me days earlier. Her friend kindly brought up two bamboo high-backed chairs and we felt like royalty as we sat in the most comfortable seats watching the world go by.

We had such an amazing view over Pushkar, the rooftops and the surrounding mountains. It was such a wonderful experience. I felt very honoured and most humbled. I really didn't want this afternoon to end and took great solace in the fact that I would be seeing him again tomorrow morning. Simply the fact that he had requested to spend more time with me, made it clear how much he too had enjoyed our precious afternoon together.

Time had passed so quickly and we were both amazed; if not slightly disappointed when the sun began to set. I had already explained that I was travelling with Duncan and had promised to return by six o' clock. From our vantage point it was such a perfect way to end the afternoon. It was certainly something that I will never forget.

Jay agreed to walk me back to my accommodation. I truly didn't want this moment to end. As we turned the corner to the guest house, I felt so sad knowing we would soon be parted. Hugging each other good-bye, he allowed his hand to run the length of my right arm and then very slowly over my hand and my fingers. As we said 'Good-bye' I realised that I felt he was a part of me.

Duncan was asleep when I returned and I was incredibly relieved that I didn't have to talk to him. I was also a little angry too, as I wished I had spent more time with

Jay. I made my excuses as I rushed to the front of the building, though could see no trace of him in the tiny street. My heart felt as though it was doing somersaults in my chest, as I tried to digest the afternoons' events. Needing time alone, I decided to spend a few minutes on the rooftop. I couldn't believe the strength and the power of the connection between us. Tears fell as I realised I was already in love with this man, who only hours earlier had been a complete stranger. The emotions were very powerful and this had been completely unexpected. Blissful doesn't come close to the feelings I had experienced from the very moment we met. I was already counting down the hours to eleven o' clock the following morning.

I smiled from ear to ear whilst I was having a shower the next morning. I had left some washing soaking in the bucket overnight and once dressed, I loved to put the damp clothes on the washing line of the rooftop to dry. The views from here were spectacular at any time of the day. I felt I was honoured to witness life from here.

We had arranged to meet at eleven, it was now a little after eight. I still had almost three hours to wait. As I bent down to lift the bucket with the water and the washing, I felt my back click. The pain was barely tolerable as I tried to rinse the clothes under the shower. I had suffered two prolapsed discs in my lower back about five years earlier and was so grateful that although very painful, it was not excruciating. As I limped up the stairs and hung the washing out to dry, I wondered what Jay would think when he saw that I was struggling and in extreme pain whenever I moved.

I had to leave earlier than I needed to that morning. I found it hard to contain my emotions as I was so excited. Once again, I had agreed with Duncan that I would return around six o'clock. It was approximately a fifteen minute walk to the bridge where we had arranged to meet, though I left about forty-five minutes earlier. I found it very difficult to contain the ecstasy that I knew awaited me when I met him again. It had been well over five years since I had been in a relationship and felt such intense feelings for anyone. I was still surprised at the power of our connection and the ease of the previous days' conversation. I had no expectations and was happy to allow the day to unfold. We had agreed to have breakfast together. I was more than happy; as Jay had seemed to be the previous day just to share time together again.

I was delighted when I saw him walking towards me in the distance. I could clearly make out his huge smile. Then he disappeared. I was surprised that after a few moments, he still hadn't reappeared. I realised that he must have been 'grabbed' by one of the priests from the ghats and taken for a blessing down to the lake.

Sure enough, as he appeared I got dragged off to the lakeside too. The priests were very capable of holding your attention and forcing the blessing on you; regardless of how much you bleated that you were meeting someone and had already had too many unplanned blessings to count.

The relief when I finally mounted the steps and we hugged one another was very powerful. It was clear that he too had been looking forward to seeing me. The connection was very strong as we walked to the nearby restaurant. Jay noticed my slow paces and realised I was in pain with my back. Sitting in the gardens of the café whilst ordering breakfast, Jay kindly rolled up his shirt and placed it in my lower back. It certainly helped my posture and eased the pain a little. Conversation was easy once again and we discussed so many aspects of spirituality; rather than religion. The look in his eyes spoke volumes to me about his feelings as we shared our personal circumstances. The similarities between us were numerous.

Jay suggested that we go to his hotel, rather than walking around the town, in order that I could rest my back. I was grateful for his understanding. My back had bothered me since I first arrived in India. I assumed it was due to lifting and manoeuvring the luggage. We were more than happy to chat and listen to music. The coincidences and synchronicities continued to unfold and we were both surprised by how many there were in both our personal and working lives.

Time passed so quickly and inevitably the sunset approached far too soon. Jay kindly walked me most of the way back to the guest house and parting once again was even more difficult than it had been the previous day. We had agreed to meet the following morning. Once more I found myself counting down the hours.

Sitting with Duncan that evening and sharing a meal was difficult. I didn't feel I could share what I had experienced with Jay and I didn't wish to do so either. I had respect for this man sitting across from me at the restaurant table, but I secretly wished I was sat with Jay.

Two blissful days had passed and Friday would be our last meeting in Pushkar. We agreed to meet at the bridge once more the following morning and again I had left the guest house far earlier than I needed to that morning. I couldn't contain my feelings. I bought some flowers from the old lady by the steps and she smiled a knowing smile at me.

I sat quietly by the lake holding the roses and the marigolds. I was grateful that I wasn't interrupted by one of the many priests, as I quietly prayed for the strength to cope in the coming days. Jay was leaving early the following morning and I was dreading being here without him. The thought of being parted was very painful; despite having known him for only two days. I knew and felt the power of our connection.

Duncan and I were due to leave Pushkar the day after Jay's departure and in a strange kind of way I was glad that I wouldn't have to face being here any longer than just one day. Jodhpur was our next destination and we would be travelling by train on Sunday. Jay had already visited the 'Blue City.' He had clearly loved his time there visiting the fort and the markets. It gave me some solace that I would be able to imagine him with me when we visited.

I checked the time as we were meeting earlier today, it was almost 8.45am. There were still a few minutes remaining before nine a.m. I sat on the steps wondering how I would cope without seeing him every day. Being in the moment is a challenge to master, though I was determined to enjoy each and every moment that today would bring. My back was still incredibly painful, although it had certainly eased considerably from the previous day.

Once again Jay approached me and he was smiling a huge smile. As we kissed and greeted each other I knew for sure that this man had certainly got under my skin. Our embrace felt so powerful, we were completely at ease with each other. We walked hand in hand, making our way to the restaurant overlooking the lake. We sat together sharing breakfast and thoroughly enjoyed watching the wildlife in the trees overhead. Our conversation flowed as the connection deepened. There was now a tangible love between us that I had not experienced to this degree before. I loved being with this man. I loved everything about him; his touch, his eyes, his voice and being with him was awakening something deep within me that I hadn't experienced for many years. I was surprised that the power of the love didn't frighten me in any way; especially knowing that we would be parted very soon.

We had agreed that we would venture out of the city today and visit the surrounding mountain that I knew I needed to visit. The light and the energy that I had noticed every time I had seen it from the rooftop was incredible. Neither of us had any idea of the road layout. We simply trusted that we would find the mountain road easily. Walking hand in hand, passing the many locals who were farming or mending their vehicles, they were obviously very surprised to see us. White people evidently visited this area very rarely. It was nice to be away from the hustle and bustle of the town. The countryside had a much clearer energy and using the mountain as a landmark it wasn't long before we arrived. We loved the change in the scenery. It was so different to the concrete jungle we had become used to. The scrub on the mountain side was a welcome sight as were the exotic desert flowers. There was a huge energy surge here and a feeling of deep peace. We knew there might be snakes in the area so we were cautious as we approached. This was not a place to hike up the mountain, nor to sit on a rock in the sun.

As we turned a corner, we were surprised to see a car park and several buildings directly ahead. There was no-one around; or so it seemed as we neared the buildings. We could smell incense and soon realised it was the site of a Hindu temple. As we approached it seemed quite out of place. It was certainly off the beaten track and unless you knew its exact location, finding it would be quite difficult.

We found a suitable place to sit, welcome of the respite after having walked in the bright sunshine and the heat of the late morning. Although sore my back had certainly eased. It was so quiet here. Within minutes the priest walked up to us and asked if we would like to view inside the temple. He seemed to have appeared from nowhere. We were both wise enough to know that we were meant to come here and followed his welcoming gestures.

The temple was simple in its design, the altar most basic and yet I felt it was probably more powerful than any I had seen in Pushkar. He kindly allowed us a few quiet moments to ourselves. Several minutes later he explained he needed to lock up and was looking forward to his lunch. He passed us a tiny card detailing the temple. We thanked him and were happy to offer a donation. He quickly disappeared and we were truly amazed and questioned whereabouts he could have possibly gone.

We were very contented to sit and be that particular morning. Being in each-others company was bliss enough. I had purchased some oranges earlier and we sat happily sharing them with the monkeys. It was such a simple joy to watch the baby monkeys approached with such extreme caution when Jay placed the segments a few feet away.

How long we stayed by the mountainside was testament to our connection and friendship. The moments of silence we shared were so comfortable and we both knew we were blessed to be there. Lunchtime was approaching and we reluctantly left this beautiful, remote location to head back to Pushkar.

We found our way back easily enough after passing the camels at the top end of town. It was clear that we were both saddened by the fact that this was our last day together and yet somehow we managed to maintain a very balanced mood between us. Sharing lunch was wonderful and we were glad that we had placed our order moments before a large group of Japanese tourists arrived. We watched the tiny birds as they flew between the trees and laughed at the fact that we had both ordered the same items from the menu. The synchronicities and similarities between us were becoming more evident as the day progressed. As the heat of the day was reaching its peak, Jay wisely suggested we return to his hotel to rest.

Van Morrison has always been a favourite singer of mine and Jay introduced me to a few songs that I had not previously heard. The wisdom in the lyrics held deep, profound wisdom. 'Enlightenment' touched me deeply, as did 'Into The Mystic'. The day had been so simple and the sharing so wonderful. Sunset was nearing and neither of us wanted to be parted. Jay had previously requested to meet Duncan and I suggested that we walk up to the guest house together. I would then ask Duncan to join us, otherwise we would find a local restaurant ourselves.

Duncan suggested a Tibetan restaurant which none of us had previously sampled. It was clean and the menu quite reasonable. Jay and I were acutely aware of the little, very precious time we had left. Immediately after the meal we said our 'Goodbyes' to Duncan and walked around the town. The atmosphere at night was totally different to that during the day and I was pleased I was not alone. We enjoyed a coffee in a café which overlooked the lake from a high vantage point. With little artificial light the stars looked stunning against the black background. I felt blessed to be here enjoying the moment as we discussed the power of our connection on every level; mentally, physically, spiritually and emotionally. Jay took my hand as he promised to keep in touch, looking at me with a deep, profound and abiding love in his eyes.

Those last three hours together were incredibly special. We decided to walk around the sacred lake which was clearly so dear to both of us. It looked different in the evening, lit only from the lights from each of the temples. Watching the light reflect on the water was stunning and beautiful. I found it comforting to a heart that I thought would surely shatter into a million pieces, now that our parting was imminent. It was so much quieter here in the evening and we were both grateful for the peace we shared. We were amazed when people who passed us kept requesting us to remove our shoes; even when we sat almost out of sight around a concealed set of steps. Eventually we gave in to their requests and carried our footwear as we continued to chat and share. Jay knew he had much to sort when he eventually arrived home. I was still being moulded by this spiritual pilgrimage and we both understood and respected that I had to complete this journey.

As we kissed and enjoyed our last hug at the end of the tiny street that led to my accommodation I suddenly found my trust was evaporating from me. Uncontrollable tears fell and I was sobbing. Taking my face in his hands, Jay reassured me that he would keep in touch and reminded me that time is not linear. He also reminded me of the power of astral projection and that none of us are ever really separated as we are all joined by a golden thread.

"This is not good-bye, we can pick this up anywhere in the world."

As we released our final hug and I walked to the doorway of the guest house, I turned to see his smiling face watching to ensure that I arrived safely. Duncan never uttered a word when I returned sobbing.

I was completely devastated at our parting and had no other choice than to trust that this love would be strong enough to endure the coming months. Leaving Jay that evening was definitely one of the hardest things I have ever done in my life.

We both knew we had been put together for a reason. We also knew that we respected each other completely. The fact that we both had our individual roles to play within our light work meant that we needed our freedom; at least for the immediate future. Duncan and I had a six month visa to travel India alone, not to mention Nepal, Bali and New Zealand. We had no idea when we would meet again and neither of us felt it necessary to make arrangements for the future. We had met purely through synchronicity and trusted that if we were to meet again the Universe would make it so. All we had was the present moment.

Chapter Twenty Seven

The rain hammered down the following morning. The wind howled relentlessly. It was so cold. Duncan and I walked through the streets of Pushkar. They were empty that morning. Even the cows had huddled together for shelter and warmth. The whole place felt soul-less without Jay's presence. The weather was truly appalling and it was the first day that I felt really, really cold. I wanted to cry as the rain droplets pelted against my skin; at least the rain would have disguised my tears. I was acutely aware that my heart felt cold in Jay's absence. The weather mirrored my emotions.

My back was extremely painful. I winced with every single move I made. Duncan and I had planned to visit the local temple which was situated on top of the mountain surrounding Pushkar. The weather had turned for the worst and the cable cars had been grounded for the day. The whole scenario reflected my feelings as the wind howled and the rain continued to fall heavily.

Knowing we would be travelling again the next day; that lifting the suitcase and the hand luggage would probably aggravate my back again, I suggested that a massage might be a good idea. The weather was so poor that there was very little else to do. As we sat waiting for a massage there was a sign hung on the wall that read;

'NOTICE'

- Respect the Holy Lake and the town.
- Photography on the bathing ghats is prohibited.
- Ladies and gents should be properly dressed while walking through the town.
- Do not kiss or embrace while walking through the town.
- Fishing and Hunting is prohibited in Pushkar.
- Any kind of drug and alcohol is prohibited in Pushkar.
- You should open your shoes 30 feet above from the lake.

The last one read;

- You should follow all the above rules otherwise you are responsible for your punishment.

The focus of my thoughts was inevitably on Jay. He would have laughed at these rules; especially number four. We were both guilty as charged. I photographed the notice and made a mental note to forward it to him later in the afternoon. Reading it had managed to put a smile on my face at least.

I wondered how he was feeling. Had he managed to get the transport he needed? Was he missing me as much I was missing him? Did he intend to message me? How did he feel about returning home? He would soon be heading to his home country after travelling Mother India for six weeks. We would soon be thousands of miles apart. How would I manage to get through this? How would I cope if he didn't contact me? I hoped the massage would not only ease my back pain, but also quieten the 'Monkey Mind.'

Mother India had called to his soul in November, roughly around the same time that Duncan had asked if I would like to travel with him. We had both visited several of the same places and he had recently left Jodhpur before arriving here in Pushkar. We were due to arrive in the city the following day.

Now all I had was trust. I had agreed that I would message him and wondered if he would reply. He had promised he would after all. Would I ever hear from him again? It was all I could do knowing that I had to push the negative, doubtful, nagging thoughts away.

Duncan was wise enough to keep his counsel, recognising that I was unusually quiet. When he did eventually mention Jay; knowing how much I felt for him, he casually explained that he had lost touch with so many people over the past few years during the time that he had been travelling outside of the United Kingdom.

I thought it best to keep my opinions and emotions to myself. I was far too fragile and far too distraught to enter into a conversation that would no doubt conclude with Duncan needing to be proved right. I simply did not have the strength. Nor did I have the inclination. Instead I decided to focus on all that Jay and I had shared. I hoped this would allow trust to bring us back together again at some point in the future. I hoped beyond any words that the love, hope, faith and trust would be enough to create a reality where we would indeed meet again. I sighed as I knew I had to resign myself to the well-known saying that 'only time would tell.'

Chapter Twenty Eight

The following morning we packed early in order to catch the bus to Ajmer. Instinctively I looked for Jay as we neared the bus station. With all the luggage and Duncan's faithful guitar, it was clear that we needed a taxi. There was no point even attempting to board the already overcrowded rickety bus. I was most grateful, as I was still in physical pain in my back not to mention feeling lost too. The thought of facing people made me feel even more crushed.

Ajmer railway station was absolutely packed as we waited for our train. I found it strange that I was now accustomed to this manic chaos and was no longer intimidated, nor frightened. The noise alone was deafening, not to mention the sheer amount of people rushing to get past us.

Finally sitting in our allocated seats on the train, I felt incredibly emotional. I took some reassurance that Jay had already visited Jodhpur and in a strange way it brought me a feeling of connection with him. I was also relieved to know that the city would be much quieter than Mumbai.

There was a lovely young couple on the train seated next to us. They had a new-born baby girl. As usual Duncan climbed on the top bunk of the sleeper carriage and slept most of the journey. As I watched the couple, it was obvious that they were very much in love. I was touched and felt incredibly honoured to witness them passing the baby between themselves. (I never saw a pushchair in India; the babies and toddlers were always carried by their parents). They acknowledged me with great kindness as I smiled over to them. I was so surprised when the father spoke to me in English. I was inevitably reminded of my own treasured granddaughters, whom I missed daily. They were several thousand miles away and combined with the fact that I was missing Jay, I was grateful when the babies' aunt exercised discretion when she saw me crying. Wiping my tears away, I managed to ask; without showing too much emotion in my voice, how old the baby was.

She had been born only six weeks earlier. We had now been travelling for five. As the mother offered her to me, I gladly accepted. It was an honour. As I held this precious child in my arms something began to still inside me. Her presence as a newly born child seemed to represent a part of me. I felt that this pilgrimage so far was bringing me a re-birth, a re-set and a deepening connection to all things; particularly myself.

When I eventually handed her back to her besotted mother, I listened happily as she sang Indian lullaby's to her as she rocked her to sleep in her arms. I was aware and so thankful for the many things that touched me in those precious hours we shared on the train journey. I will be forever grateful.

Jodhpur was chaos itself when we arrived later that afternoon. The exits on the railway stations in India are not clearly marked; or at least not in English. Lifting and pulling my suitcase was agonizing as we attempted to force our way through the masses. I was so relieved when the taxi finally arrived. The physical pain alone had left me exhausted. The emotional pain still lingered, threatening to engulf me on occasions.

When the driver stopped outside the city walls, he tried to explain that no cars were allowed beyond this point, as the roads were far too narrow. Duncan was furious and we were both agitated that we now needed to hire a Tuk Tuk; knowing that it meant unloading and re-loading the luggage, not to mention bargaining once more in order to get a reasonable price.

The hotel was situated on a main road, right in the centre of Jodhpur. The traffic was constant here and the noise pollution horrendously loud. The honking was awful as we desperately tried to unload the Tuk Tuk; which was holding up all the traffic. As the endless stream of motorbikes sped past, I truly wondered if I could cope in a busy city again. The streets here were so tiny. I knew I had to find the strength to adjust to another environment and quickly.

The hotel was very basic. When we were shown to our room we explained that it was far too small for two people, two suitcases and a guitar. It was situated right above the main road and the noise was deafening. He swiftly showed us to another room at the rear of the property. I failed to notice that it had no window in either the bedroom or the adjoining bathroom. I was pleased to see bunk beds and settled my personal belongings on that side of the room. I didn't feel comfortable here at all. I decided under the circumstances I would give myself time to adjust and hoped that I would feel better after a good night's sleep.

Although there was a restaurant on the rooftop of our accommodation, we decided to walk a short distance around the corner to a nearby hotel. The name 'Heavenly Blends' made me smile and the decision to eat there was made. As we ordered our meal, I happened to look to the left and was truly amazed to see Jodhpur fort in all its glory. It looked splendid against the evening sky with spotlights positioned at various intervals. I knew instantly that I had seen this fort before in another more ancient time. It was truly majestic and breath-taking. I loved feeling its connection and was glad as it seemed to bring peace to my troubled heart.

As we sat waiting to order, I remembered that Jay had glowed when he spoke about the 'Blue City' and the fort. Now I could see why. I looked forward to visiting there in the coming days. It was even more beautiful than I imagined. Even the photographs, I had seen, didn't do it justice. There was a power and tangible splendour to this place. I was already looking forward to seeing the fort in the daylight.

The menu was extensive and the food was lovely. Aladdin the manager introduced himself and I was delighted that he spoke excellent English. Conversation flowed easily between us. Looking up at the stars before we left I said a quiet personal prayer of thanks.

The following morning I ventured onto the rooftop of our hotel. I was so excited to see the fort and the surrounding area in the daylight. It was very early and I was pleased it was relatively quiet. The view was truly spectacular. The fort was huge and spanned the length of a huge cliff edge. There were some towers and it was clear even from such a distance, that the workmanship was exquisite. I was in awe of this place and such craftsmanship. The planning and construction of the whole project must have taken years, if not decades. To the right hand side was a white temple and from my vantage point I could see a palace way off in the distance. It was clear why it was named the 'Blue City' as many of the buildings were painted blue. They looked stunning in the early morning sunlight.

Standing on the rooftop looking out over the concrete jungle was very thought provoking. It was a city which was far bigger than I had first thought. There was obviously much to explore and appreciate here.

I suddenly realised that I was really hungry and was pleased when I noticed a waiter. As usual, I ordered a chai and a paratha. I sat quietly alone at the table wondering what the coming days would bring. By now it had become clear that Duncan was not a 'morning person,' unlike myself. I had learnt to leave him be for at least an hour or maybe two, before he was ready to start the day. I was quite keen to take a look around and was certainly gaining my confidence in India. I sat quietly and meditated before breakfast arrived.

Duncan was still asleep when I returned to the room, so I returned upstairs to the rooftop again, taking my laptop. As I re-read my first novel; 'Reflections Of A Hummingbird', I remembered how much work, commitment and passion I had put into her creation. I loved this project when I was writing her and was so delighted that I had continued with a determined effort to finish the book. Recollecting the memories of the numerous times that I had very nearly quit writing her made me smile. As my first novel she had proved to be quite a challenge as the characters and the storyline unfolded in my mind. I was humbled at my own work and pleased with my effort too. It had taken me so many years to acknowledge my skills as a writer. I was deeply humbled. Writing had brought passion into my life in a way that I could never have anticipated. I sat experiencing the extreme gratitude and appreciation that I had been able to share with so many people who had enjoyed reading my first work of fiction.

Many of my friends and clients had hinted that I would write another novel while I was away; potentially about my adventures in India. My intention was to write the sequel novel to 'Reflections' and then maybe write about my pilgrimage. Sitting in a quiet space, I was touched when I realised how much passion I truly possessed for the written word. The reason I had written my first book was simply to inspire people. Now, several years later; having published four books I have had the pleasure of inspiring hundreds, if not thousands.

My thoughts changed from the book to gratitude in all aspects of my life. The sun felt warm against my skin and I was grateful to be here. I was missing Jay though confident that he would indeed be in touch. I realised that something had shifted in me during the train journey, or was it being here in Jodhpur? Maybe it was fear that had melted away? Maybe it was simply honouring the trust and the loving connection between us? I decided it really didn't matter in the greater scheme of things and was happy to enjoy the peace and the stillness it brought.

Duncan and I wandered down to the market later that morning. It was so busy and overcrowded. The narrow streets meant that we had to navigate our way carefully with every step as sewers lined the side of the roads here. The market was far bigger than either of us anticipated. There were spices, teas, fruits, vegetables, shoes, trainers, clothes, pots and pans but when we saw old irons, radios and other out-dated electrical equipment I was really surprised. It made me realise how much I had taken for granted in the United Kingdom. It was obvious that they were grateful for everything they had here and were happy to re-cycle as much as possible.

There was a real buzz around the market place though we were very aware of potential pick-pockets. I loved getting amongst the people and seeing how they lived in their day to day lives. Everyday brought a new level of humility.

Returning to the hotel I suddenly realised there were no windows and the room made me feel claustrophobic. The whole place didn't have a positive atmosphere at all and there was a heaviness and a dullness to it. I left Duncan to sleep and wandered to 'Heavenly Blends,' with my laptop.

I loved sitting in the sunshine and enjoyed the spectacular view of the fort and the surrounding area daily. I knew how lucky I was to experience this journey. Later that evening Duncan and I found a new restaurant and we thoroughly enjoyed the meal. My back was once again very painful and the waiter kindly offered me some ice wrapped in a towel to ease the pain. It was a random act of kindness that I can still recall fondly; at least it allowed me to sit more comfortably to eat.

Combined with the searing heat, the itching from the numerous mosquito bites and the pain in my back, sleeping was proving to be difficult. I made a promise to myself to find someone who could massage it the next day.

The following morning I ventured alone to 'Heavenly Blends', while Duncan slept. I always loved chatting to Ali and his staff. We all shared conversations about religion and the Indian way of life. One morning, as we all sat together, he shared that he had been in love with a woman who was a Hindu. He was a Muslim which meant that they could never marry. I was deeply saddened as he explained how much he loved her. It was obvious throughout the conversation that he was still very much in love with her. I felt honoured that he had chosen to share his story with me and it touched a deep part of my soul. He was separated from the woman he clearly loved; as I was separated from Jay. I was blessed that they had welcomed me into their private lives. There was a huge trust between us all and I was so grateful for all we shared in subsequent days. Listening to their stories of love, life, travel, work and relationships felt like an honour.

I was ecstatic when I noticed there was an email from Jay in my inbox. He had finally arrived home after many hours travelling and was pleased it was so green and blissfully quiet. I cried with relief. My heart and soul were finally at peace. He was safe and our connection could continue - even if it was from a distance.

There were far fewer cows here in Jodhpur than there had been in Pushkar, which surprised me in a strange way. The dogs in India were far less healthy than those in the United Kingdom and I truly disliked seeing any of the animals here scavenging through the many piles of rubbish. There was no infrastructure in India; at least not in the places we had visited so far. Rubbish was simply left littering the city.

Walking around the many streets I had noticed a female dog feeding her three puppies. They were only weeks old and I loved watching them play amongst themselves daily. They looked reasonably healthy which was a blessing here. One morning after another wonderful chat and great food at the restaurant, I happily wandered back to the hotel. I was amazed when I rounded the corner to see a car in the street. It was such a surprise and I wondered how they had even managed to turn into this tiny road. As I kept close to the wall I noticed the black puppy; one of the litter right under the car. He turned to return to his mother and his siblings. There was an Indian man a few yards in front of me and even from a distance, I could see that he had noticed the puppy too. The inevitable happened and the beautiful puppy was squished under the wheel of the car as it drove off. The Indian man turned and we both shrugged our shoulders at one another. He too was clearly upset and we both knew we could do nothing more. He waited for me to catch up to him and we both shared a knowing expression of sadness mixed with a feeling of 'maybe it was for the best after all'.

Very early the next morning I cried when I saw the pups limp body at the other side of the road. I'll never know whether the mother, or a kindly passer-by moved it. Looking more closely, its sibling was snuggled into its lifeless body. The whole scene was incredibly touching and it reminded me that love is universal; between humans, animals and all creatures. The image will stay with me forever.

I desperately wanted to visit the fort and Jay had suggested I look out for the singers around the archways who performed their music. It was so much bigger than I had anticipated. The entrance gate towered above me. The stone arches were magnificent.

I truly loved it from the moment I neared the fort in the Tuk Tuk. The heat of the day was not due for a few hours, so I decided to explore while I could still enjoy the relative cool of the early morning.

Lined with cobblestones and the most beautiful stonework I felt truly blessed to be here. Now I was actually inside the fort, I could at least begin to understand the magnitude of the work needed in its original design and construction. I was truly amazed and appreciated each and every minute detail. I looked around for the musicians, as Jay had suggested, though those I saw certainly didn't fit the description that he had shared.

I wandered up to the fort walls anticipating what the view would be like. It took my breath away for several seconds. It was absolutely spectacular. The city was a huge sprawling mass. The desert surrounded the fort in the far distance. I could clearly see why it was called the 'Blue City.' The colour looked amazing against the backdrop of the ordinary concrete buildings. I felt truly blessed and it was such a powerful, sacred moment in its own magical way. The sprawl of the city stretched as far as the eye could see and was far bigger than I had first thought. How long I stood there admiring the view I will never know, as thoughts of how the fort had been essential in protecting against the invading armies amazed me. I absorbed it all, the architecture, the history, the breath-taking views and the barren desert in the distance.

Although I had a map of the layout of the fort, I followed my intuition which led me towards the edge of the complex. The pathway and the stairs led to another path which I followed to a simple, yet beautiful temple. Many of the temples here had an armed guard; (which initially freaked me out when I had first seen them). Now it seemed perfectly normal that at least one guard should stand at the temple with a huge rifle. This guard was certainly not like any other I had seen. He was a gentle soul with a genuine smile. He had a light-coloured aura with flecks of gold. It was rare to see such colours; representing a powerful, deeply spiritual, connected person. He was here because he was genuinely spiritual and enjoyed this sacred space. I was touched as he smiled at me.

I watched the priest as he gave blessings for the offerings on the altar and was delighted to see that his aura was also large and bright. I felt honoured when I caught his eye and he smiled at me. Had he seen my aura? I was a white woman in a Hindu Temple after all. I was always surprised to see a bright, white, sparkling aura. This man was genuine and very heart-centred. I prayed in my own quiet way and was feeling a genuine peace and connection to the Divine in this sacred sanctuary.

I hadn't realised the time; it was almost eleven. There were only a couple of people here and when the security guard requested me to ring one of the four bells I was delighted. It felt such an honour as I rang the bell in tune with the other three people. Each of us smiled at the other; the priest and the guard too. The whole scene made me feel very welcome and privileged. As the bells rang out, I could feel the Divine connect with each one of us. I knew that my prayers were being heard. It was a truly blessed and most sacred moment. After the bell ringing, I moved to the rear of the temple to meditate and to digest the power that those precious minutes of bell ringing had brought to me.

I allowed many tears to fall following that incredibly simple, yet most powerful experience. I was forever grateful that I had tissues in my handbag. This was a truly sacred place; it was certainly not what I had expected to find in a fort where battles had been fought and lives lost over the centuries. When I looked out over the surrounding gardens I was even more amazed to see a beautiful statue to the God Shiva. I could feel the elementals and I delighted in their presence.

Grateful that the tears had now stopped, I was busy taking photographs when the security guard approached me and kindly offered to take mine with the sacred statue in the background. I felt humbled once again to experience the power of human generosity and the power of the human touch. It was an act of random kindness from one human being to another; without expectations, conditions or attachments. As I thanked him and started to make my way towards the exit, an elderly lady who was at least eighty years old offered me some chai tea. I had grown very partial to chai by now and was certainly grateful for her offer considering the intense heat of the day was now becoming almost unbearable. She refused to let me pay for the chai. It tasted absolutely delicious. Had she seen the energies and all our collective light? Her smile was so touching and it shone through her eyes. I felt blessed to have shared such a powerful experience in such a short few minutes. I bowed to her and gestured 'Namaste'. Both the guard and the priest smiled a knowing smile at me as I mounted the exit stairs. More treasured memories.

Duncan and I were happy to continue to give one another space. He was much less concerned about my welfare now as my confidence was increasing. I felt more comfortable in India and was confident enough to barter alone. However, coping with the local men staring at me was still a work in progress.

We had visited several temples in the city centre though he mentioned that he had found one that was situated on the edge of the city. My whole body was covered in Goosebumps before he had even suggested that we visit.

The following morning we set off after breakfast and walked out of the city. It was so busy and I was once again surprised at how many people there were here in India. Crossing over the dual carriageway was quite a challenge and Duncan had taken to holding my hand; rather than waiting several minutes until I felt safe enough to cross. I found the whole scenario of crossing the road hilarious. The Tuk Tuks, bikes, honking and general bedlam of the whole transportation system in India seemed like madness and yet it worked; in a crazy sort of way. I was used to seeing a whole family ride on a motorbike; maybe with a goat too. I was used to seeing a Tuk Tuk loaded with up to eight people and was now used to people driving on the wrong side of the road, or even on the pavement. My mantra, 'expect the unexpected' served me well in these moments of utter madness.

The temple was located in a really quiet part of the city. The further we walked away from the main road, the quieter it became. It was such a welcome relief and we were both really surprised. When we finally arrived, we were given a warm welcome and cushions so that we could pray in our own time. We were not hurried, nor watched over by an armed guard. The peace, love, connection and respect were tangible in this sacred place. I was pleased that we had journeyed here; despite having walked several miles in the heat. I was amazed to see the paintings of the gods and the artwork that was hundreds of years old. The intricate stonework in the ceiling was a true celebration to Indian craftsmanship. It was lovely to enjoy a much needed rest too. Something touched my whole being in that sacred, most holy place. It was something I hadn't experienced previously. I felt as though I was glowing with energy and yet felt grounded and a deep stillness of peace within my whole being.

The old lady who showed us into the temple was happy for us to wander around the whole site; even though much of it was used as a school. The pupils looked on as we soaked up the whole experience in the midday sun. We offered a donation and each gave a gesture of thanks to her when we were leaving. I could still feel the power of the place running through my veins.

Following on from our visit here, we had planned to travel to a nearby lake that was located a short distance away. We were in need of refreshment and found a suitable café where we ordered fresh orange juice. The local men asked where we were headed as we certainly weren't on the usual tourist route. I found it hilarious as the language barrier created havoc in the conversation. Today however we were in for an unexpected surprise. Duncan explained that we planned to visit the lake and the Indian men chatted between themselves. They stated quite clearly that it was too far to walk in the heat of the day and we would need to hire a Tuk Tuk. Once we had finished our drinks and rested, the Tuk Tuk was duly ordered.

About thirty minutes later we arrived at a palace. We truly had no idea whereabouts we were in the city, though we decided to follow the breadcrumb trail. Once we were through the huge iron painted gates, the whole scene was surreal. Only moments earlier we had been in busy streets full of rubbish, noise and all of India's craziness. Here it was absolutely stunning with beautiful, lush greenery in every direction. There were tree-lined avenues and some of the most immaculate gardens I have ever seen. It was like walking into a scene from a fairy-tale. The pleasure of seeing the green grass, the trees, the shrubs, the flowers, the peacocks and the parrots was wonderful. As the fragrances and the magnitude of Mother Nature touched my senses, I breathed in the most beautiful freshness of the palace gardens. I was stunned. The whole place was pristine. I loved it. It was a blissful haven away from the noise, the pollution and all that India now represented to me. There were very few people here; it seemed there were more staff than guests. What a joy it was to have lunch with a quiet table, a clean tablecloth, beautiful chairs and waiters in uniform.

We were asked if we wanted to see the accommodation here. I was very keen to see what lay inside the guest rooms. It was lovely and very modern. The furniture was based on an English cottage-style theme, with cushions and throws. The attention to detail was clearly evident in all the furnishings and I was surprised when he mentioned the price. It was the equivalent of fifty English pounds per evening. I guessed that had the accommodation been located in the United Kingdom, the price would probably have been in the thousands.

After lunch we were happy to stay for the whole afternoon in the grounds. I was keen to explore and was so pleased to be away from the mayhem outside these walls. Being able to walk barefoot on the grass brought such a wonderful, joyful feeling of connection to the earth. It was something I had sorely missed. Here there was no need to be concerned about what we might be stepping in; nor to check where we were walking; looking out for various pieces of rubbish, excrement or broken pieces of glass.

I was surprised to see how big the palace grounds actually were as we wandered along an avenue of trees. I was absolutely amazed and delighted when I spotted a huge fountain in the distance. When we approached it was clear that it had several tiers and several stone staircases arranged in zig-zags. Nearing the fountain the sound of the water touched my senses. Each of the tiers were carved in white marble, shaped like a peacock's feather. I gasped in surprise. The whole structure stood about fifty, or sixty feet high and the view from the top fountain was breath-taking. The perfectly clean avenues, the immaculate lawns and such a variety of exotic colourful flowers made it seem as though it were a botanical garden.

I sat happily that afternoon for over an hour simply watching the water cascade and spray between each of the tiers, remoulding itself every time over the 'peacock-shaped carvings.' I watched the green parrots and the peacocks in the distance and gave thanks for the misunderstanding with the Tuk Tuk driver, which had brought us here. I felt blessed and was so incredibly grateful for an afternoon of peaceful bliss amongst nature.

As the heat of the afternoon progressed I was becoming extremely thirsty. Duncan was asleep and had used the rucksack as his pillow. The bottle of water was in the rucksack and although I didn't wish to disturb him, I knew I risked dehydration and possible sunstroke. Seconds later, I was amazed when a young man approached me and offered me a bottle of water. We chatted easily as he shared that he was waiting-on at the wedding that was taking place in the palace building to our left. He was only in his twenties and as we discussed his life, he shared his love for his girlfriend and what his dreams were for their future. I felt honoured as I listened. His passion and courage to break the mould of a normal Indian life were immense. This was a magical place and together with the sound of the water from the fountain, I said a quiet prayer that he would fulfil all his wishes.

I also said prayers for my beloved family and for myself. I prayed that I would cope without Jay; that we would hopefully meet again, sooner, rather than later and that our conversations would provide us with all the sustaining love and support we would need for whatever our lives would inevitably bring. I still had no idea what would become of me. I knew nothing of where I would eventually settle, or what opportunities I would encounter. All I knew was what this particular day had brought. It was such a blessing and I was incredibly grateful and humbled knowing that later that afternoon we would return to the chaos outside of these palace walls.

Chapter Twenty Nine

Sitting on the train as we waited for the other passengers to board, I wondered what new adventures awaited us in Jaipur. I thought back to all I had experienced over these last few months. Jay was in touch daily which was a blessing and a relief. I loved sharing my experiences with him. It was clear that he missed me, as I missed him and he loved and appreciated our email conversations. My friends and family were still in touch which gave me a great sense of love and connection.

I felt happy and contented within myself as I watched more passengers' board and eventually settle themselves. The Indian trains were always so busy and chaotic.

When a man sat across from me with a lovely, light, bright aura I was pleased when he smiled over to me. He immediately introduced himself and shook my hand. He was clearly soulful and open-hearted. I felt blessed and honoured. This was going to be quite an interesting journey. He explained that he lived in an ashram in the city and was returning home after visiting his fiancée in Jodhpur. I loved listening as he described her and the love shone with such passion from his eyes. They were both devotees of one of the Hindu gods and I was keen to hear more about his beliefs and philosophy; not to mention his future wife.

Throughout the train journey he noticed that I was struggling to sit for any length of time due to the intense pain in my back. He said he knew a natural healer in Jaipur and also a physiotherapist who could assist me once we arrived. I was so grateful for his help and advice as the pain had brought tears to my eyes on more than one occasion throughout the journey

Conversation was light and flowed easily as he shared his life story. I loved listening to each and every minute detail. We promised to keep in touch and we hoped to share some time together at the ashram.

Duncan and I had booked a self-catering apartment in the city. We both had a feeling that it wasn't quite what it should be as soon as we arrived. The whole place looked like a building site. When we were eventually showed into the accommodation our fears were confirmed. It was absolutely filthy; the bathroom, the kitchen, not to mention the beds and bedding too. The owner kept reassuring us that it wasn't that bad and that it could be cleaned easily. We were definitely not staying here. Ever!

By now it was late afternoon we had to find a room quickly. 'Tripadvisor', 'Booking.com' and 'lastminute.com' had proved to be of great help already so we quickly looked for alternative accommodation. Jaipur was such a huge city and we felt we were on a wing and a prayer at this late hour. We came across a hotel which was only slightly more expensive than this crappy apartment.

We were so relieved when we arrived. I was delighted that there was a wonderful rooftop and in the remaining daylight, I was pleased to see that there was a beautiful fort several miles away. I immediately felt at ease here and knew we had made a good choice.

My backache continued and by now I found the pain excruciating. The healer that Shaz had suggested was right at the other end of this huge city and in desperation I phoned the local physiotherapist. He agreed to travel to our hotel and would give me some stretches to do. I knew it needed manipulation and I was in so much pain that I was on the verge of collapsing into a heap of tears. Every move I made sent a sheering pain throughout my body. I felt so weary and worn out with it after all these weeks.

I was struggling to sit down once again, as I drank chai on the rooftop when I noticed a beauty shop, located directly across from the hotel. I hobbled downstairs and asked if she was free to massage my back. Experience and getting amongst the locals had made us aware that the local cost of a massage would be approximately three hundred rupees. We were being charged over four times that amount. I was more than capable of bartering, though the pain had worn me down so much that I was too exhausted. The Indian custom is always to barter; regardless of the situation. I had no choice if I wanted a massage. When she finally agreed on a price and began to massage my back, I cried as the pain began to ease slightly.

Walking back to the hotel I was ready to rest. I had slept so badly in the last fortnight. Jay had suggested that resting was probably the best remedy. I certainly didn't feel like visiting any of the temples, gardens, or the fort. The mere thought of being jostled about in a Tuk Tuk made me feel quite nauseous.

I was grateful that we had a nice clean hotel and a rooftop where I could simply be. I had started writing again with suggestions to amend 'Reflections Of A Hummingbird'. I was happy most days to sit quietly, re-read and re-write the relevant chapters. I realised more and more each day how much I loved writing. Although I had written the novel, I was amazed how the characters became even more alive on the pages as I continued to read. The writing bug had definitely got under my skin once again and I wondered whether this had been a huge part of the reason that I had backache. Only time would tell.

If I hadn't been forced to rest, I would probably have spent most days visiting various temples and tourist attractions, soaking up the vibe of the city. I had meditated as to the origin of the pain in my back and recognised it was all about establishing new roots. I was uprooted from everything I had known in England. This journey had already changed me so much; especially meeting Jay. Resting gave me time to ponder what 'roots' meant to me personally and the possibility of establishing new ones. I knew I had a sponsor in New Zealand and that settling there could definitely be a possibility. I intuited that there was more.....much more. This was certainly the journey of the unknown. I needed to allow it to unfold and stay ever present, allowing and following the breadcrumb trail.

I loved this hotel and the staff were always very welcoming. They soon got used to me in the restaurant; knowing that I loved a cup of chai first thing in the morning. There would always be a welcome smile as I worked on my laptop. I would sit at my favourite table and order paratha in the morning for breakfast. I found that I was happy to rest and simply be here. The rooftop provided space for me and Duncan to do our own thing which proved to be a blessing. Spending twenty four hours together seven days a week with someone who was a virtual stranger was becoming very challenging.

One afternoon in the hotel lift, I met a fellow guest and we instantly clicked. Over the coming days we got on easily and chatted about many things. One morning whilst I was sat writing he greeted me with the usual 'Good morning.' I had a knowing that we needed to sit together. I quickly saved my work onto the hard-drive and switched off the laptop. As we sat sharing our breakfast, he explained that he had been widowed only weeks earlier and was clearly devastated. There are times when no words are necessary; just the ability to listen and hear someone, acknowledging their pain. This was one of those moments and simply sitting with him was enough. I felt honoured that he was comfortable to share his life story with me.

He was travelling to Varanasi later that afternoon. He asked if I would like to accompany him. I explained that Duncan and I had agreed that we would visit Varanasi in the coming weeks and suggested we meet there. We exchanged contact details and I promised to keep in touch. Several hours later, I messaged to wish Lee a safe journey and thanked him for his company. He sent a 'Thank You' emoji back to me and I smiled with gratitude knowing that I had made another new friend. As I smiled, I felt a tap on my shoulder and turning around, there he was, arms outstretched ready for a huge hug. I was so grateful for that wonderful 'Good-bye' hug; knowing he was leaving only minutes later.

Resting proved to be the solution with my back. Jay had been right. Several days later Duncan knew I was finally well enough to visit the Monkey Temple. It was quite a long journey out of town and I was grateful for a comfortable taxi ride, rather than a rickety Tuk Tuk that would have inevitably jarred my back; even over the slightest pothole.

Finally arriving at the Temple, I was amazed to see how big the complex was. It was set against a backdrop of hills. Located well away from the city, it was so quiet. The numerous buildings were incredibly old, with very detailed artwork. The energy here was so peaceful mixed together with a tangible sacredness and a divine connection. I wandered off to explore and was delighted to see stone steps leading towards more temple buildings. I felt a powerful energy pull me upwards like a magnet. I was very surprised when I sensed something towards the top of the stairs. I knew Duncan would find me and I was so thrilled to be finally out and about that I simply followed the pull.

Alongside the stairs were sacred bathing pools which were full of pilgrims. I loved listening to their laughter and watched over them as they shared their obvious joy at being here. The green water reminded me of Pushkar and inevitably I thought of Jay. I missed him daily, my feelings for him were growing stronger and stronger.

I was still feeling a powerful pull to reach the top where I could 'see' a bright light glowing. When I reached the light at the top of the stairs there was a very simple small temple to the left. The priest welcomed me inside and offered me a blessing. His aura was stunning and he was clearly 'the real deal.' He was open-hearted and empowered by his pure soul. I felt really blessed to be in his presence. As he said the prayers, light danced around my whole being and touched me deeply. I allowed the tears to come as he continued to pray. I had no idea where this journey would take me and during the prayers I cried as I felt the incredible gratitude for all that I had experienced thus far. Tears of appreciation fell for the love I shared with those back in England; especially my granddaughters. Here I could feel the distinct presence of my beloved sons in New Zealand which would be my final destination, and I cried at the unknown. I knew nothing of what lay between now, this very present, incredible moment and my visit there.

I remained silent for some time after those prayers and his powerful blessing. They had brought an immense lightness to my whole being. I was humbled and deeply touched to have met a 'real' priest and to be in the presence of the Divine Oneness. Eventually I walked back to the top of the stairs and saw Duncan waiting for me.

Chatting, we agreed to visit the Sun Temple further up the mountain. Walking up the many stone steps I was amazed to feel such an ease in my back. In fact my whole body felt lighter. Was it the priests influence?

Was it simply because I had rested? I couldn't be sure. All I knew was that I loved the feeling and I pressed on despite the steepness and the heat of the day without even a slight pain from my lower back.

The Sun Temple was right at the top of the steps and stood proudly overlooking the whole city. It felt as though it was like a guardian, with almighty wings spread over the surrounding area. There was an elderly gentleman sat outside on the wall and I knew when he saw me that he had seen my aura. We smiled at each other and communicated what we needed to; despite the language barrier.

After Duncan and I prayed our silent intentions in the temple, I found the elderly gentleman was waiting for me outside in the courtyard. He approached me, hugged me and planted a huge kiss on my cheek. All three of us remained together for some time as we enjoyed the view over this huge sprawling city.

It never ceased to amaze me how vast these concrete jungles were and how they spread right across the landscape, consuming everything in their path. There were random areas of green; I guessed they were public gardens or maybe school grounds. I was sad as there were so few, providing a precious green sanctuary for the whole area. The pollution from the fumes hung like a cloud over the city below us and I quietly asked The Divine for a solution to this situation. How had it come to this? How did people survive their daily toil in this place of constant noise and ever-growing pollution, especially without nature? The whole place seemed to have abandoned itself, or at least a part of itself in some way. I decided to ponder these questions and sent love to the whole sad and seemingly abandoned, soul-crushing scene.

I was pleased to be out and about again. Jaipur was such a huge city and it seemed to spread in all directions. There was so much to see and do in the next few days before we moved on. We had agreed to visit a huge temple which was dedicated to the God, Ganesh.

I was surprised when we arrived to see many market stalls outside and throngs of people. It was clearly another day of celebration in the Hindu calendar. The temple was incredibly busy with people making many offerings and gathering for their prayers. We were hustled and bustled inside where we eventually found a quiet spot to admire the details of the temple ceiling, the statues and the artwork. Although it was lovely I sensed something more spiritual outside.

I was drawn to another temple on the left hand side and I could feel a sense of true Divinity here, even before I mounted the steps. I was grateful that it was far less busy than the previous temple and I found a quiet spot to sit and simply be. Closing my eyes, I instantly felt light surround me and was aware of a very powerful connection. It was similar to that which I had experienced three days earlier. I simply sat absorbing the light and feeling immense gratitude for whatever was happening to me. A few minutes later I knew that whatever had just happened had been completed when the light around me dissipated. I sat for a few moments before leaving the temple. I smiled as I rang the huge brass bell as a gesture of thanksgiving.

As I descended the steps several ladies were dancing in front of me in what looked like a town square. They had painted their faces and were so happy singing, dancing and chanting. I had rarely seen women in India. The waiters and hotel staff were always male. When they invited me over I was absolutely delighted to join them in their dancing. They threw marigold petals all over me and despite the language barrier, they showed me that as they painted my face, I should in turn paint theirs. The bright colours were vibrant and I loved the connection with them as we smiled, laughed, danced and hugged each other. The music was touching my soul and as many people approached for selfies of the crazy Englishwoman with a painted face, I was only too happy to oblige. We danced for quite a while together with several other women being invited up to join us.

Duncan moved further and further away as he had no intention of joining the mayhem. I was thoroughly enjoying each and every precious moment. It felt sacred and divine, dancing in thanks with strangers who had welcomed me into their unique circle. We were happy to smile, laugh and hug; despite the language barrier. The whole experience felt wonderful and I was truly blessed to be a part of whatever it was that they were celebrating. The armed security guards looked over at us all and smiled. The whole scene was surreal in a weird sort of way. Security guards at a sacred temple in a deeply religious, spiritual country always seemed very odd and peculiar.

As I motioned to them that I needed to leave, it was clear that they wanted me to stay. It took me at least another twenty minutes of hugging and more selfies before I finally made my way to Duncan. He laughed at my painted face. I was so happy and still felt such a huge glow from the afternoons' experiences.

There was another temple less than a five minute walk away that we had also planned to visit. As we walked outside on to the surrounding streets I got lots of strange looks from the many passers-by. Duncan thought it was hilarious. I simply soaked it all up as part of the afternoons' joy.

As we approached the next temple, a friendly Indian man explained that I needed to wash my face as a sign of respect. He kindly showed us where the soap was located and I guessed I wasn't the first painted lady to visit here. Watching the water run with bright colours, I smiled to myself as I had to keep going out to Duncan to check if my face was clean. Several washes later, I was finally ready to enter the gardens of the temple.

India never ceased to amaze me. Here we were right in the heart of the city surrounded by one of the most prestigious gardens I have truly ever visited. I was bombarded with colours, fragrances and exotic flowers, some of which I had never seen before. I thought of my mother when I saw the roses. I desperately wanted to walk barefoot on the grass. I was so disappointed when I noticed signs saying; 'Please keep off the grass.' The temptation was intense though I knew there were armed guards here.

The white marble statues of Shiva were stunning in the bright afternoon sun. I felt blessed to be here as we walked around the huge white temple. This felt so different to the previous two temples; it felt more connected to the earth rather than the Gods, or maybe somehow it was a go-between? When we went inside and I noticed the most stunning stained glass windows I was delighted. They were all brightly coloured and I could feel intuitively that they were all sighted on energy points, or vortexes. This place felt like it was holding the light for the whole city and for the fort above too.

In the middle of the immaculately tiled floor was a brightly coloured exquisite mosaic in the shape of a huge star. I could feel the powerful energies there which came from many different directions. I decided to sit and meditate right in its centre. I could feel the earth beneath me, feel her power and a most beautiful, pure connection ran through my being. Maybe this was in fact where heaven and earth met? Whatever this feeling was I loved it and I soaked it up, basking like a lizard in the precious sunshine. I was so pleased we had agreed to come here and felt my soul celebrate with me. Of all the temples we had visited thus far, this one was truly the most sacred.

Chapter Thirty

Holi Day was approaching and a couple of my new friends had asked me if I would like to meet them in Pushkar for the celebrations. There they would be celebrating in style and I was most tempted. Unfortunately, Duncan and I had already agreed to travel to Vrindavan the following day; as we were due to meet his friends there. Although I was confident enough to travel alone, I was unsure whether or not I would be back in time to catch the train the following day. I was happy enough to return to Pushkar, despite knowing that Jay would not be there. I looked through the details of the public transport and intuitively knew I would be on a wing and a prayer if I decided to go ahead. Something didn't quite feel right intuitively so I reluctantly declined their kind offer.

When we first arrived in Jaipur we met a man who offered to take us to a renowned psychic in the city. I tuned into his energy immediately and I knew I was destined to meet him. At the time my back was far too painful to travel any distance, so I followed my instincts, trusting that we would meet at a later date. Two days before we were due to leave Jaipur, Duncan and I visited the Palace Of The Winds. It was stunning and once again the déjà vu was powerful. I 'knew' I had walked through these many passages before and felt a real connection with the place. As I looked through the tiny latticed windows they were so familiar to me.

Duncan and I had a blazing row the previous evening and later when we stopped in a lovely café for refreshments he apologised profusely. We were both struggling having little space apart. I knew I would soon be travelling alone as the differences between us were vast. The cracks in the proverbial mirror were becoming deeper and more numerous by the day.

We visited a temple further down the main road and spent time in there separately, praying and meditating. Duncan went in first and he loved it, recommending me to visit. When I came out he was chatting to a man we had met earlier that day who suggested we meet a well-known psychic. We were both wise enough to know that we needed to follow the breadcrumb trail and finally meet him.

Within the hour we walked into his shop and as soon as I saw him we both knew that we were both healers and psychics. He mentioned numerous things to me and we shared a lovely few minutes together. He knew I would soon be travelling alone and described my children, ex-husband and so much more. He advised me to continue with my creative work and intuited several more books around me. There was so much more that was mentioned though much of it was private and deeply personal to me. One thing that did stand out was that he mentioned I needed a sacred mantra to help ease my throat chakra. I agreed with him and said I had been searching for many months. My throat had been my weak spot and I had frequently suffered from sore throats and coughs which affected my vocal chords. He said I would find one sooner, rather than later. I felt the meeting was a success and was happy with all we had shared.

When we eventually arrived back at the accommodation the celebrations for Holi Day were in full swing. The streets were so much quieter and many of the restaurants were closed. It was quite odd after being so accustomed to the usual days' craziness, as the streets were normally filled with cars, bikes and Tuk Tuks honking at each other. On rare occasions the odd camel could even be seen carrying loads on this ever-crowded road. The local people were happily gathered and evidently loving the celebrations as they stood around small bonfires on the streets. It was such a humbling sight as they shouted 'Happy Holi Day' to us. I was more than happy to reply with a huge smile. If this was the night before the huge celebrations, then I guessed we were in for quite a treat the following day.

Waking up the next morning to almost complete quiet was incredibly strange after being so used to noise, noise and more noise. As I looked out from the hotel window the road was full of many colours from the powder paints. There was no sign of anyone; the man with the vegetable cart was no-where to be seen, neither were any of the taxi drivers. It was certainly strange. It felt almost ghostly.

Holi Day was a celebration of good over evil and the coming of springtime. The quiet was celebration enough for me. No more would I have to answer to at least five taxi drivers, all asking if I required a taxi before I had even walked to the end of the road where the hotel was situated. Quiet meant bliss. As I ventured out for a walk it was almost surreal. Most of the hotels and restaurants were closed and there was hardly anyone walking on the streets. None of the shops were open and none of the usual street vendors selling cakes, samosas, fruit and vegetables were anywhere to be seen. I was amazed as I crossed the road for the first time, without fearing I was taking my life into my hands.

A few days earlier I had spotted some beautiful villas with stunning architecture. I loved my early morning strolls although today was extra special. There was hardly anyone to be seen at all and I soaked up the peace without any interruption. There were some children playing in the street, they were covered in many different coloured paints, happily smiling and playing with water pistols. They all shouted; "Happy Holi Day" and I shouted back the same greeting. A little girl made it clear she wanted to paint my face. I was happy to oblige and I painted hers in return. I felt a connection with her, as the other children looked over and giggled. It was such a lovely feeling of communal silliness.

Laughter is such a universal language. I wondered what I looked like with a painted face; probably as wonderful as I had done only a few days earlier. My intention was to witness and absorb this day as much as I possibly could. I rounded a corner and could hear so much laughter from the garden of the property. Within seconds I was ushered in and welcomed by a huge Indian family; and the dog who refused to leave my side. They each painted me in turn as I returned the favour. There was something truly magical about being painted with bright purple, green, blue, yellow, orange and red powder paints. They spoke excellent English and I was humbled when they shared vast amounts of home-made food with me. It was truly such a lovely gesture and once again I felt a huge sense of their genuine welcoming gestures and my connection with them.

Returning to the hotel I was happy to sit on the rooftop to enjoy the city view. Most of the other hotel guests were there and we all laughed at one another as we were all covered in so much paint. It was a great talking point and such a great way to meet and greet people. By now I was covered predominately in pink. It was in my hair, up my nose and in my ears. The rooftop floor was a mass of powder paints and I loved it. Chatting easily to the other guests and listening to their life stories was such a wonderful sharing. Duncan was still in bed and I was sad that he was missing all this frolicking.

Watching from my usual spot on the rooftop a man approached me with two of his male friends. In turn we painted each other. As his friends wandered off to sit in the shaded part of the rooftop he smiled at me and said; "You need a mantra for your throat chakra."

"Yes I do", I replied.

"*Ram* would be my recommendation. Say it three times a day."

I knew he was very spiritual as his aura was so large, light and bright. I let him continue as he explained that he was deeply soulful, though in no way religious. As the conversation continued he mentioned that he knew (as I did), that we had shared many other lives together. I was definitely in agreement and we spent the rest of the afternoon chatting about all things spiritual and sharing our experiences and beliefs. He had been born a Brahman and he clearly hated the Caste system. It saddened him how it created such separation. Perhaps the most poignant point he raised was when he expressed his philosophy.

"A dog from India can meet a dog from another country and they understand one another's language. They might sniff one another and bark, yet they communicate all the same. A bird may well do the same, a sparrow eats crumbs and is happy to share with the other sparrows and yet a human cannot communicate and share with another human if they are from a different country, with a different culture and a different religion. We have lost our ability to communicate and connect without the need for language." Having taught spiritual awareness for so long I agreed completely and this saddened me too.

I loved listening to his life story and we shared many happy moments, before we eventually left the hotel to share a fabulous evening meal. Walking me back to the hotel he was surprised as almost everyone we met greeted me. He asked if I knew them and I explained that I spoke to most of the locals here. He was clearly stunned to see how well I had settled into the area. We agreed to keep in touch and since that day we have shared so much friendship and deep wisdom through our many messages.

Holi Day proved to be such a wonderful day. Lee sent his photographs from Varanasi. His granddaughter Sonali, had painted his face silver. It looked awesome. He messaged several times to say that everyone there was thoroughly enjoying the day. Prince, Samber and

Anita forwarded me the photographs of their celebrations from Pushkar. They were amazing and the streets were completely filled with people laughing, dancing and of course all covered in paint. It looked truly spectacular. They had certainly celebrated in style. Looking at their pictures I realised how much I missed Pushkar and my friends too. I was sad that I had missed being there although I had thoroughly enjoyed myself in Jaipur.

Chapter Thirty One

Duncan and I were already packed and ready to order a taxi to the station the following morning. It was to be another railway journey though by now I accepted that the toilets would be incredibly smelly and had taken to carrying a bottle of antiseptic hand wash in my bag. Much of India's craziness was normal to me now. It was quite a huge admission. I wondered if I would, or even could, cope with the Western way of life ever again.

Vrindavan was located several miles away from the railway station and when we arrived we soon realised that getting a taxi to our destination was not going to be easy. It took us over twenty minutes of bartering between the local taxi and Tuk Tuk drivers before we were finally ready to set off to the ashram.

It had been a long day and we were delighted to find an amazing restaurant after we had settled into our separate rooms. After yet another row, I knew it was time to go solo. I hadn't yet managed to find the necessary courage to inform Duncan; though for now I was absolutely delighted that at last I had my own space. It felt like heaven. I could sleep knowing that when I awoke I wouldn't have to creep around quietly, or wait to have a shower until he was up and about. I could read in bed and put the kettle on without being concerned that the noise, as it boiled, would wake him from his slumbers.

The following morning I ventured into the streets to find some cleaning products. The bathroom was reasonably clean though in desperate need of a really good scour. The language barrier had brought many challenges in these last few months and finding some 'Flash' or 'Jif' proved to be no different; neither did trying to seek out a scouring sponge. These many learning curves inevitably brought such laughter; I loved the experiences.

As I cleaned the sink, toilet, walls and the floor I reflected that this seemed to represent how I felt in myself. It reminded me of how much I had cleaned my emotions and the past hurts in my personal life. Once cleaned this space represented a sacred space within myself. I felt cleaner in so many ways; mentally, physically, spiritually and emotionally. Perhaps that was why I had to go solo now?

Lee was still in touch from Varanasi. The wedding photographs of his adopted Indian family were truly stunning. The bride and groom looked beautiful. I knew I had to visit there next. It felt as though it was a priority. I thought it odd that I knew I would travel with Duncan to Vrindavan; though could never 'see' beyond that point in our travels. The weight of telling him still overhung my shoulders. I was aware of it each and every day, as I pondered the decision about how and when I would tell him. I had to be diplomatic and kindly to him. I also knew I had to be assertive; as he would probably try to talk me into remaining with him, which was by now absolutely out of the question. I prayed to The Divine and asked for assistance as to when and how to chat with him. We hadn't spoken properly for several days; we merely exchanged pleasantries and essential conversations. In one way I hoped that he had guessed what my plans were.

I was tired of the concrete jungle now. I longed to walk in greenery or in a park under the trees. The constant assault on all my senses from the various noises and smells were taking their toll. I was fed up having to watch each and every step I took to avoid walking in cow dung, falling down a hole, or stepping on a baby monkey. The sight of the cows feeding from the local rubbish pile on the streets sickened me.

I was missing Jay and my loved ones in England. I was glad to finally experience some respite in my own private room and the local restaurant. It was amazingly clean with such a nutritious healthy range of foods on the menu. To the rear it had a huge garden which was stunning. It was covered in green, lush grass and was such a welcome sight. The flowers and the roses were abundant and looking out across the garden often brought a tear to my eye. I dearly missed Mother

Nature; the grass, the trees and the beautiful flowers. As the monkeys darted from one tree branch to another, I thought how lucky they were and wondered if they cherished this garden as much as I did.

Desperate to visit Varanasi, I needed to ask about travel options and I said a quiet prayer to the Universe for assistance. Within the hour I found a local book store and chatted so easily to the vendor and his family. He was a very soulful and clearly a most humble man. As the conversation continued, I felt comfortable enough to ask his advice about my intentions to travel. He explained that his friend Dennis had a local taxi business and would be willing to take me to Delhi airport. From there I could fly directly to Varanasi. The relief was intense and it was all I could do to refrain from crying a tsunami of tears. The thought of being near the Holy Ganges River felt as though it would bring me completion in some way. I was desperate for open space and to see flowing water again.

While we chatted I asked his advice about which of the local temples I should visit. Looking at my list he kindly explained that some were located on one side of the city and many others were located further away. He grouped together those in the different regions. I was so grateful for his assistance.

The following morning I approached a Tuk Tuk driver with the list of temples that I wanted to visit. As I was bartering a price, within less than two minutes seven men surrounded me. They were all making their own suggestions as to which I should visit first. It was most unnerving. My whole body space was surrounded, invaded and they were so close that I could smell their breath. I felt incredibly uncomfortable. Panic began to set in as I tried various self-hypnosis techniques; 'Breathe, breathe, breathe, they'll soon be gone. Visualise yourself surrounded by a bubble of light... you are safe and secure, you are safe and secure, you are safe and secure.' I was at ease when all of them; apart from my driver, finally left.

The temples were stunning and all were incredibly busy, despite the early hour. I was glad I hadn't left it 'til late morning to start my journey. I enjoyed visiting each of them in turn. As we journeyed through the narrow streets I was amazed at the drivers' ability to manoeuver between oncoming bikes and other Tuk Tuks. He was kind enough to wait for me outside each of the temples to ensure my safety.

Suddenly we turned a corner to the left and we were in an open space. I gasped loudly when I caught sight of the river. He obviously heard me and asked if I was okay. I explained I hadn't seen a river for several months. I was amazed when he kindly reversed the vehicle and stopped, allowing me to spend a few moments alone by the waterside. He explained that he would get something to drink from a local market stall and that there was no need to rush, I should take my time. I wondered if he had known how dear water has always been to me. I had gasped loud enough for him to notice after all.

As I walked down to the river I cried tears of joy and relief. I was so relieved to see flowing water again. It was reasonably clean and so many people were enjoying boating across to the other side. I had to catch my breath as I stood and felt Mother Nature around me. I must have stood there for several minutes, taking in the wonder of it all. By the time I returned to my driver I felt a peace which I had not felt since being with Jay. Now I was in no doubt that my time in Varanasi alongside The Ganges was going to be amazing. It was as if seeing this river confirmed it all.

PART THREE

Chapter Thirty Two

Making the decision to travel without Duncan was such a relief. However, I was honest with myself and I acknowledged the feelings of fear as I now faced travelling Mother India on my own. Only Jay was aware that I would be travelling alone and he was confident that I had made the right choice. He trusted that I would be safe; knowing that I had the necessary skills and the strength of character to complete the journey eastwards. Eventually I knew that I would also need to inform my family back in the United Kingdom. Knowing that they would be concerned; especially my mother, wasn't the most pleasant thought. Trying to convince and reassure others when we are taking a leap of faith ourselves and having our own doubts and 'wobbles' can prove to be quite a challenge. I decided that for now at least, I would keep this between Jay and myself. His support was endearing and very much appreciated during this time.

Very early the next morning I opened the tiny ashram door and found that manoeuvring my suitcase and hand luggage through was quite a feat. I had told Duncan that I felt I needed to travel alone. We both accepted that we had learnt and shared so much. We had said our 'Goodbyes' the night before and knowing that he wasn't an early riser, I was relieved that I would be leaving without any more tears and a whole heap of emotions. The taxi was waiting in the side street which was such a relief. The previous day there had been a huge amount of confusion relating to exactly which ashram I was staying at.

I didn't look back as Dennis pulled out onto the main street. I had felt really oppressed and deeply unsettled here. Within minutes we were on a dual carriageway and the relief I felt that I would soon be with my friend Lee was intense. I was so looking forward to seeing the famous Ganges River. I had looked forward to visiting Varanasi for several years and now I was thrilled to be finally on my way.

Sitting alone in the rear of the taxi was an incredibly powerful feeling. I felt empowered that I was actually travelling India alone now. As I watched the sunrise behind us, tears of relief poured out. My heart centre felt sore inside my chest, as I allowed my body to let go of the stress I had experienced these last few weeks.

I was grateful that the roads were so quiet at this early hour. We passed many tractors piled high with produce from the surrounding fields. I was amazed at how overloaded they were. Seeing was definitely believing here. When we passed one which had actually tipped on its side due to the sheer weight of the load, I wasn't at all surprised. This was such a crazy place where crazy things were the everyday norm.

It was a three hour drive to Delhi and I was relieved when Dennis, asked me if I would like to get some breakfast. The marsala chai was most welcome, as was the paratha. I was aware that the restaurant staff; all male, were staring at me. After a quick visit to the toilet, I returned to the rear seat in the taxi. Whilst Dennis re-fuelled the car, the staring continued. I watched him as he began to notice each of their stares in turn, and then looked back at me in the rear of the car. I mentioned it when we re-joined the dual carriageway. His English was excellent and I was interested to hear his thoughts. He expressed his surprise at their behaviour and was most apologetic.

I was delighted to see so many open fields along the route. As the morning progressed the traffic inevitably increased. I was glad that I had at least enjoyed some respite from the noise. I was intrigued to see the Indian version of 'motorway services' as we drove along. Many were simple cafes lined with tables and plastic chairs. When we drove past a 'Subway' and a 'McDonalds' I was truly surprised. They looked so out of place here amongst the potholes, the rubbish and the whole background tapestry that represented Mother India. It saddened me as I thought back to the UK, where the services are modern and filled with the big food outlets. Here there was a culture and a uniqueness to India. The thought of these people losing their identity touched me deeply.

Approaching Delhi I could clearly see the vast, dense cloud of smog ahead. I had seen so many people wear face masks in these past two months and now I wished that I had purchased one. Within minutes the traffic ground to a halt and immediately, once again all of my senses were on full alert. So, this was Delhi. We were still miles from the airport and I was so grateful that we had allowed extra time.

Arriving at Delhi airport was one of the most amazing experiences of my journey thus far. As we entered the complex the roads were absolutely immaculate, there were numerous staff in smart green uniforms sweeping the grass. There was not a single piece of litter in sight. There was no smell, no crazy driving and everyone had a wonderful smile. It was almost surreal.

Inside the airport was breath-taking. Spectacular, stunning sculptors of elephants, various palms and exotic flowers greeted me. The cleanliness was amazing. Checking-in was quick, smooth and incredibly efficient. I had assumed that it would be similar to the dreaded, over-crowded, chaotic railway stations. I was delighted to be proved wrong.

The plane was one of the cleanest I have ever seen. Even the seat belt was laid out ready. The staff were dressed immaculately with beautiful, genuine smiles. I had to pinch myself. As I made my way down the plane to my seat, I noticed a Tibetan monk sat across from me. My seat number was 16C and his 15F. He smiled across at me and started chatting. “Is this your first time in India?”

“Yes”, I replied.

“But it’s not is it? You’ve been here in many lifetimes.”

With that comment and his beautiful smile, I invited him to sit with me as the other two adjoining seats in my row were empty. Throughout the journey we discussed soulfulness, compassion, the power of unconditional love and forgiveness. He explained that he taught Buddhism and meditation all over the world and that his family were exiled from Tibet many years earlier. It was so inspiring and humbling listening to him and we agreed to keep in touch. I was delighted that we had met and shared so much.

Chapter Thirty Three

Lee was waiting for me at the hotel when I arrived. His welcoming hug and huge smile were just what I needed after my journey. I had decided to stay at the same hotel as it made sense; at least for the moment, until I found my way around the local area. The gratitude I experienced when I was shown to my room was truly immense. I had a lovely, modern bathroom, comfortable bed and the most beautiful wooden furniture. It felt like heaven.

Glad of good company and great conversation we planned to eat at the local Japanese restaurant. He was looking forward to introducing me to his adopted Indian family. He had told them a little about me and I was greeted with such incredible warmth. They were truly soulful people and I felt truly humbled to be welcomed into their home. This family of six lived in two simple rooms. As Lee had recently been widowed I was delighted to hear their stories about his late wife. Their love for her shone brightly and I was both pleased and relieved that everyone was comfortable talking about her. It was so refreshing; most English people rarely talked about death, or their dead relatives, or loved ones. I felt instantly at ease with them. If I needed confirmation that I had made the right choice by coming here I had certainly found it.

The following day Lee had several personal things to take care of with the Indian family. He was leaving the following morning so time was precious. We planned to meet up later that afternoon. He had recommended a local café; simply called 'The Aum Café.' Walking inside, I received a lovely welcome smile from the waitress. It reminded of the well-known 'hippie' cafes at Hebden Bridge in England. The owner introduced herself and was clearly very spiritual. As it was busy she asked if I would mind sharing a table. I was delighted when I was introduced to Samuel. His aura glowed radiantly and I felt I knew him. We chatted easily and were soon laughing and giggling like children. I had been here for less than twenty four hours and yet I felt so at ease.

The friendship between Samuel and I was instant. I was delighted, as I knew Lee's leaving was imminent. We added each other through 'Facebook Messenger' and agreed to meet up the following day for lunch, after his music lesson. He was learning to play the sarangi and was clearly dedicated to his 'Guruji.'

To celebrate Lee's last evening we had been invited to share a meal with our Indian family. It was lovely sharing home-made pizza and chai. They all made it clear that they wanted me to visit daily; even after Lee had left. These people had so little and yet so much. The laughter and conversation continued for many hours and I was grateful to be a huge part of the whole scenario. I felt blessed and those moments were very sacred.

Lee's leaving was emotional and we promised to keep in touch. I wanted to find another hotel after he left. It wasn't the same without him. Arun, the head of the Indian family assisted me. I was thrilled to find one which looked directly out over The Ganges. I felt most settled and loved my balcony overlooking the sacred river and the area below.

Watching the sunrise and the sunsets were amazing here in Varanasi. There was the opportunity here to travel by boat; watching the sunrise whilst travelling on The Ganges. I knew I had to be up at 5am though it felt very much that it should be a part of my pilgrimage whilst I was here. Getting into the tiny, wooden hand-made rowing boat was a humbling experience. Connecting to the earth through the wood, the water and the early morning sky touched something deep within me. It was one of the most precious memories I have of my time in India.

As the sun began to rise I felt peaceful and loved to watch as the other boats moved past us. The oarsman steered easily and I felt completely safe as the oars moved us through the green water. I loved the sound of the water lapping against the boat and the fish jumping in and out of the river.

Watching the locals swimming and washing their clothes here brought another connection too. We were all sharing the same beloved river. We were all reliant on the river for different reasons and as smiles were exchanged between fellow travellers, swimmers and those on the shore, there was definitely a feeling of one-ness. As the sun rose the heat was unbelievable. A rich tapestry of colours began to fill the skyline with pinks, reds, yellows, and oranges. It was a perfect time to pray, to celebrate and to feel Mother Earth at her absolute best. It was a truly sacred experience and one that will remain with me forever.

Samuel was delighted that I was so settled and we continued our daily laughter sessions at the café. I loved listening to his stories and meeting his valued friends. So many of them stayed for several months in the city; some learning music, yoga or other spiritual practises. The 'Aum' was definitely the place to attract spiritually evolving and evolved souls. The company was wonderful and the food was definitely the best in the area.

Walking alongside The Ganges was such a beautiful experience each and every day. I felt very privileged to be here. These many weeks had changed me. My gratitude and appreciation had grown daily, as did my connection to all living things.

Before sunrise, each and every day the Puja Ceremony would take place directly across from my hotel balcony. Waking up in the morning to their sacred chanting was blissful. I would often get up early to walk a few yards to the riverbed. There I could watch as the five Brahman celebrated their thanks for the river, Mother Earth and for the whole community. Sometimes I simply lay in bed listening and feeling cosy; knowing that our planet was being honoured. I loved to listen to the sound of their bells ringing and the crowd clapping too. This was such a sacred way to start the day and it always touched a part of me.

Duncan and I kept in touch and he was now settled in an Osho ashram further upriver. He loved it and would share details of his treks into the mountains and his daily swims in The Ganges. I was delighted that we had put our differences aside and remained friends. Without him I might never have experienced Mother India; except through the very small window of a holiday package deal. I will be forever grateful.

It was quiet here by the river and I felt incredibly settled and safe. I was so grateful to be away from the constant noise of the Tuk Tuks, motorbikes and the loud honking. They were not allowed by the riverside and the road was several hundred metres away. It was such a welcome relief.

I knew that I had made the right decision to travel alone. After journeying for several weeks now, I was experiencing an ever growing peace within myself. I had learnt to trust that I would be okay whatever the day brought; be it a new friend, or a sense of grace and appreciation as I walked alongside the river. I loved it whenever I found a new temple, or a wonderful new restaurant. I felt like a child experiencing the world for the first time.

I was now writing again daily and learning to trust in my ability with the help of a dear and beloved friend. He supported me as my writing evolved and continued to improve. I was finding more faith and trust in my still-unknown-future and allowing each of the days to unfold at their own pace. There was no rush here, no timetable and no forced agenda. I was simply be-ing and I loved it.

My usual day began around dawn, listening to, or attending the Puja ceremony. A few minutes later I loved watching as people gathered for their daily Laughter Yoga in the square below my balcony. I would then begin writing. Around 8am I would walk by the sacred river.

One morning as I took my usual stroll, I noticed that the restaurant where I had eaten a wonderful meal the night before was open for breakfast. As I wandered up the stone steps I received a warm welcome, as I had done the previous evening. In the last few weeks, I had become rather partial to either aloo, or gobhi paratha for breakfast. I loved it with curd and preferably without pickle. (The Indian pickle had the ability to turn my stomach at any time of the day; especially in the morning). The waiter served the very best paratha and marsala chai that I had ever tasted. I felt spoilt though the tiny tea-cups were never enough to satisfy my thirst first thing in the morning. I always asked for a refill or a teapot.

Over the coming days, the waiter was so used to me that he rarely asked what I wanted for breakfast. We would smile, exchange greetings; as I would with all the other staff, then I would sit in my usual chair overlooking this most sacred river. The day he brought me my very own green mug of chai I was delighted. He said it was ‘my cup’ and would not to be used for anyone else. I was so thrilled and certainly felt connected as he knew the depth of the appreciation I had for him. It was not only because he made the very best chai, but also because that cup represented so much more. I felt valued and it personalised the service in a very touching way. It saddened me when I watched other guests as they placed their orders: often without a simple ‘Please’ or even a ‘Thank you’. Some would rarely even look up and acknowledge the waiters presence.

Appreciation for me was a perfect way to continue my morning and I loved that particular restaurant, knowing that each and every day would be a real treat. Sitting overlooking the Ganges River, I could watch the local guru chatting to his students, the ladies selling their garlands of marigolds and the old men pottering by the river. I loved to watch the people washing their clothes, swimming and bathing, laughing and often splashing one another. The simplicity of the whole river scene felt sacred. Each morning I looked forward to my walk down here. I loved to sit in the bright sunshine under the parasol, whilst I enjoyed each of the morning's gifts.

From this perfect position I would send a daily message to Jay and my loved ones. I was happy and felt blessed to be a part of this community. Writing to Jay always brought a warm glow to my heart and I loved sharing my experiences. He loved hearing from me and we shared so much in each precious email. By sharing our wit and humour the support and our connection grew daily.

One morning after enjoying my usual breakfast treat I wondered back towards the hotel. It was another beautiful day of sunshine and quiet. There were many steps leading upwards towards the main road and I planned to visit my Indian family. There was a man with a young toddler, a bicycle and a huge shopping bag walking up the steps towards the road above. The steps were far too steep for him to manage alone and without a single word I took the little girls tiny hand in mine. He looked across at me in silence with a look of complete trust. The child held my hand tightly, not even glancing towards me.

As I helped her up the steps and he manoeuvred the bike and the bag, the three of us walked in absolute silence. Nearing the top of the steps, I could see that the road was flooded with several inches of water. It was plenty deep enough to soak a child's shoes. I looked over to him and swiftly gathered her into my arms, staying close to the man and his bicycle. She was completely at ease with me and the trust that was exchanged between the three of us was tangible. I felt honoured that he had allowed me to help. As we rounded the corner, we were now away from the deep water. I placed her down next to him and we both exchanged a knowing smile.

The simplicity of that meeting was incredibly powerful. I missed my granddaughters daily and have always loved children. Being able to help him that morning and being trusted with the care of his daughter brought such treasured moments into my world. I will be forever grateful.

My days here were very simple, usually after breakfast I would eventually wander back to the hotel. I loved to sit on the balcony to begin writing again. Once inspiration faded, or I knew I needed time to rest, I often wandered to visit my beloved Indian family. The days were precious and everyday sacred.

Lunch with Samuel; usually around two o'clock would often be salad. We shared stories of our loved ones and our beloved grandchildren. We would laugh at the little things in life; which were clearly the most important to us. His friendship was something I will treasure forever. Our conversations were sprinkled with lashings of laughter, as we shared a piece of calorie-free chocolate cake and stole potato chips from one another's plate. It was incredible, simple fun. We frequently made both the waitress and the owner laugh. Newcomers were soon at ease in our company too. That was the beauty and the depth of the connection between us. We loved to take the piss out of each other over the simplest of things. We would often watch other customers in the cafe and were greatly saddened if they never even smiled, or looked up from their mobile phones.

By the time we left 'Aum' the water buffalo would be making their way down to the river. Samuel loved them and would chat to them as we walked side by side. They were such huge creatures and yet so very gentle. Watching as they held up the traffic I would delight being in their presence. I loved watching them walk past my hotel and taking photos of these majestic Godly creatures. Sometimes I walked alongside them and watched as they cooled off in the water, while the locals carried on washing their clothes.

One evening after I had watched the puja ceremony I settled down in the room of my hotel to continue editing 'Reflections of A Hummingbird'. I was awaiting more suggested edits from a treasured friend when I noticed an email arrive from him. Indian WiFi was notorious for its slowness; the email had been received although I was unable to open it. I needed to go outdoors in order to get a better signal. I could then open the email attachment and read his suggestions.

I ventured outside into the busy evening with nothing more than my iPhone and hotel room key. As usual it was busy alongside the riverbed and full of hundreds of people. This place never ceased to amaze me; every day and every night was different. Crowds of people thronged everywhere, the noise and the tremendous vibrancy of the evening were absolutely stunning. I wasn't sure what the celebration was although it was bigger than that of the previous evenings.

I found a quiet space to sit down, open and read the email. From here I could also reply if I needed to query anything. I was always delighted and grateful to receive an email and I read it happily. I was about to reply with a 'Thank You' when I was approached by a young girl holding some red balloons. She requested ten rupees from me for a balloon. This was the only occasion when

I had left the hotel without my handbag. I didn't have any cash with me at all. I would have gladly given her a hundred rupees.

She looked at me as I held out both of my hands; one with my phone and the other with my key. I wasn't sure if she spoke, or understood English at all and had learnt over these months how effective sign language could be. As I looked into her eyes, they held a deep, deep sadness. There was such a deep well of hurt and pain. It seemed she had known no respite and very little, if any peace. Her aura was confirmation of everything she spoke in volumes to me through her eyes. She looked back at me, looking very deeply into mine. It was clear she was grateful simply to be acknowledged, rather than being brushed off, or ignored. It was such an incredible connection. It seemed at that very moment that our souls touched. It felt like we were in our own bubble. She looked so sad; as though she was held in a black, empty void. It was obvious, even to the most hard-hearted of people that life had been challenging and was very difficult for her.

"Do you speak English?", I asked gently with compassion and grace.

"Yes", was her immediate reply.

As I looked further into her eyes I simply said; "It's a hard life."

It was more of a statement that a question. It was so clear to see her pain in those dark brown eyes. Here it seemed the light in her world had gone out.

"Yes", was her simple reply.

There was no further need for words. It was crystal clear that she appreciated being acknowledged.

We were both completely in the moment. As she looked into my eyes again it was as if the whole world ceased to exist around us. It was just the two of us. We sat together; just sitting, sharing and being present in that moment. I held her space with love, compassion and I simply acknowledged that she was there. I didn't feel pity for her – merely a powerful compassion that one human being is truly privileged to share with another.

The bubble continued to hold us together. I wasn't sure what the bubble was; whether it was peace, grace, love or light. Maybe it was all of them, or something else. I watched her as she began to relax. No more words were exchanged. There was simply no need for them. The words; any words, would have spoilt those incredibly precious moments.

How long we stayed in that particular most comfortable, humble and connected silence I will never know. It was evident she felt safe with me and I was touched and honoured to provide her with that feeling on that memorable, treasured evening. Somewhere in the distance fireworks went off and we watched the bright colours fall from the sky together. The whole scene touched something deep within me. We both knew we were so blessed to share the evening together. I still feel the power of that connection. It has brought me to tears once again with its depth

The silence, the essence and the bubble that held our connection was eventually broken when two young men approached me for a selfie. They then asked to buy some balloons. She looked across at me with complete and utter disappointment. The moment was instantly gone. Within seconds she had disappeared into the crowds.

Had I made a difference in her life, simply by acknowledging her presence? Had I touched her soul as much as she had certainly brought something to mine? I gave thanks and gratitude in a quiet prayer to the divine. Watching the young men wander off into the crowds I noticed the balloons had 'Love' written on them.

I still feel her presence now, as clearly as I did that evening in March. Whenever I think of her, I send intentions of loving kindness and gratitude for a few precious moments of human connection, absolute humility and the chance to share, despite our very different backgrounds and futures. What would life hold for this young woman?

One afternoon whilst Samuel and I shared lunch, he introduced me to Paige. She was English and lived in Lancashire, only a few minutes' drive away from my previous home. The three of us shared much laughter that afternoon and Paige and I promised to keep in touch. She had been travelling for several months and was loving the experience of witnessing different cultures, languages and religions.

After we had taken a walk by The Ganges one afternoon, she said she felt incredibly emotional here in Mother India. She had frequently burst into tears at random moments and these moments took her completely by surprise. Often she was unaware what it was that she was crying about. She said she had never experienced it anywhere else throughout her travels. I shared with her that I had felt the same and now I simply allowed the tears to fall whenever they arose.

Paige was due to leave within the coming days. We agreed to share the Puja ceremony later that evening. She loved watching the Brahmans as they performed the sacred ritual. We were both in awe of the feeling the prayers and the chanting gave us. I had lost a dear and most treasured friend a year earlier. Today was the anniversary of his death. We purchased baskets of marigolds as offerings to the Gods. After the ceremony we placed them in The Ganges, each of us saying our own private prayers. Sharing that evening was such a treasured experience and we both agreed to keep in touch.

Several days later I met a beautiful lady in the café. I had called in early that morning after walking directly from the nearby bank. We chatted easily and she shared that today was her birthday. She was a well-known Russian model and had travelled extensively with her work. She explained that she had visited approximately forty other countries; though none had caused her to cry without reason like Mother India had. As I listened I was deeply touched to hear her raw honesty. She was so spiritual and, like me, had been 'called' here on a personal pilgrimage. I shared that Paige and I had experienced the exact same feelings. Wishing her 'A Very Happy Birthday' I suggested that we celebrate her birthday in style with herbal tea and the famous 'Aum' chocolate cake.

I met so many lovely people in that wonderful café. I often wondered whether it simply attracted them with its light aura. One afternoon as I chatted to Shivani; the owner, she shared that she looked after her staff; watching their energy levels throughout the day. I wondered what the rest of the world would be like if every employer took such care over their staff. She was such an inspiration to me for many reasons and I was grateful for everything I experienced in that particularly magical café.

The Indian family were so kind to me. I was always greeted with a smile and a most welcome cup of chai. Usually Reeta would cook me something; regardless of the time; day, or night. She was definitely a 'feeder' and no matter how many times I said I was full, she would appear with yet another spoon full of delicious curry, or whatever else she was cooking at the time.

Their house was always full of love, laughter and connection. Children and family members wandered in and out frequently and always shared a smile with me. Despite the language barrier we always managed somehow. Their daughter Sonali had recently married a beautiful Japanese man and their love was a wonderful thing to witness. They were so in love and full of respect for each other. Both had a wonderful sense of humour and both spoke excellent English. We shared many wonderful conversations and the two of them managed to copy my laugh perfectly. I only needed to hear one of them start mimicking me and I was in fits of laughter once more, then the cycle would continue until my belly hurt. Each of them adopted me into their family unit and I was named 'Grandma' as a sign of endearment and respect.

I loved visiting the many Hindu temples alongside the river. I had also studied Buddhism for many years and loved learning about the life of Buddha; his teachings of compassion, forgiveness and profound wisdom. Sarnath in Varanasi was where Lord Buddha had taught his first sermon after being enlightened. It was pulling at my soul and I was looking forward to visiting the whole site with the stupa and the many statues and temples.

My adopted Japanese grandson and Arun came with me that memorable Sunday. It was an incredible place and the feelings of peace and tranquillity were tangible everywhere. Everything felt vibrant here, everything radiated pure love and connection. I was touched as we wandered towards the powerful huge stupa (Buddhist monument) and the many relics. Everything Buddhism represents was very apparent here. Unconditional love oozed from everything and I certainly felt a deepening of my inner peace. All three of us felt the connection here and we cherished the whole day.

It was around this time that I had a profound dream where I received a blessing from Buddha while sitting under the famous Bodhi Tree with a dear friend. I had already made the decision to visit Bodh Gaya and this sacred tree, where he was enlightened. When I awoke from the dream I remembered it so clearly. I was surrounded by light and had no doubt that I needed to visit. The daily temperatures in Varanasi were now in the forties and although I wanted to stay longer, inevitably as the monsoon season approached, I had no other choice than to move north.

The last day that I saw Samuel, before leaving for Bodh Gaya, we had shared lunch and as usual we walked to Assi Junction together. Although we planned to see one another the following evening, there was a remote chance that I might not make it. I was going out with my dear Indian family to a remote village many miles away. I may or may not, make it back in time. As usual we hugged as he turned right to go to his apartment, I was turning left to return to my hotel. Instinctively I hugged him again. I am forever grateful that I followed my intuition that afternoon. It proved to be the last time we shared the magic that only a sincere hug can bring. We both knew we had known one another in many other lives and possessed a profound respect and regard that is very rare and unique. Through social media, that connection continues. Friendship is a true blessing and a most sacred gift.

Varanasi brought me joy and much needed respite. It was indeed stunning with the huge variety of temples alongside the river. Although The Ganges itself was filthy and polluted with rubbish from upstream; particularly from the open sewer river which was less than a mile away, overall I had loved my time here. I would certainly take many treasured memories with me of friendships and connections.

Watching the Brahmans perform the Puja ceremony daily to honour the river and Mother Earth had been such an absolute joy. The feeling of unity and community with the audience chanting and clapping through most of the ceremony was incredibly sacred.

And yet, the street beggars continued to sit, continued to beg at the passing people and just sat, seemingly unaware of the sacred prayers and the intentions that were being offered to the Gods. It would always leave me pondering the duality of life. Here the lower caste appeared to know nothing of light – or so it seemed. It was as though their light had been extinguished, if indeed, it had ever been there? Watching the tiniest of children as they walked the streets barefoot, holding up their hands for the 'magic rupees.' It was as if they believed the rupees would solve everything. Simply everything.

Where was the love here? Where was their love for one another and themselves? Where was their mothers love? Were they simply too exhausted and humiliated by life? Were they just zapped of life-force? Soul-force? Connection? Did they feel part of the community? Did they even hear the ceremony? Did they clap with the rest of the group at the right times?

Many strangers; despite the language barrier, found it such a joy to participate in this incredibly beautiful, touching, sacred and blessed ceremony that had taken place daily along the river for thousands of years. Did they even know what it represented? They had the advantage that they spoke the language after all. And yet, they seemed completely trapped in their inner worlds of poverty and emptiness. Their worlds consumed with inner pain and deep, deep suffering.

There were so many of these seemingly abandoned souls. Without fail, each and every morning I would get mobbed by the children; sometimes clinging to my dress, or my skirt. As hard as it was to see them, nothing would be solved, or resolved by handing over rupees. I sent love, light and healing in the hope that at least they would have an opportunity to welcome the light into their lives.

I often felt saddened as I thought back to the fountain in the park where I had first made my decision to change my life and travel. As I stood by The Ganges one afternoon watching the water buffalo, my thoughts deepened. Could these people really grasp a chance to escape from that muddy puddle and realise and welcome something different, or would they rather accept their caste system?

My thoughts took me to a faraway place. So, was it true? It seemed that one water particle was more favoured or more privileged than another. Was one more likely to be destined for that dirty, muddy puddle? Had the choices already been made? Did it really depend on which way the wind blew on that particular day? In that exact moment in time? Or was life just one big, muddy puddle for some and for others it was always the ever sparkling diamond, ever beautiful. The diamond was not afraid to show itself, or its colours. In that muddy puddle life could dry out in an instant. Life was uncertain and unsafe. No-one ever admired a muddy puddle. And yet everyone always loved and enjoyed the fountain.

The design, the water droplets, the sound of the spray as it touched the water below as it was enveloped to safety. All of it mattered in some way. Each and every individual water droplet had the ability to look like a pure diamond. It was only a matter of chance that the sunlight might happen to catch the water at the exact, right, perfect moment. On a really good day, the cascading water would look as though a rainbow had woven itself into the spray. What a joy to see. The beauty of that one ray of sunlight which could easily split into all seven of its intimate colours. As gentle as the kiss of the butterfly on the petals of a rose, the light would gently touch and join with the water.

As my thoughts continued I pondered on the depth of life's meaning. How could it be that some lives were simply more colourful than others? Did some people have a right to shine more than others? Were some destined to stay in the darkness?

Thinking back to the muddy puddle, it was simply that. Nothing more, nothing less, just plain mud. No light, no colour. Just a dark, muddy puddle. I pondered what the molecules of water trapped within the mud, might be thinking if they were asked about the light?

"Rainbows here? You must be joking." That's what they would probably say I thought and then realised that I had said it out loud without even realising that my lips had moved. 'This was certainly turning out to be a deep, philosophical debate' I thought.

"Do you think we deserve light? Do you think we deserve colour and maybe to be part of a huge brightly coloured rainbow?" I imagined what the water molecules would say if they were asked if they deserved the light.

"We thought we were destined to be here." As my thoughts continued further, I became aware that the water molecules which were offered the light simply embraced it and yet the water molecules trapped within the mud, merely accepted their miserable fate. Had these people lost all hope?

"No-one escapes from here. No-one. We are waiting to die as the puddle evaporates, or as we get washed away somewhere else, maybe into the drain, or the sewers. It's our fate. We were born that way."

‘An age old struggle’ I thought. The things that made the myths and the legends of eons. The yin and the yang. Black and white. Night and day. Male and female. Just polarities….or were they? Was it true that some people had a right to the light and some simply didn’t? Whose choice was it anyway?

As my mind wandered further into the abyss, I pondered more deeply. Had those choices already been made? Whether we were each to be like a sparkling diamond shining in the sunlight or whether we would be a part of that muddied puddle.

What if…? What if, one of the water molecules in that muddy pool asked the question?

“Do we deserve the light? Do we deserve colour in our lives? Do we deserve to be admired? Can we actually allow ourselves to receive the light? To receive the joy? To receive laughter and happiness?”

I was rolling my shoulders and continuing to stretch out my limbs, as I stood by The Ganges. I thought of what it would be like to be a water molecule who could at least *welcome the possibility* of changing from the dark to the light. How much courage would it take to even think differently to the others and consider a different life? What would the other water molecules think if one decided to think differently from them? After all, water changed its form constantly and the water cycle was simply that, a water cycle. A cycle of continuous and continuing, never ending change. It was like the wheel of life. The cycle of karma and dharma. The fact was that change could bring about magical things. It could transform everything with the right environment and circumstances.

India was rather like that for me. To seek out the diamonds and the rainbows. To be aware of the mud too and the mudded waters. I felt as though those thoughts related to me also. I was finally allowing myself to shine and to sparkle.

Varanasi by The Ganges is known as 'The City Of Light.' Indeed as I prepared to leave, this place had certainly brought me light and had guided me on my way as a lone traveller. My writing style had changed and was becoming more professional. I had recognised many changes in myself.

It was now time to head to Buddha country.

Chapter Thirty Four

Booking in at the hotel that the Tibetan monk had recommended was easy. I had said ‘Good-bye’ to many of my Indian family that morning, though Arun and my ‘grandson’ travelled with me to Bodh Gaya. The journey had taken about six hours and we were all glad to have eaten and rested on route.

Saying my final ‘Good-bye’ to them felt most odd. Now I was alone in this town. It felt very strange. As I unpacked my things, making my room my personal space, I felt a huge range of emotions. I only planned to be here for two more days, then I would be heading to Patna. From there I was due to fly to Delhi. My time in Mother India was coming to its natural end and I thought it appropriate that I should now spend time where Lord Buddha reached enlightenment.

I took an afternoon stroll in the searing heat. The temperatures were now in the high thirties. I was drawn towards a bridge. I wasn’t quite sure what was pulling me to walk this way though simply followed my intuition. I chatted to a lady and we walked together sharing stories of how we both came to be in India. She mentioned that the original Bodhi Tree was further down the road and she gave me directions. The tree was obviously pulling me towards it, though by now it was approaching sunset. Without natural daylight I knew I was being incredibly foolish to continue to walk on the path into the remote villages. I vowed to return the following day.

Later that evening I met a lady called Marie and we shared a meal together. She worked here for a well-known charity and we chatted easily about Buddhism and spirituality. She had been coming here for many years and recommended me to visit Mahabodhi Temple early the following morning.

The Mahabodhi was magnificent and surrounded by beautiful gardens. There was a tangible peace here, similar to the peace I had experienced in Sarnath. The different temple structures were splendid and I was delighted that I had taken her advice. The tree where Lord Buddha was enlightened was said to be here. After yesterday's intuitive walk I couldn't be sure which one was the original Bodhi tree. I loved it nonetheless and meditated alongside many other pilgrims and monks of many different nationalities. The Mucalinda Lake was also beautiful and I sat there quietly meditating for some time before I moved to sit in the International Peace Garden. Two huge bells hung there to commemorate world peace. Reading the inscriptions I was very tempted to ring them. This place touched my soul; the fact that Lord Buddha and his teachings were spread across the world encouraging peace, forgiveness and compassion are a true testimony to a holy, enlightened wise master.

The other temples in the town were stunning. The numerous Buddhist temples each with their own unique designs from across the world; Tibetan, Chinese, Japanese, Thai to mention only some of the splendid buildings that were erected to celebrate the life of Lord Buddha. They were absolutely amazing and in their own way each of them simply took my breath-away. Walking around in the extreme heat, despite the fact that it was still morning was an uncomfortable experience, though it proved to be so worthwhile.

It was far too hot to venture outdoors in the heat of the midday sun and I was aware that I still wanted to visit the Bodhi Tree near the remote villages. Once the afternoon sun had cooled a little, I walked hoping to find a taxi to take me to the sacred tree. I had literally journeyed around the corner from the hotel when a young man asked if I wanted to visit the well-known, most sacred tree.

Travelling in the same direction as I had the day before, I was delighted when we eventually arrived. It was quite a way from where I had turned back the evening before. The tree was amazing and even bigger than I had anticipated. It was such a beautiful sight. The tree was wrapped in multi-coloured prayer flags with a beautiful statue of the Buddha alongside it. There were four sets of huge roots which towered above me. It was approximately eighty feet high and perhaps fifteen feet wide; a set of roots at each corner. As I stood inside the tree, I felt something move within me. It was almost as though something was set alight - rather like a candle for the very first time. Whether this was the original tree or not, its power was intense. I was honoured to be here and glad I had listened to my intuition. I sent a quiet prayer of thanks to this particular tree and to all the trees across the world.

Later that evening after sharing another meal with Marie, I awoke feeling nauseous. Within minutes I was vomiting and felt quite ill. My flights were booked for my journey to Delhi from Patna, I needed to recover quickly. I became very concerned that I might have to cancel them.

As the night went on into the early morning hours the sickness and diarrhoea continued. It finally began to ease towards lunchtime the following day. I rested in the hope that I would be well enough to travel the next morning. The edits of 'Reflections Of A Hummingbird' were almost finished. I prayed that I would feel well enough in the evening to complete the book before I was due to leave early the next morning. Several hours later when I awoke, I was delighted to finish 'Reflections'. I had not eaten all day though I was able to drink water without vomiting.

I was so relieved that I was fit enough to travel by taxi the next morning. Arriving at Patna airport I realised I felt hungry for the first time. Eating a toastie very slowly and listening to my bodies signals, I was pleased that I actually felt well.

The flight to Delhi was straightforward and I had booked an overnight hotel as I would be flying to Kolkata very early the next day. From there I was due to fly to Kathmandu in Nepal. Giving the name of the hotel to the taxi driver I was amazed when we arrived at a most beautiful luxurious hotel. I re-checked the name and thanked the Universe that the Indian hotels are so much cheaper than in the United Kingdom. The taxi driver agreed to collect me at 5am promptly. As I checked in, the hotel staff could find no booking under my name. I decided the Universe was playing a joke at my expense and as the early morning taxi had already been ordered and payment made, I decided to stay and enjoy my time here. The hotel room was amazing. It was so comfortable and a fantastic way to celebrate my last night in Mother India. I found it quite ironic that it was raining heavily outside: another reminder of England before my imminent departure north to cooler climates. I was looking forward to my early morning flight to Kathmandu. Another place and new adventures awaited.

Chapter Thirty Five

Phill and I had kept in touch throughout my months of travelling. He had suggested I stay in the 'Yak and Yeti' hotel in Kathmandu. After my arrival, thankful for a smooth flight, as I walked towards the taxi, I suddenly started to feel incredibly nauseous again. Opening the taxi window for some air, I breathed and used some self-hypnosis techniques to assist me. I was pleased when I arrived in my beautiful room which overlooked the most splendid gardens. The swimming pool looked so inviting. I had already fallen in love with the place, especially when I saw the fountain and the brightly coloured koi. I looked forward to a lovely swim as I started to unpack my suitcase and located my swimming costume.

Suddenly the nausea returned and within an hour I was vomiting much worse than I had done two days earlier. Sweat poured from every pore as I lay writhing in agony on the bathroom floor. I was grateful that it was so clean and hygienic. Diarrhoea soon followed and it was several hours later before I actually managed to crawl into bed, praying that if I needed the toilet again I would make the journey; rather than vomiting on the beautiful wooden floor.

As I lay sweating I was surrounded by bright white light. I had experienced this before many years earlier when I had been hospitalised with a serious kidney infection. I surrendered, knowing that if my time was up, there was nothing I could do about it. I have never feared death as I have always known where souls go. I was surprised when I awoke the following morning.

The sickness and diarrhoea continued and that evening unable to control the retching I heard people walking past in the adjoining corridor. I guessed they might have thought I was hung-over from too much alcohol. Too weak to move, I allowed the shower to run warm water all over my body to wash away the sweat and the vomit.

Two days later I was completely exhausted. Too weak to leave my room, I was glad to be able to sit in the window seat and watch the other guests enjoy the pool and the magnificent gardens below. I had only booked in the hotel for three days and was far too weak to relocate. I phoned reception and explained the situation. I was so grateful that I could stay here another night.

The following day I wandered tentatively to reception to pay for yet another evenings stay. I felt so weak though was determined to sit and enjoy the garden; even if it would only be for a few minutes. I found a quiet bench by the fish pond and was simply grateful to be out of my room.

Jay was so supportive. He suggested tea, toast and bananas - the thought of the latter did not appeal at all. I looked dreadful and was glad I could order simple toast from room service. Being ill gave me even more time than I normally had to reflect upon life, my family and my travels. As our emails continued, Jay suggested that maybe there was something I was being shown? Maybe there was a learning to this experience? I had already decided to write again and 'The Dance Of The Mosquito' was birthed in the beautiful hotel grounds on the final morning of my stay. I never did get to enjoy a swim in the pool.

Moving from this incredible luxurious hotel to a reasonably priced one which was situated on the busy main road felt like a real let down. The first room I was shown was dark and something about the room really gave me the creeps. I returned to reception a few minutes later to request another room. I had decided that I would leave if no other was available; despite being so weak and weary. The next room they showed me was much lighter, with a huge window and it certainly felt more homely too. I was glad that I had spoken my truth with assertion and refused to stay in a room that was so oppressive.

The following morning I was still weak though had already booked my accommodation in Pokhara. I had looked forward to visiting the temples in Kathmandu with great anticipation for weeks. I knew I'd had many lives here previously and was so disappointed that since my arrival I had been unable to visit any of the cities many sights.

The next day I booked a taxi to the local square where I could at last visit the temples. Looking at the map the drive was only fifteen minutes away. The driver was still journeying across town over thirty minutes later. I intuited that I was obviously meant to be somewhere else.

Arriving at Bhaktapur Square certainly proved to be a surprise well worth waiting for. It was absolutely amazing. The temples were not like any others I had ever seen and yet the whole area felt so familiar to me. The sacred chanting of Snatum Kaur played in the background and I felt a part of me had come home. I was so pleased to be feeling better. My guide spoke excellent English and he was a kind, humble young man. Looking at the hand-made brick buildings and the incredibly detailed wooden windows I was astounded at such craftsmanship. The windows were intricately latticed and the love that had gone into their creation was obvious.

The earthquake damage was substantial here and many of the temples had fresh flowing water running through them before the fatal earthquake struck. Now the water table had been damaged the fountains were without water. It saddened me greatly. The earthquake damage was clearly evident. Many buildings had been left with only one main wall standing. It all represented the fragility of life and those that had been lost. Other buildings had no roof or had simply become a heap of rubble. Most of the temples had been damaged too, some were being rebuilt and some seemed to have been left abandoned. Others stood tall and elegant in the main square. It was an incredibly humbling sight. My guide explained how many people had lost their lives and their loved ones. He too had lost friends and family. I was grateful that I was safe and well.

The shops were filled with all things spiritual; singing bowls, statues of the Gods, crystals, music CDs, stunning sacred artwork and tapestries. It was a cacophony of colour and music as I walked between the tiny streets. Walking towards another part of the square a woman was making earthenware pots. Watching her as she sculpted the clay was truly amazing. Her gift and experience allowed her to produce so many pots within minutes. She clearly loved her work. I was mesmerised watching her mould the clay.

Jay and I had discussed so much about how we can choose to live through the soul, connecting to our original self and how we also need to be grounded to Mother Earth. We both thought it interesting that soul and sole were pronounced the same, and yet were two very different words. The clay came from the earth and I could feel the earths' connection in each and every piece of the earthenware that was laid out in the square. I thought about pottery which is now mass produced by machines and felt our modern world to be such a sad reflection of what was once a normal and key part in people's lives across the globe.

Walking further to the right an elderly man was operating a potter's wheel, making a beautiful vase. I wondered if he had done this most of his life as I looked at his clay engrained skin. There was a tangible sadness to these people who had lost so much in the earthquake and yet there was also a feeling of gratitude and renewal; a sense of survival and connection where death and the living are at one with each other. The reminders of that earthquake were everywhere for all to see.

My guide mentioned another temple which was one of the oldest in the city. It was on top of a nearby mountain. The drive was stunning as we passed through rice paddies and so much greenery. I appreciated it all; especially as we were now well away from the pollution of the city. It was still quite a walk up to the temple from the car park and when we arrived in the heat of the afternoon sun it was no easy task. When we finally arrived, we were greeted by two armed soldiers with huge rifles. No photographs were allowed in parts of the temple. I wasn't about to argue with armed guards.

Phill had mentioned that he had intuited a sacred bell which I needed to touch, or ring. Here there were so many and I was pleased as I walked about the area touching them all. I was delighted that this temple had escaped the earthquake although parts of the path were still being re-built. The gold on the roof was stunning. The whole place seemed even more sacred than the temples we had visited only a little over an hour earlier. It felt such an honour to be here.

Driving down the mountain on our return journey was pure bliss as we passed so much natural beauty of the region; the scenery was breath-taking. However, once we neared the city I was saddened to be amongst the traffic and the pollution once again.

The following day I had arranged to meet my guide for more sight-seeing. I would be leaving within two days, time was precious. We visited a beautiful temple though I was disappointed that I was unable to visit some parts; as they were only open to Hindus.

Watching bodies being prepared for cremation was quite an experience. My guide explained the whole process of laying the bodies out on a slab of stone so the soul could be released from the earth. I was amazed at the respect and the way the dead were honoured. A few minutes later we crossed over a bridge and witnessed a woman's body being cremated. As the kindling was set alight, the priest attended the service ensuring the soul travelled straight to heaven. I watched on; as did many other westerners; in awe of this deeply touching and most humbling ceremony, marking the end of someone's life; not as a loss but a celebration of all they had shared. When one of the legs moved due to the heat, I could clearly make out a woman's foot. It brought a sense of fragility to me; especially after witnessing all the earthquake damage the previous day. Listening to a family member of the deceased wailing also deepened these feelings.

The whole scene and the emotions it stirred were most powerful. I thought of my beloved granddaughters in England and was grateful that I had enjoyed each and every precious moment that I had shared with them. I was grateful for family and dear friends alike and was glad that I had no 'loose ends' in the United Kingdom. They were all very aware that they were loved and it was a sobering thought that if I died whilst away, they would know exactly how much love I had for them.

Boudhanath Stupa was to be our next destination. It was stunning and steeped in history, culture and Buddhism. The hundreds of brightly coloured prayer flags danced in the wind. I loved the whole setting which was surrounded by cafes, restaurants and delightful shops selling all things spiritual.

As I wandered around I met a Dutch girl and her grandfather. We had chatted in the airport over a week ago and it was lovely to share a few minutes catching up with them and wishing them well; especially as they would be leaving for home the next day. Peace and love oozed from this place and it was a great honour to share these feelings with the other pilgrims. Saying my prayers and intentions as I turned the prayer wheels, it felt as though they had been heard and were in the process of being answered. I prayed for many things; health, wisdom, grace, inspiration, enthusiasm, courage to continue this unknown journey and of course for my loved ones across the world. Now that I had re-written 'Reflections', I realised how much writing fulfilled something deep within my soul. I prayed for my books to reach the masses; be it through finding a book publisher, an agent or by whatever means available to inspire and assist people through their lives.

Arriving back at the hotel I sat gathering my thoughts on the balcony. I had felt the bed move earlier that morning and wondered whether or not there had been a small earthquake. My guide and I had chatted whilst we were en route to our various destinations and he had mentioned that there had in fact been two tremors that morning. It was all incredibly sobering; especially after seeing the cremation. My son and his wife were expecting a new arrival; a daughter, the following day and a Caesarean Section had already been arranged. Life and death were utmost in my mind. I sent a prayer for her safe delivery

After everything I had already experienced here in Kathmandu and the fact that I still felt below par after being ill, I was grateful that I could rest while I considered the fragility and balance between life and death. The whole purpose of this journey was to allow myself time to travel alone as a spiritual pilgrim; allowing the heart and soul time to grow and hopefully to experience some of the most sacred, spiritual places in the world.

That night I considered connections and how many people I had connected with throughout my life. I pondered on the many lives that I had been privileged to touch in my personal and my professional capacity. I thought about how others had touched my life and had brought so much to me; both the good and the bad. Wise enough to accept and appreciate life lessons and disagreements, broken promises and conflicts as part of life's rich tapestry were all food for thought. The perfection was in appreciating the imperfection. Gratitude welled up inside me from the bottom of my belly.

Checking my phone later that evening I wished my son and his wife 'good luck' for the pending birth. I drifted off to sleep knowing that tomorrow would be my final day here before I travelled to Pokhara.

The following afternoon photographs of baby Phoebe arrived. It proved to be quite a celebration. Mother and baby were fine and I was once again a most proud and delighted grandmother. My Indian 'grandson', Yuya and Arun, the head of the Indian family were here in Kathmandu. Yuya was hoping to visit the embassy to acquire his work visa. I was so surprised and delighted to see them again as we shared a lovely meal together on my last evening in the city.

Chapter Thirty Six

I hadn't booked a ticket on the coach to Pokhara and trusted the advice of the locals that I would find a seat on one of the many buses when I arrived at the depot. I had made enquiries at the local travel agents who had quoted a price of over two hundred English pounds. I was grateful that 'Tripadviser' had listed the price at approximately twenty pounds. When the conductor asked for payment of seven hundred rupees I was amazed. It was the equivalent of approximately eight pounds sterling. He stated that we would arrive in the early afternoon; dependent upon traffic and landslides.

The coach was soon full and a young man called Niklas sat next to me throughout the journey. He was from Germany and had been travelling for several months. We chatted easily and I enjoyed his company. The journey took us through the mountains. Often the road was right on the edge of the mountains; drops which were several hundred feet below. The river in the valley beneath us was stunning as was the rest of the scenery here. I was relieved to be out of the city. Niklas and I looked back at one point and could see a huge cloud of smog from all the pollution. It saddened us both deeply.

The rice paddies lined the sides of the mountains in their glorious splendour and were so beautiful they actually looked as though they were sculptured terraces in a magical garden. As I watched the local's farm the land and the children swim and play below in the river, I felt blessed to witness life here. It was obvious the people were incredibly connected to the land. We passed men who were cutting marble by the roadside, people chopping vegetables and children sitting with their grandparents, men playing chess and people drinking coffee simply watching the world go by. It was such a beautiful, connected way of living and I loved the whole journey. While so many other travellers slept, I was delighted to get an insight into these people's lives. I didn't want to miss a single moment.

We arrived over seven hours later. It had started to rain and as we waited to get our luggage out from underneath the coach we got soaked in the downpour. The rain was lovely and quite refreshing. We knew we would soon dry off in the afternoon heat. Niklas and I shared a taxi and hoped to catch up in the coming days. His accommodation was at the other end of the lake to my hotel.

Arriving in my hotel I felt an immediate depth of connection. The whole place seemed to welcome me. When I was shown to my room, I was thrilled when I saw a bath in the bathroom; rather than just a shower. I hadn't had a bath for months. What a simple pleasure it would be to enjoy a soak in a hot bath. I was delighted to have a balcony, as I had requested. Looking out across at my new view I almost cried. Not only was this place quiet but I had mountains to the left, to the right and in the far distance. The trees covered most of the mountains and they looked absolutely stunning. The World Peace Stupa sat proudly perched on the top of the mountain to my left, overlooking the whole valley.

I took a deep breath, I took another. The air here was so clean. I instantly felt so much gratitude. My heart expanded as I breathed again and the connection with Mother Nature was tangibly strong. It was certainly a place I needed to be after being in a noisy city with very few trees. Seeing the mountains from here brought me such joy.

Boiling the kettle, I was grateful to be able to make a cup of my usual weak black tea. I sat on the balcony in the afternoon sun, just being; taking in all of this natural beauty. I had certainly missed the trees and the mountain views these past few months. Although I hadn't yet visited the lake, I needed to be present in this one particular moment. The intensity of the relief now that I had escaped the concrete jungle made me cry.

I have no idea how long I sat there. I simply sat on the balcony listening to the people chatting below and absorbing it all. The quiet surprised me the most. There was no honking, much, much less traffic, and only the occasional sound of a power tool way off in the far distance. Silence, silence, silence. I finally had silence. The lake would have to wait; as would my unpacking.

Gratitude touched every single part of my very being and oozed from each and every cell as I sat there. I absorbed it all. The view, the mountains, the sight of trees in abundance, the hillside villages and the Peace Stupa.

I love looking out over towns, cities and villages at night when the last of the daylight is finally gone and night time descends. I wondered what this valley would look like as night fell. I wondered how the lights would pepper the mountain side and I smiled knowing how lucky I was to experience all that this pilgrimage had brought me. Watching the colourful prayer flags as they blew on the adjacent rooftop in the afternoon breeze was blissful. The simplicity of allowing the wind to catch their intentions, to carry them off into the universe to be heard by God. I knew I was blessed. These were such sacred, treasured moments in a most sacred, treasured valley.

I sat and absorbed all this intimate beauty for almost two hours, now I could feel the lake calling. Locking the bedroom door I asked at reception for directions to the lakeside. The hotel was located up a side street. I had no idea whereabouts the main town; or the lake were located from here. As I ambled outside, I felt something I hadn't felt for quite some time. It took me a while to put my finger on just what it was. Safe. I actually felt totally safe and secure. In that one, single moment I realised that I hadn't felt this safe for weeks. I breathed out a deep and lasting sigh. I breathed in safety. Was it the mountains? The trees? The whole valley? I hadn't even arrived at the lake yet? I simply enjoyed the feeling.

Following the directions I had been given I was so excited. The English Lakes always held a special place in my heart. I wondered what this one would be like. The pollution of the waters in India and Kathmandu had saddened me greatly and although it had eventually become normal to me, the thought of seeing a clean lake was something that brought joy to my very soul.

I gasped when I saw her. I started to shake a little too with sheer delight. There she was, in all her splendid beauty. The lake, this beautiful, vast expanse of clean water, as far as the eye could see. My eyes filled with tears once again, as they had done so many times on this journey. Although there were many people milling around, I managed to find a quiet spot where I breathed and absorbed the surrounding beauty.

The mountain to the left where the Stupa was located seemed to fold itself into the lake with such grace and a powerful, majestic elegance. There was a tiny island a little off-shore with a beautiful temple. Many rowing boats were tethered there, awaiting the return of their pilgrims. Once again the quiet touched me. Despite the volume of people here no-one was shouting, talking loudly, or generally making noise. No-one played loud music and I wondered if the peace and safety I felt had also touched them. I made a vow that I would come here daily during my seventeen day stay.

There was a path to the right which seemed to lead along the shoreline. As I followed it, it was lined with restaurants and bars. There were so many different ones; a combination of modern, old, Nepalese, Italian and one with a model of the Eiffel Tower, Paris. Everyone seemed so friendly here and the smiles genuine. I had grown tired of smiles being used as a means to get business and custom. I felt like a young child watching in awe as more and more of the scene opened up in front of me.

I could see even more mountains to the right and they continued to the end of the lake as far as the eye could see. Once again a wave of gratitude and peace swept over me. It was late afternoon now, the sunset was due about 6pm. I knew it signalled that the mosquitos would soon be ready to dance their dance. I was well aware how much they loved to dance on me. I knew I didn't have long to get back to the hotel.

As night time fell I watched in awe once more as the whole scenery changed. Lights from the local mountain villages looked stunning as they shone in bright clusters amongst the trees. The Peace Stupa looked absolutely amazing. It stood with a distinct sense of pride and was the most brightly lit building to be seen across the whole valley.

I knew I had to visit the Stupa. I was so contented here that I was happy to wait and decided to allow it to unfold in the coming days. I felt at peace here. It was a complete and abiding peace combined with serenity. Whether it was the peace Stupa, the sacredness of the valley, the lovely hotel room, or something inside of myself I couldn't be sure. I enjoyed the feeling as I closed the curtains on what had definitely been a memorable day. I drifted off into a world of dreams.

The following morning I was excited to visit the lake. I had promised myself that I would spend most of the day alongside the water's edge. Delighted that paratha and chai tea were listed on the breakfast menu, I ordered my favourite meal to start the day. The staff were incredibly friendly here and I found that I was so relaxed. The manager introduced himself; his name was Deep. His humble mannerisms reminded me of my late grandfather. There was a depth of character and a profound sense of grace to this man. He asked if I had plans for the day and I explained that I was looking forward to spending time by the lakeside.

When I arrived at the lake I was surprised to see armed guards and Ghurkhas on patrol. I was not aware of the political situation in Nepal. Regardless, I found it odd that armed men would be in attendance here. I had a choice to feel the fear the soldiers represented to me, or to simply ignore them and move on. I decided upon the latter as I walked through the gate to the path which ran alongside the lake.

The water was clean and covered with stunning, sacred water lilies. I could see an abundance of fish and was tempted to swim. The path could be seen quite a way ahead and I had many landmarks which I could use as markers; beside the path, ensuring that I wouldn't get lost. I followed it for over a mile before I came to the roadside.

The water was a stunning, exquisite turquoise. I loved it. By now, the heat of the day was rapidly increasing and I stopped at a café by the water's edge for refreshment and a well-needed toilet break. It looked like a setting from Robinson Crusoe and it felt magical as I pulled up an old tree stump to use as a stool. The menu was quirky too; 'Swampy Juice' or 'Paradise Smoothie'. As the wind chimes played their song as the morning breeze breathed life into them, I was feeling very comfortable enjoying my 'Swampy Juice' while watching the gentle ripples at the water's edge. I welcomed the quiet here and the simplicity of be-ing. I felt truly blessed and all the stress of India and Kathmandu simply seemed to melt away.

Wandering back to the hotel I was amazed when I saw the water buffalo in the water alongside children who were swimming, and fishing. Nature was at one here with humanity and it seemed respect for everything was plentiful.

The next morning Deep asked what my plans were for the day. I explained that I was happy to be by the lakeside and would be taking time to write daily. He mentioned that he was very happy to take me up to the Peace Stupa in the coming days. I was so delighted to be invited.

Three days later we travelled by bus to the other side of the mountain. When we left the bus we hoped to catch another which then led directly up to the Stupa. Each bus that drove past was full of passengers. Now in the midday sun we had to walk up the mountain, another kilometre or so. Dripping with sweat we found ourselves laughing at every stop we made on each of the many bends. We both struggled with the steep climb. Looking down over the terraced rice paddies and the surrounding mountains I was stunned by the beauty of the whole valley. There were many eagles soaring above us. It was a powerful reminder of untouched, unspoilt Mother Earth.

The views were well worth the climb when we finally arrived at the top. I was amazed to see how busy it was with tourists of all nationalities. The lake looked tiny from our vantage point and the adjoining mountain tops stood in all their splendour. Seeing a sign that read 'No Jumping' at the edge of the cliff made me smile. The stupa was magnificent; a white mound which radiated unconditional love. The whole place resonated peace and I felt blessed to be here in a truly sacred space. It overlooked the whole area and I could see clearly why it had been named 'The Sacred Valley.' Meditating alone at the side of the stupa was a wonderful, sacred, touching and memorable experience.

Deep led the way as we ambled down the many steps to the lakeside below. I was grateful that he had made time to bring me here. We shared a beautiful walk through the forest to the lake. The trees provided a welcome canopy from the sun.

His friend was waiting for us by the water in his canoe when we arrived at the waters edge. This day was just getting better and better. Being out on the open lake was a perfect way to end the journey, as the oars rowed us gently to the other side of the shoreline. I loved listening to the two men laughing and chatting easily in Nepalese. It was a great testimony to their friendship which had begun many decades earlier. I had wanted to travel on the lake since my arrival. However my rowing skills were completely inadequate. I now felt rather spoilt. It was an honour to share the whole experience and even though I offered to pay; neither men would take any payment. Friendship was given freely that day; without expectations or attachments. I will remember it for the rest of my life. Arriving back at the shore I noticed the magnificent wisteria tree, its lilac splashes were beautiful set against the background of greenery. I thanked them both for such a blessed, memorable afternoon as I made my way back to the hotel.

The following morning whilst in the shower, I noticed the sorry state of my feet. After walking for months in flip-flops, the dirt was now ingrained; despite having used a scrubbing brush frequently. I decided to treat myself to a much needed pedicure. As I walked along the main street, I was surprised to find that many beauty spas were still closed.

I had walked almost a mile before I located one that was reasonably priced. I was amazed to find a man on reception who spoke with a Canadian accent. He explained that the beauticians were getting ready for the day and asked if I would mind waiting. We chatted easily and I asked how he had come to be here in Pokhara;

"I have been visiting for over a decade and I love it dearly. Me and my father survived when the earthquake struck several years earlier. It was a poignant moment and I realised that I had a choice whether I would ever return. I've loved hiking here and the whole area has felt like a second home. I met my wife here and we connected easily. I proposed a few months later."

I was so delighted to hear his story. He explained that this was her salon and he helped to run it. He spoke the language fluently and recognised the connection between them immediately.

I was in awe of this man who had followed his heart and was clearly incredibly happy and settled here. He was a delight to listen to and when he mentioned that there are no coincidences in life, the conversation swiftly changed to sharing stories about how we both used the law of attraction and our intuition as tools to guide us through life. I was delighted when he mentioned that he was collating information for a book that he was about to begin writing. I offered my help and was so engrossed in sharing that when the beautician came through to begin the pedicure I was rather disappointed that we had to close the conversation. Louis suggested we chat later and I happily agreed.

The pedicure was amazing and the service I received was exceptional. My feet looked wonderful after the treatment. I thanked her and sat happily in reception once more chatting to Louis. He mentioned that there was a wonderful restaurant towards the end of the lake. I suddenly realised I was hungry and making my way to the main road, I ordered a taxi. I thought it odd that the driver resembled Freddie Mercury. The restaurant was quite a way from my hotel though it was located along the lakeside. It would be easy for me to wander back later that afternoon. The food was absolutely delicious, the service excellent and the views breath-taking from this magnificent vantage point overlooking the lake. It was everything he had said it would be and I could see clearly why he and his wife loved it here. The restaurant became a favourite of mine and although it was a long walk from the hotel, I loved the views.

The vendors along the lakeside path soon became used to me. Within a few days of my stay most of them greeted me daily. I felt so alive here and so connected.

A few days later I returned to the salon. Louis and I chatted easily once more about life, religion, philosophy, and so much more. He clearly loved his wife and I was looking forward to meeting her.

"Love is a choice" he said with much assertion. I was surprized by his passionate outburst.

"I choose to love her, and I chose to be here. I had known someone previously for seven years and in all that time we never connected on this deep level." I thought of my love for Jay and the gratitude I had for our connection. We both agreed that love was a very powerful thing to share and enjoy with another.

The following Sunday I was sat enjoying the view at 'Gusto' while chatting to my son-in-law on the phone. I heard someone say 'Hello' and was delighted to see Louis and his wife standing behind me. We all hugged and the love these two people shared was touching.

The thunder storms here were becoming more frequent now. I soon became used to reading the weather as the clouds began to change their colour and formation. Usually I knew I had thirty minutes to either take shelter, or return to the hotel.

The thunder storms were the most spectacular I have ever seen. I loved to watch as the rods of lightening lit up the sky, stretching across most of the valley. The sound as the rain pelted down on the roof was incredible and deafening. The storms were spectacular. With each and every storm the electricity would go off until the weather had calmed again. I captured so many stunning photographs and the ferocity of Thor, the mighty God of thunder. Each and every one was breath-taking and I loved the experiences of witnessing Mother Earth's mighty power as she lit up the whole sky. After the storms the sky would return to normal so quickly, even if the streets were still running with water.

On the Wednesday before I was due to leave Pokhara I took my usual walk by the lakeside. I decided to try a new restaurant on the road which ran parallel to the lake. I sat in the restaurant and was enjoying the view across the lake when I saw a small plane on a rooftop. Thinking I was seeing things, I looked again. Then again. There it was, a small plane on the rooftop of a hotel, or restaurant a few minutes' walk away. There was a motif on the plane which looked familiar. I took a photograph so that I could enlarge the picture. It read: 'Bohemian Rhapsody.' Then to the side I noticed the four faces of each of the band members who made up the rock group 'Queen'. I still couldn't believe my eyes, so I turned away and then looked back again, taking yet photograph. The plane was still there. It was definitely time to finish my drink and investigate.

I was surprised that it was relatively easy to locate. I had to stop for breath when I saw that the sign to the restaurant was indeed named 'Bohemian Rhapsody'. I was stunned. Freddie Mercury has been a hero of mine for many decades. Here I was in Pokhara, Nepal about to go into a restaurant which had a plane on the rooftop dedicated to him and the band. I hoped I would meet the owner as I suspected there had to be a story behind it all. As I walked into the garden there was a huge painting of Freddie on the whole of the wall. I wanted someone to pinch me. I considered that I might have sunstroke from the heat. As I ventured nearer there was a huge music hall with a stage. Pictures of 'Queen' hung on all four walls. I stood mesmerized by this phenomenal site when I was approached by a young man in his twenties.

"Can I help you madam" he asked.

"I thought I was seeing things and had to come and take a look to see if it was real."

I hoped I didn't sound like an over-excited schoolgirl.

The guy explained that he had always loved 'Queen'. He came into some money and had purchased the plane and then brought it here. The restaurant wasn't quite finished though he hoped to complete the project within the coming three months. I was amazed at his story and his passion. He offered to take photographs of me by the plane. I was delighted by his offer as I could then prove to myself that I had visited their private plane.

When he suggested I look inside the aircraft and see for myself what it was like I felt faint for a moment. It was amazing and although most of the cockpit had been stripped of the controls, the rest was still very much in its original state. It was truly a day to remember as I exchanged my love for Freddie with him and suggested that he might like to visit Switzerland to stand by Freddie's statue. He vowed he would, once this project was completed. I wished him great success and thanked him for his kindness as I sat and enjoyed a most welcome lunch, sitting right by the side of this treasured plane.

I loved this town. Often I took a different route towards the lakeside though I spent time there every day. One morning I found a stunning temple quite by chance. It had Hindu statues and a huge statue of Buddha too. The peace was incredible and I found myself visiting for a few moments most days for a quiet prayer of gratitude.

I enjoyed each and every precious day in Pokhara. It was testimony to a beautiful town with beautiful people. I received a warm welcome wherever I visited and I felt incredibly settled here.

Visiting Tibet had crossed my mind though Louis had stated that I would not be able to visit the sacred sites unaccompanied. He explained that my only option to visit would be to purchase an over-priced package deal. It didn't feel right. I decided against the idea.

When I visited the local Tibetan refugee camp which housed hundreds of Tibetans I was deeply saddened. As I read the posters in the information centre I found myself wiping away several tears as I read about the plight of these people. They had escaped over The Himalayas and there were many testimonies relating to the dire circumstances these people endured during their journey. Many had sadly lost their lives and inevitably much of their culture was also lost.

As I witnessed the women in the refugee camp making hand-made woollen carpets and material being woven on hand operated looms, I was touched and humbled. I said a quiet prayer for these people who had suffered so much when their country had been invaded by the Chinese. I felt honoured to share time with them and was relieved that they were now safe here in Nepal.

In the last fortnight, this place had brought me peace, an ever-deepening grace and an inner stillness daily. I had made so many friends and they had genuinely touched me in a simple and most powerful way. Each and every morning there was always a friendly smile awaiting me from the lady on reception. She was genuine as she wished me 'a lovely day'. As I walked from the hotel to the restaurant two doors down, there another greeting would await me. Deep always had a genuine heartfelt smile for me, as did the rest of his staff. The camaraderie was evident as was the respect between each of them: for their work and for each other. Over these last two weeks I had loved watching them through the window in a quiet moment, when they would frolic about; laughing, joking and playing piggy-back with each other. Their work was completed and the customers were happy. Once again I was witnessing and feeling the joy of human connection and it was such a powerful, deep pleasure.

The monsoon season was approaching and Deep had explained that the mosquito bites were far worse during this time. It certainly didn't feel right to extent my visa. I considered flying directly to New Zealand, although I had thought of visiting Bali first. My sons had been expecting me since I left England in January. I was so excited to see them again and looked forward to spending time with them. I pondered whether or not I should skip Bali altogether when I heard a very strong 'No' intuitively. The decision was made. It was time to book my flight to Bali, as my visa would soon be expiring.

The morning I was leaving, my breakfast was ready at 6.30am promptly. All the staff knew that aloo, or gobhi paratha was my favourite, together with a teapot of marsala chai; without sugar. I'll always remember each of those precious mornings. I was due to leave at 7am, travelling by taxi to the local bus station, then on to Kathmandu. From there I would get another taxi to the airport finally en route to Bali. As I said my final 'Goodbye' and expressed my deep thanks, I knew that I would miss them and that this feeling was mutual.

Pulling out of the bus station, I offered a prayer of appreciation and gratitude for all this wonderful place had given me. Some of the locals called it 'The Sacred Valley.' I had to agree that this place was now very sacred to me, in many ways. Here I had experienced grace, and an even deeper peace than I had ever known, a serenity and an abiding contentment beyond words that felt like it had somehow integrated itself into my very blood, maybe into my DNA too. The depth of the connection from the surrounding mountains and the lake had truly touched my very being. Each and every day here had brought me joy.

Some places touch our heart. Pokhara had certainly woven itself into mine and seemed to have done so on many levels of my essence. I felt it in every step I took, whether it was beside the lake, sat in a café, or a restaurant, or in the temple. It felt as though it was actually in the very air that I breathed and it touched against my skin daily.

I had witnessed the power of very heavy rain here in Nepal. Listening to the giant hailstones pelt down on the rooftop was deafening. Here, passing by on the bus, I was saddened when we passed maize crops that had fallen due to the heavy rain and the winds. I wondered whether that would mean these people would possibly go without food, or a livelihood. I watched from the window of the bus as some farmers were trying to salvage what they could and resurrect the battered plants. As we passed the corn, I said a private prayer for them.

From the window of the bus the humility I experienced as I watched men and women laying individual stones;

like cobbles to construct a road was a powerful feeling. And yet, manual labour here, wherever I had witnessed it never seemed to be a chore. When I had watched the locals wipe the sweat from their brow, I never recall hearing an argument, or hearing them moaning about the hard work. Whenever I had watched them work on the construction sites, they would all work together and there was usually much laughter too.

Women worked moving bags of concrete and mixing the mortar. As one lady shovelled the mixed concrete, another pulled on a rope which was tied to the spade to assist her when she lifted the heavily laden spade. At the same time her son played with the hose pipe, adding water to the concrete mix. Health and safety had no place here but common-sense and dignity were clearly apparent. The women and the men simply wore their flip flops, rather than steel toe-capped boots. There were no hard hats to be seen, nor high visibility jackets. Everyone worked together, they all knew when to eat, drink and rest, knowing with a simple nod of the head, when to return to work. It was a joy to witness and incredibly refreshing after often seeing so much discord in the United Kingdom. Respect and regard for each other was so evident both in the smaller and the larger tasks.

I held that feeling throughout the journey on the bus. Travelling through the valleys with the mountains on either side was such a powerful reminder of Mother Earth's beauty. As the bus weaved through the small villages and the towns, I watched the local people; some were working in the fields, women were chopping and peeling vegetables sat in a small group by the roadside, boys fished in the river, stone masons carved stone into statues of the many Gods and Goddesses. I loved watching the mechanics repairing pushbikes, motorbikes, cars, or huge trucks. I smiled to myself as watching them made me think of my late Grandfather. He would often be seen repairing and mending something.

The humility deepened as I watched the goat herders walking at the side of the road, or in the valleys. Other people were cutting marble to size, laying bricks, rendering, building homes, or simply sitting with their children watching the world go by. I saw men sat around a table at the side of the road, drinking coffee, playing cards or chess. I pondered the meaning of the simplicity of life and human connection.

These people clearly appreciated everything they had, from the food on their table, to the clothes on their backs. They knew where everything had come from originally. The wood from the trees, the stones from the riverbed, the crops from the soil and the fish from the river. Was that why they were respectful? Perhaps it was because they spent time in nature and certainly having seen the devastation the earthquakes had caused in Nepal, many of them knew Mother Earth's power and respected her.

Whenever we passed children I would often find that a tear would appear as I thought of my beloved granddaughters back in England. That feeling was probably the most prominent when I saw a young child, or a baby being cuddled by a grandparent. Now having eight granddaughters of my own, the emotion of love for them is so deeply ingrained within me. I was so grateful that I had the opportunity to share the feeling of simply being present in the world of a young child.

Here from the window of the bus, life in Nepal could be seen, from the seed to the plant and then to the food on the table. The carpenter sat by the roadside carving wood to make the table, or a chair. From the huge pieces of bedrock to the much smaller stones used to make roads, or in construction. The goats herded and used to provide milk, cheese, or to make wool from their coats and possibly be eaten. The chickens in their coops providing eggs and of course the cow: sacred here and used for precious milk.

There was a feeling of deep connection to the earth and all her bounties. Passing field upon field of rice paddies, I thought of how much rice on occasions I had wasted; when I had cooked too much. These people watched over their rice plants and took care with utmost respect daily, watering and tending to the small shoots. I doubt I will ever waste rice again.

It was a truly humbling feeling to witness the lives of the Nepalese people. It was a simple yet incredibly connected life; to the earth and to each other. It made me realise that we all have our place, we each have a niche. In some way, shape, or form we all need one another's skills. Was the stone mason more valuable than the farmer, or the weaver, or the taxi driver, or the chef in the restaurant?

I was grateful to have witnessed these things here in Nepal. As the bus neared Kathmandu the scenery changed to that of a concrete jungle; a crazy, busy city with noise, traffic and fumes.

I was pleased to be heading to Bali, the last destination before I was due to see my beloved sons and daughter-in-law Rachel in New Zealand. My journey was coming to a close. Or was it a new beginning?

Chapter Thirty Seven

Waiting to board the fight to Denpasar, Bali, I hoped that my loved ones trusted that I was okay. I had hoped to message them at the airport, though the WiFi was unavailable. They knew I had an overnight flight and was due to arrive in the early hours at Kuala Lumpur airport and from there I would fly to Bali. It would be several more hours before I could contact them.

As nightfall descended I watched a very impressive thunderstorm through the window of the plane. I was humbled as I reflected on the trip so far. It had certainly changed me.

Travelling had given me more time. There were no distractions such as work, phone calls, emails, opening post or concerns with my business. The everyday things like trips to the bank, washing, shopping, ironing, cleaning, tidying the garden and the general planning of the days' necessities were simply no longer a part of my life. Each and every day was a blank canvas. I've always been an early riser. Usually I was up between 6am and 7am. In my; (what seemed like now), 'other life', I usually started the day with a lovely cup of Lady Grey tea. I would often meditate, maybe do some T'ai Chi or possibly go for an early morning walk in the local park. If I was writing a book then I would use my time wisely.

In India and Kathmandu it was very different. I usually started the day sitting on the rooftop; often the only place where I could get some peace and quiet. Looking out over the surrounding area would often provide inspiration. Sometimes that might be a sprawling concrete jungle and I was wise enough to know that I had to make the most of my surroundings; regardless. In Jodhpur I treasured each morning as I loved to look out over the majestic fort and the White Palace.

I truly felt blessed and very lucky if I could listen to the birds. This was always a pleasant start to the day; much more preferable than my senses being overloaded if I was forced to listen to the seemingly endless honking of the Tuk Tuks, motorbikes and scooters. The noise pollution was dreadful and invasive. Spike Milligan had once said that noise pollution was probably one of the worst things we can ever experience; it always took away our peace. I definitely agreed.

Each and every morning I would think back to the quiet I used to love and treasure in my beloved home in Preston. Each morning I would think of my dear family and send a quiet prayer of love. Connecting to the morning itself was always important to me; the gratitude of the first morning sunlight and the birdsong. Connection also meant gratitude for whatever the day ahead would bring. Whilst travelling, the appreciation would certainly include my first cup of weak black tea.

As a writer over these many months, I had become more observant, and more and more, I was finding that I would watch as other hotel guests would order their meals, or simply a coffee. I watched connections between couples, between parents and their children, the connections of the single traveller with the waiter, or with fellow travellers. Over these last few months, I had realised with great sadness that it was rare to see a genuine connection; not impossible, just rare.

Eye to eye contact has always been of the utmost importance to me. Many people would place their order without even looking up at the waiter. If one person had already sat in the restaurant and their partner came a few moments later, they would rarely look up, or even greet one another. I found this particularly sad and quite disturbing. I would often ponder the question that if this was how people started their day, what would it be like as the day progressed? The simple gift of acknowledgement from one human being to another was always appreciated.

I pondered on an old Buddhist proverb; 'You cannot walk in the same river twice'. Life was ever changing. Nothing ever remained the same. Then I considered another proverb; 'The only thing in life that's guaranteed is change'. India and Nepal had changed me. It was now time to allow Bali to find its place within my pilgrimage.

Sitting alone by the window in my row of three seats on the plane, I thought back to all the people who were dear to me and those who had supported my decision to sell my home and travel. I was grateful for the messages, texts and phone calls from loved ones. They sustained me daily. Some were now very far away and, as I reflected I also thought of the many new friends I had met on my trip. It had challenged me on several occasions, Mumbai in particular. I was grateful to all those I had the pleasure of meeting along my journey.

Coming back to the present I thought of Matthew, Philip and my daughter-in-law Rachel who all agreed I would love the tropical island of Bali; otherwise known as 'Paradise Island.' They had certainly loved it when they had visited previously. I hadn't seen a beautiful beach since we left Goa in February. Having lived near the sea throughout my entire life, I had truly missed everything about beaches. Everything.

I was grateful for the quietness on the plane that evening, as I thought of all the things I had left behind in the United Kingdom. Letting go of my home; a huge four bedroomed detached house and leaving most of my treasured personal possessions. I was thankful for all the essential things I had with me. I had managed with nothing more than a suitcase and a small bag since January. I had lived quite comfortably in a one-bedroomed hotel room with a bathroom, washing my clothes in the shower. I hadn't always slept in a comfortable bed, nor always had a clean, comfortable pillow. Neither had I had as many fruits and vegetables as I would have preferred. I had very few of my previous luxuries such as biscuits, crisps, cakes or hot chocolate and I rarely even ate chocolate now. All these things had been thoroughly enjoyable treats beforehand. Now they seemed to pale into insignificance.

As the lights were dimmed on the plane, I pondered further on my ever deepening experience and my dance with gratitude and grace, as I considered what I had actually needed throughout my travels. Whilst away, I had purchased a new pair of flip-flops when my other pair had broken in Goa. I had also bought myself some new walking boots ready for New Zealand. Some of the clothes in my suitcase I hadn't even worn. Others were washed and dried in the warm climate within the same day. What was it that I needed?

In the various messages from friends and relatives in the United Kingdom, I had been asked occasionally what I missed. I certainly missed my loved ones the most: especially my granddaughters. I missed watching them grow and evolve, changing into little people with their own personalities. I missed their laughter. I missed sharing their adventures and listening to their stories. I missed taking them out and without a doubt, I missed

'Grandma cuddles' the most. Each and every time I had seen grandchildren together with their grandparents during my trip, I had always sent a quiet prayer back to England for their well-being. Sleepovers with my granddaughters had always been such fun. I was sad that I had not yet seen my latest edition; Phoebe, who had been born recently whilst I was in Kathmandu.

Thinking of dear old England, I also missed the greenery, the snowdrops, bluebells, daffodils and the trees, the rivers, canals, the ocean and walking on the beach; either alone, or with loved ones. I really missed eating Great British fish and chips. I missed sharing so much laughter and great conversation with those I loved; friends and family alike. I was thankful that through messenger, email and WhatsApp, I had managed to keep in touch with so many of my loved ones.

I had learnt the deep appreciation of having electricity and therefore WiFi. In India and Nepal, particularly Pushkar, Jodhpur and Pokhara, it would frequently go off randomly; without any assurance as to when it would be back on again. Most of all, I had learnt the value of water; which like the electricity, would either be on, or off, in certain places. It was also water in all its forms such as a river, a lake, or the ocean.

Since the start of my travels in January, I had certainly learnt about gratitude, humility, connection and appreciation, eating a meal from a clean kitchen was probably one of the top on the list, as was a clean, comfortable bed and definitely a clean bathroom; especially the toilet.

Continuing to think of what I actually missed, I began to think of what I would be able to enjoy in New Zealand. The thought of being able to wash my clothes again in an automatic washing machine which had once been a normal, everyday thing, now brought joy in a simple way. My white trousers, shorts and white dress had taken quite a 'battering' while I was in India. I was grateful that most hotels offered a laundry service. The thought of being able to brush my teeth once more using tap water; rather than having to use bottled water was appealing.

It was almost time to sleep. My last thoughts were of how much I treasured the sacred valley of Pokhara. It brought peace to a soul that was exhausted from constant noise. I smiled as I remembered a conversation I had shared with two sisters over lunch on my final day there;

"India vandalises ALL your senses!" Liz laughed as I replied: "Well, I would have said assaulted!"

The three of us howled with laughter whilst we ate the most delicious green bean curry. Although our meeting was short, we each knew we were meant to meet and we were grateful for the opportunity to share great conversation and much laughter. As the connection flowed we shared that it would soon be all of our birthdays. I would be fifty-two years old on the 4th of June. Liz was celebrating her fiftieth a week later and Louise her fifty-second birthday shortly afterwards. With the synchronicity of our connection, we each had a knowing that it had been pre-destined. Little did they know the personal significance to me of their names: Louise and Elizabeth. As we hugged one another, departing before yet another wonderful thunderstorm, I thanked the Universe for what we had all shared in that simple meeting over lunch.

My last thoughts took me back to a conversation I had with my dear friend Tony before I left England. He is incredibly intuitive and I asked him if he thought I would ever return to live once again in the United Kingdom.

"Whatever happens, the journey will change you. If you do return it will be a different version of you. If you don't, well, enjoy the journey." Enjoying the quiet on the plane I looked at my ticket number '18A'. I knew he was right. One plus eight equals nine and according to the principles of numerology, nine is significant of endings; creating space for new beginnings. I curled myself into the foetal position on the plane, grateful that the adjoining seats were empty. I drifted off to sleep with nothing more than a smile and feelings of immense gratitude.

Chapter Thirty Eight

The relief when I finally arrived in Bali around noon was tremendous. I had been travelling since 7am the previous morning. I was exhausted. Making my way through the airport, I noticed that the queue for the thirty day visas was huge. I prayed I would soon be through it, so that I could exchange my cash into the Indonesian Rupiah. Finally I would be able to get a taxi to my hotel. I definitely needed sleep. My whole body was wondering which way was up!

Grateful to the hotel staff for their swift efficiency, I was soon booked into my room overlooking the very inviting swimming pool. After quickly messaging loved ones to say that I had arrived safely, I gladly crawled into one of the most comfortable beds I have ever slept in. To be honest even if it had felt as though I was sleeping on a few bricks; (as had some of the beds while I was in India), I would have slept.

Ninety minutes later, I felt much restored. The hotel was quiet and the view across the surrounding area included a mosque only a few yards away. I knew I would be awakened by the early morning prayers. The sacred prayers always reminded me of the importance of gratitude and thanking The Divine daily. To me it was not about religious beliefs; rather beginning the day with a healthy habit that included appreciation for a new chapter.

Gratitude was once more uppermost in my thoughts. As I made a cup of piping hot black tea, I sat looking out over the trees and the surrounding city. It was so very different to my view of the magnificent mountains and the lake at Pokhara. I knew that I had to be here. The statue of the Garuda Wisnu Kencana stood majestically in the distance. It was huge and towered over the highest of buildings. I wondered how big it actually was; since it was located several miles away.

The pool downstairs looked very inviting though I was aware that my body was still recovering. I had learnt not to push too hard after suffering from Chronic Fatigue Syndrome several years earlier. Tempting as it was, it would have to wait until tomorrow.

I ventured downstairs to the dining room and ordered a seafood pizza: an absolute favourite of mine. It was delicious and I was grateful for all the food I had eaten whilst away. I hadn't cooked a meal for months. Peeling a banana, or an orange was the nearest I had gotten to preparing food. Returning to my room after a little walk around the hotel, I was aware that my body was crying out for more rest. I messaged Jay and settled down for the night as a deep peace descended upon my whole body.

The following morning I ventured into the hotel lobby straight after breakfast to see if there were any local buses, or taxis to show me around the island. My sons had recommended several places for me to visit and I had also checked on the internet. There were several overlaps and using my intuition, I had a comprehensive list of the local attractions.

I noticed a taxi stand near the huge hotel entrance and was greeted by a young man with an impish grin. His prices for either a full or half day touring were most reasonable. I agreed to be ready within a few minutes and was looking forward to seeing the sights of Bali.

Several friends had mentioned that the Balinese temples were stunning. They had all said how amazing Bali had been in their experience. My dear friend Karen had lived in Ubud for many years. She always glowed with so much passion as she told me how incredibly spiritual it was in the town. I intuitively knew I had to stay there at some point and decided I would look for accommodation in the coming days.

The taxi driver was a most humble man and he clearly wanted to ensure my stay here in Bali was both comfortable and memorable. I was quite taken aback at his genuine interest in what I would like to see and experience here. His aura glowed brightly as I explained that I loved the spiritual aspect of Bali: both the Buddhism and the Hinduism. I mentioned my love of the ocean and water generally; be it waterfalls, fountains, goldfish, or simply a river, or a stream. I briefed him on my time in India, stating how much I had dearly missed the ocean and the rivers. I explained that my whole journey since January, was solely focused on experiences to feed my soul; I had concentrated on visiting the spiritual towns, the temples and the various spiritual sites.

Passing through the streets, everywhere I looked I was astonished to see such beautiful stonework and the most exquisitely detailed wooden carvings. I was truly amazed by the many different statues and the quality of the intricate workmanship. I have always appreciated art and craftsmanship. Here it was so clearly evident that there was also a profound and incredibly tangible respect for artwork.

The streets were quiet in comparison to Kathmandu and India. They were incredibly clean and the roads were in much better condition. Greenery was so abundant and I could breathe in the freshness, just as I had done in Pokhara. As he listened to my personal preferences, he suggested we visit a famous temple nearby, then maybe a waterfall. The trust was established between us and I was delighted that I was in such capable hands. I knew this part of my trip was going to be the pinnacle.

I felt deeply contented as I watched the beauty of the island unfold before my eyes. It seemed everywhere I looked there was something inspiring. The artwork; statues, canvases, carvings and glassware as we passed the shops drew my attention as I visualised various pieces of furniture in my new home. The incredible skills of these native people were evident everywhere. I was once again deeply humbled

Arriving at the temple and putting on the sarong felt as though the island was welcoming me in that one simple gesture. Everybody was dressed so smartly – men and women alike. The temple itself was stunning and unlike anything I had seen before in its unique design. Taking photos to send to loved ones, I was grateful to be able to do this journey. My soul was certainly growing and being enhanced. I felt it was such a privilege.

As I looked around, my inner child almost fell into the pool where the koi were swimming contentedly between the lotus leaves and the flowers. How beautiful it all was; a delightful temple, colourful and brightly painted with various fountains and pools full of the most colourful fish. Gratitude oozed from this holy place. It was a very deep reverence and an absolutely undeniable connection to ALL living things. I felt truly blessed to be present in such sacredness. Everything was in immaculate condition. A photograph can rarely capture the essence and the presence of a place so majestic, though I certainly tried to capture it in the pictures that day. It struck me while I was walking around that the whole place was actually quiet and this silence was restorative, allowing a deepening of my connection to the island; and indeed to myself.

Handing back the sarong to the ladies, I was thrilled to feel a tangible sense of belonging here. It was also nice to see women as I had seen very few in the Indian, or Nepalese temples. The Balinese ladies were very smartly dressed and so welcoming. The whole experience had touched something very deep inside of my being. Up to this point on my journey I had never experienced such a memorable, deep, abiding connection to my surroundings. I needed to breathe it in and accept it as a massive and very warming welcome.

The taxi driver was keen to please and impress me. At the time I reassured him that I was delighted so far. Journeying to our next destination; he mentioned that it would be a waterfall. My heart skipped a beat. My inner child felt like skipping and jumping around. I was giddy with excitement.

We chatted easily throughout the journey. He explained that most of Bali is geared towards tourism. It is the islands main industry. I was amazed as it was evidently very well-organised and I was actually quite taken a back. In both India and Kathmandu, chaos had by now become so familiar to me; it felt as though it was ingrained. Here this quiet, efficient order, despite the busyness, seemed so peaceful and was definitely refreshing and most welcome.

Arriving a few minutes later, there was no effort needed as we were guided to a parking space in a very busy car park. There was no rushed pace to purchase an entrance ticket. Neither was there any pushing or shoving in the queues. Everyone and everything was relaxed. I could breathe easily here. It was such a welcome relief. Like most things we can become conditioned to different situations and experiences, the very fact that I could relax here made me realise how stressful it had been in both India and Kathmandu.

As we viewed the waterfall from a distance, it was all I could do to hold back the well of tears. Although there were hordes of people there was a huge viewing space big enough for everyone to simply enjoy the magnificence of the waterfall. As I listened to the sound of the water thundering about eighty metres down into a pool below, I completely embraced the feeling of absolute joy in my heart. It felt as though it would surely burst at any given moment.

Since early childhood I have loved water in all its forms. There is truly something very special about a huge waterfall that pours gallons and gallons of water over a rocky edge. I was mesmerized. Down below to my left, I could see the crowds too, loving being so close to the waterfall. There were people of all nationalities here. I hadn't seen so many white people for quite some time. It all felt odd and surreal in some way. Some were swimming, others paddling and some were climbing up the many stone steps to the waterfalls origin.

Walking carefully down towards it, I noticed several small piles of rock cairns which people had built. They reminded me of my many walks in The Lake District. These were often built in memory of those who we had lost in our lives, our current loved ones and perhaps those who had died during a mountain rescue attempt. Respect was the first word that came to mind. I pondered building one myself as a representation of those I loved, my current experiences and the sheer pleasure; despite the challenges of everything I was and had already experienced on this trip.

As we neared the water and the sound increased, I soaked up each and every wonderful moment. The taxi driver was happy to watch over me, as I walked happily on the make-shift rickety bamboo bridges making my way to the other side of the river. I soon found a comfortable rock to sit on, whilst I kicked my feet in the water. Blissful ecstasy are words that *almost* describes how I felt.

Goa Ganga Temple was next on the day's list of venues. Watching the world go by through the car window was once again such a wonderful experience for me. The coconut trees, huge ferns, palm trees and the bamboo stood so tall against the background of a beautiful clear, blue sky. This certainly was even more beautiful than the brochures, it was truly a most magical, very special tropical island. It was touching something deep within my core. Despite everything I had experienced in India and Pokhara, this place held a spirit, a soul perhaps of its own. I couldn't put my finger on whatever that feeling was, so I simply continued to watch through the car window and embraced each and every wonderful moment.

Goa Ganga was more breath-taking than the first temple we had visited. After coming out of the cave, I noticed the statues with the natural spring water pouring out into the pools below, I felt I had been here before. The déjà vu gave me Goosebumps everywhere on my body. A part of me was saddened, as I thought back to Kathmandu. The statues there no longer oozed water following the earthquake damage. Swiftly regrouping my thoughts, I was so delighted when I saw the elaborate exotic carvings and the surrounding jungle. I realised that I had already fallen in love with this island.

I was grateful to Komang, my driver, as he assisted me in navigating which pathway I should take as the temple opened even further into a huge forest below. Here was another much smaller temple and I was introduced to an elderly lady who offered to do a blessing for me. I prayed with her quietly. I could certainly feel the power of the prayer. It was tangible and it touched my core. I knew the prayers had been heard for my many loved ones and for my yet unknown future. As I turned to thank her; despite the language barrier, it was clear in her eyes and her expression that she knew exactly what I wanted to say. Komang would willingly have translated those feelings into words though I declined his kind offer knowing that it would have diluted their power. I was happy simply to bow and express my appreciation.

And this was only my first day here!

On the way back to the hotel the feeling that I needed to connect to the sea was most powerful. I asked Komang if he would please drop me at a local quiet beach. He agreed and I asked if he would mind if I had a quick walk barefoot in the sand and maybe a paddle. We had only arranged a half day trip, as I was still quite tired.

Once I felt the sand underneath my feet and the sea breeze on my skin, I asked him to please come and collect me in a few hours. The sound of the sea, the waves and the smell of the ocean touched my essence. I had missed this so very much. I was so grateful that I had listened to that earlier whisper from my soul. As I paddled along the beach in the bright sunshine and looked across at the distant ocean waves, I felt a deep contentment and a powerful connection to Mother Earth. In all my months of travelling, nothing had touched my being quite so much. I walked several miles up and down the beach, smiling with a huge grin as I paddled and splashed like a child.

Chapter Thirty Nine

Arriving back at the hotel I was absolutely knackered. Despite the tiredness, I was feeling blissful and deeply contented. In the last few months, I treasured watching the sunsets across a variety of skylines and would often take photographs. I loved to share them with my loved ones. As I lay on the bed and listened to the evening prayers from the mosque, I offered mine for one of the most memorable days I had ever experienced; not just on this trip, but in my whole life.

Another half day touring was booked for two o'clock the following afternoon. I was happy to write and then swim in the hotel pool before leaving. After the joy I had experienced the previous day, I wondered what today would bring. This tropical island clearly held its own magic. My need to be by the water had inspired me to book a few hours visiting different beaches.

Once again as we drove around, I was in awe of the abundance of the many different statues and such exquisite artwork. The roundabouts and most of the junctions had displays of great creativity. The respect together with a sense of deep pride was definitely tangible. These people loved and treasured their island.

Our agenda included visiting a beach called 'Dreamland'. Little did I know what awaited me. It was set in private grounds and it was incredibly stunning.

Statues lined each of the many avenues, together with the most colourful flowering trees. It was so magnificent, clean and peaceful too. I had never seen anything like it in my whole life. The hotels on the site stood in all their splendour and glory. I was impressed with absolutely everything. I pondered how much detailed planning had gone into the whole resort. Someone certainly had incredible foresight and an abundant passion for creating such a paradise. There was a deep and very tangible sense of respect within this whole environment and the energy was very harmonious and balanced. It was something that I have rarely encountered and I felt privileged. How many amazing more places and surprises, did Bali have in store for me? I wished Jay was with me to witness this. I missed him daily and wanted to share these experiences with him so much.

Arriving at the beach a few minutes later in the resort's shuttle bus, I was grateful to experience the ocean once more. It held the same magic as it had always done for me, perhaps even more. The waves here were very powerful and despite wanting to swim; with so many rocks scattered on the shoreline I decided that I was better safe; rather than sorry, or dead! So I simply paddled. The beach was reasonably quiet, another huge bonus and a sign for me to relax and enjoy my time here. I lay in my own private rock pool and absorbed those extremely exquisite, precious moments. It was another blissful afternoon in a tropical island paradise.

The other beaches we visited were equally stunning. As we set off back to the hotel, I saw some statues that I didn't recognise. After studying Hinduism and seeing various carvings of the many deities in India, I truly did not recognise these exquisite female sculptures. Asking Komang, the driver, which Goddess they represented I felt like an idiot when he explained they were the Balinese dancers. He asked if I would like to watch a local performance. It was agreed that I would attend that evening.

Throughout our many conversations it had become obvious to him that I enjoyed photographing the sunsets. He suggested a local place where I would get a wonderful backdrop of the setting sun whilst waiting for the performance to commence. Arriving at Uluwatu Temple I was surprised to see so many people gathering for the upcoming performance. As I waited, I read the leaflet explaining what 'The Fire Dance' represented in the tradition of the Balinese people. Komang was right, I managed to get some stunning pictures of the setting sun against the horizon.

Sat in an amphitheatre packed with tourists was quite an overwhelming experience for me. I was still becoming accustomed to seeing white people and hearing the English language being spoken; regardless of the accent; be it Australian, French or Russian. I was not used to seeing so many people in one space. I estimated there were roughly about eight hundred people assembled in a semi-circle waiting for the show to commence. The feeling of excitement was tangible as the men entered the 'stage'. As they sat down I was most impressed when they started chanting, singing and toning. There were no instruments and no sign of a conductor, choreographer or a director; this was a well-rehearsed and practised performance. They clearly held a real passion for what they were doing. They were in tune with one another and the mutual respect and camaraderie was most evident. I was in awe of the whole experience.

When the Balinese dancers entered and I saw their stunning costumes, I was even more wonderstruck. The dancing was truly like nothing I have ever seen. The minute detail of each of the body movements and even the tiniest detail of each of the finger movements was very impressive. I was truly mesmerized. The way the whole performance was exceptionally well co-ordinated, with the men singing throughout and the fact that there were no instruments, all added to the magic of the evenings' experience.

Most plays or theatre productions have the 'Goody' and the 'Baddie'. This was to be no exception. I was literally sat on the edge of my seat. As the 'monkey' jumped high up on the stone entrance archway, I was impressed by both the costume and the professionalism of the acting. As he began interacting with the audience, multiple shrieks of laughter went out across the whole arena. I was completely in awe.

No words can ever do justice to what I experienced that evening, outstanding perhaps comes close. I managed to capture a little of that magic in my photographs.

Chapter Forty

The following morning at breakfast, I spotted 'Lurpak' butter alongside the croissants. I hadn't tasted butter for months and I started to drool. Tasting it was such a treasured pleasure.

I had enjoyed the previous night's entertainment so much, that Komang suggested I attend another quite different performance the following morning. This would include both Balinese dancing and instruments.

I loved it and was amazed when I heard the many different sounds of the various instruments. These performances took place daily and were enjoyed by hundreds of people. I loved this culture. It was already under my skin. It was in both my heart and my soul. These people respected their traditions and strongly upheld them. Each of the performers clearly loved what they were doing and were dressed in such beautiful, elaborate costumes. Everything here was hand-made; the elaborate head-dresses, incredible costumes and even the instruments. It all added an even deeper respect for the entire experience.

Inevitably it made me think of England and our traditions. Sadly, the only thing I could think of was Morris Dancing and I hadn't seen it performed in many years. Besides jeans, Tee-shirts and 'hoodies,' I couldn't think of any English traditional dress either. Were we more 'civilized' in the West? Or had materialism taken something from us, from our roots and from our connections?

As we drove inland towards The Monkey Forest, we passed a mix of both modern and traditional shops. The various different buildings were all interlaced with tropical trees and huge ferns between and around them. I realised how balanced everything seemed to be here. We never passed a shop with a dirty window, or a litter-strewn door-step. We rarely passed any litter at all. The other cars rarely honked at one another and none were driving past with music blaring at full volume. No one was 'Boy Racing.' Everyone here drove with respect; if someone needed to get back into the line of traffic, the other drivers simply made room; allowing them to join in the flow. There was a tangible feeling of acceptance and patience on the roads. For me it was such a welcome relief; especially after the craziness of the streets in Kathmandu only three days earlier.

It was respect and all that one, single word encompassed. Whilst I pondered further, I realised that I had never heard anyone swear here. People spoke quietly and respectfully to one another, no-one spoke over, or even seemed to interrupt another. There was a peace in every conversation that I had heard so far. I also realised that I hadn't yet seen anyone who looked miserable or unhappy.

As my thoughts deepened, I realised that the whole island itself seemed to hold respect. It was in the very land, the trees, the flowers, the birds, the insects, the animals and the very air itself. There was a tangible peace and serenity everywhere. There was a deep regard and a value for life and living; which I had never experienced before. It brought me a new awareness and a depth to the meaning to the word gratitude. It seemed people were equally grateful for both the big and the small things here. There was an undeniable feeling that everything was connected to everything else and that these peaceful people were certainly connected to their beloved island. I had never experienced this depth of serenity, respect and connection. As Komang continued to drive north, I sat pondering my own thoughts, absorbing the ambience and allowing it to filter and percolate wherever it needed to go within my being.

It felt as though my core was being cleansed and re-set. I could feel it travel to my heart and soul. It was touching my very essence. Did Bali touch everyone like this? It was hard to believe that I had considered not coming here.

Chapter Forty One

I felt the energy change as we approached the town of Ubud. Once again there was something incredibly special here, something very deeply sacred. It was something that was certainly spiritual, although there was an added extra. I couldn't put my finger on this exact feeling, I simply accepted it and made a very large mental note of it. I decided to allow whatever it was to unfold in its own time and of its own accord. I knew that I would be returning here to stay in the coming days for almost three weeks. My accommodation was already booked in a local homestay which was in the very centre of Ubud; almost directly across from the Palace. I trusted that it would become clear to me during my stay.

Rachel, Matthew and Phil had all highly recommended I visit the Monkey Forest in Ubud. Arriving we had to cross over a bridge into the visitor area which was surrounded by Koi in the pool below, it was such a wonderful setting. I radiated smiles of pleasure and delight.

I was quite used to monkeys by now, after my numerous experiences of them in both India and Nepal. They were clever and sharp, quick learners and most cheeky. I knew better than to have food; especially fruit, in my handbag. I had also removed my sunglasses and jewellery, as they snatch with lightning speed. Their bodies are mostly muscle, having had two on my shoulders whilst I was in Jaipur, I had felt their power. No longer did I think they were sweet, simple, furry, cuddly creatures. They were talented, intelligent animals and had to be respected.

The forest was just that. It was a breath-taking beautiful, natural forest, filled with incredible giant ferns, palms and banana, bamboo, papaya and many other exotic trees. The different shades, tones and hues of the greenery were like an orchestra playing different notes, yet there was a tiny variation between each of them. It felt like paradise; the connection and the balance between human, plant and animal life was evident; they were in complete harmony with each other. It touched my whole being right to the very core. Taking my breath away for several moments, it was easy to imagine the elementals at peace here. The fairies, elves, sprites and nymphs playing and simply being.

I have always been deeply connected to Mother Earth and the connection here was certainly the most apparent that I have ever experienced. Perhaps heaven and earth met here? It felt like it to me. The many monkeys were not encaged, nor were they separated from the public. There were signs advising how the tourists should behave towards the monkeys. Respect.

The humans were respecting the monkeys, respecting that we were in their environment; rather than the monkeys in ours. It was so refreshing. The many feeding stations were situated at various intervals throughout the forest, so the tourists could watch these wonderful creatures in their natural surroundings. The Balinese people want to encourage the monkeys here on the island to breed and be as one with the 'civilised' world. Such wisdom.

I loved the whole experience. The forest was well-kempt throughout the whole diverse complex and now having seen so many animals in their natural habitat in the wild, I knew I could never imagine being comfortable seeing animals in cages, or enclosures again.

Lunchtime was fast approaching and I was certainly hungry. Komang drove towards a well-known and reputable restaurant where the mountains could be easily seen. It was packed. The scenery from the restaurant balcony took my breath away. I sat eating my scrumptious lunch with stunning views of the surrounding mountains, the lake, the volcano and the most beautiful countryside. I was once again deeply touched with gratitude and appreciation for our planet. There was a feeling that I was connected to all of this perfect wonder. I felt the presence of God in that place.

The restaurant was really busy and I felt sad when my time came to leave. My magic bottle which was already full of incredibly precious memories had to find room for even more. I decided to make it bigger, much bigger as it was becoming incredibly clear that there was so much more to be experienced.

The day was not yet over, and Tirta Emple; a sacred water temple was last on the list of sight-seeing that particular day. I have an incredibly powerful love of water and I had an inner knowing that this place was very special indeed. Making our way to the sacred pools I was touched as many people were already in them, fully clothed; trusting and allowing the healing waters to work their magic.

A peace seemed to radiate all around. As the fish swam in the pools below, I embraced the feeling of serenity without feeling the need to join the other pilgrims in the water. Whilst I looked over the various pools, I experienced a vision of having received a most holy and sacred blessing here before; maybe in another life? I was stood with someone I loved dearly and the whole scenario brought me to tears. I stood in silence whilst the memory of that previous time seemed to embody itself into my present self.

There was a temple a few metres away and I really wanted to pray and meditate in silence. I felt I needed a few quiet moments to integrate these emotions and to absorb them fully. I have learnt over these many years to be in stillness with these deeply personal experiences, rather than trying to analyse and understand them; it becomes distracting from the real 'feel' of them.

Komang kindly asked if I could pray with two beautiful Balinese ladies. I felt so grateful for those incredibly precious moments that I had in the temple that day. As I received another blessing from the priest, I allowed the tears to flow as I felt the love and the connection circulate throughout my whole being. I had been touched to my core.

Chapter Forty Two

My birthday was fast approaching and I was considering what I should do to celebrate, considering I was travelling alone. I had already seen so many awesome places and decided that I might like to spend the day perhaps near a waterfall, or a beach. There was so much to see and do here. I adored this magical island. I trusted it would unfold. I knew I would enjoy my birthday regardless and Rachel had said that we would celebrate it again when I arrived in New Zealand.

My visa here in Bali was for a month. My week in Kuta was almost at its end and I had planned my final day of sight-seeing. Whilst I ate breakfast that morning, I wondered why I had crammed so much into the last few days. I still had three weeks remaining on my visa after all. I had toured many of the temples and had ticked off almost everywhere I wanted to visit; leaving only those located in Ubud; which I would visit whilst I was there.

Komang had shared that he lived in a village on the east of the island; it was approximately a three hour drive away. It was clear that although he loved his work, he dearly missed his wife and their two young sons. I loved listening to him when he told me stories about his family life. The abundance of love and connection shone through in his whole being; his eyes lit up, his voice softened and there was a distinct glow in his aura. He usually managed to visit home for a few days each fortnight. He obviously treasured each and every minute of that precious time. I was pleased for him, as I thought of the people in India; who often only visited their families perhaps once every two months.

When we spoke of the east coast, I enquired about the beaches there. He said they were mostly much quieter because they were away from the main airport. He mentioned Candi Dasa and I was covered in Goosebumps within seconds. I knew I had to visit although I also felt there was something else on the east coast that was waiting for me. I made a mental note of it and wondered whether perhaps I was meant to visit on my birthday? I decided that for today, I would enjoy my visits and allow everything else to unfold of its own accord, in its own time.

Tanah Lot was listed as a top attraction. Its history and origin intrigued me and I knew that I had to see it for myself. It is a most sacred temple, situated on the western coastline. When we visited although I loved it, I was a little disappointed that we were not allowed into the actual temple for safety reasons. Nonetheless, I was pleased that I managed to take some wonderful photos. It was another beautiful sunny day. There is a cave where there is said to be a Holy Snake. I knew intuitively that I needed to visit. The snake is said to bring good luck, though Komang had said that when he had escorted other tourists here, the snake was no-where to be seen. He was truly amazed when the priest was there alongside this magical creature. Curled up in its own space in the rock it seemed quite happy in its environment. I felt its sacred presence and said a quiet prayer. There was such a peaceful ambience and as I wandered around the beach, I smiled as I realised how relaxed and comfortable I felt. A new even deeper sense of appreciation combined with a sense of total harmony seemed to run through my veins that afternoon.

The days were passing by so quickly and tomorrow I would be staying in the town of Ubud. I wondered if I had done the right thing, as I would now be inland away from the ocean once more. Perhaps I should have booked for one week only? I had already made the full payment. I considered that maybe I might prefer a week beside a quiet beach; especially around the time of my birthday. Only time would tell.

Chapter Forty Three

Ubud would represent the end of my journey before I arrived in New Zealand. I wasn't really sure that I was entirely ready to return to the western way of life. The thought of busy shops, consumerism and materialism didn't appeal to me and actually felt quite abhorrent. I loved the peace here in Bali and the most welcome quiet.

I knew New Zealand was one of the most beautiful and scenic places in the world. I had seen from the many photos that my loved ones had sent to me over the last four years. It was truly majestic; the combination of mountains, waterfalls, rivers, forests and lakes. I took consolation that at least I would have nature all around me; if the way of the west became too much. I knew I had so much that awaited me in New Zealand; I could feel it. I was excited as my visit there now loomed. For months it had seemed as though this moment would never arrive. Sometimes I wondered if I would ever reach my 'final' destination.

I was desperately looking forward to seeing them all again; sharing hugs and lengthy conversations, catching up as they told me all about their lives and seeing how much they were settled. The thoughts of being with my sons once more and Rachel were heart-warming. I had travelled alone since the end of March, and although I had spoken to the various hoteliers and so many other people throughout my travels, finally I would have a sustaining flow of great company, good conversation and laughter.

Their love for New Zealand shone whenever they spoke about both the North and South islands. The photographs they sent were picturesque, stunning and magnificent. Now it was almost my time.

"You'll love it here mum, you'll just love it." Their enthusiasm left me in no doubt that I would indeed love it. I had met Rachel the previous summer and we had connected instantly. I had rarely shared female company while in India, apart from when I was with Sonali and Reeta's family. The Indian and Nepalese women tended to remain with their families. Besides seeing my sons, I was certainly looking forward to some female company; 'Girlie time awaited.'

Although I had the opportunity of hiking in Pokhara, I felt vulnerable travelling alone and it simply never felt right. Now I was so looking forward to hiking in the countryside and the mountains of New Zealand. It had been a favourite pastime of mine from my early teenage years.

I was aware that I was leaving a tropical island and its climate, where the average temperature was usually twenty nine degrees. In New Zealand it was almost winter; the average temperature would be eight degrees, or less. I was grateful that I had my warm, padded coat with me from the day I had left England; over five months earlier. I doubted I would need three showers daily.

Just what did await me? Would I settle in New Zealand? I already had a sponsor there and could apply for a work visa immediately. I truly had no idea what my future would hold. The phrase ‘It’s the journey, not the destination’ kept repeating in my mind. The experiences over these last few months had certainly taught me to be in the moment and enjoy each and every precious day. Things would unfold in their own time. I trusted that my intuition would guide the way.

For now I was content to enjoy these last two weeks in Bali and looked forward to my stay in Ubud.

Chapter Forty Four

Humping my suitcase up the stairs of the homestay accommodation brought so many thoughts to mind. This would be my last chance to enjoy this beautiful island and all that Bali had to offer. It was my last point of call before my final destination; New Zealand.

The owner, Wayan, introduced himself and showed me to my room. He spoke excellent English which was such a welcome relief. His aura was light and bright. I already felt comfortable here, it was lovely, clean and very quiet. I was grateful that I had a balcony where I could look out over the town.

By now I was used to re-settling myself and making each and every place a home. As I began to place my personal photographs on the dressing table, I was feeling melancholic knowing that this was at last to be my final residence. The whole scenario stirred quite a few emotions. I decided to sit quietly with these feelings, as I acknowledged and digested each one of them in turn.

Tears fell as I recognised my achievements in these past few months; especially when I had travelled alone. It had not always been easy choosing reasonable accommodation, researching local tourist attractions and finding suitable restaurants. Transport between locations had sometimes proved to be a challenge; either by bus, plane, or taxi at times.

In the last few months I had missed my dear family, especially my granddaughters and there had also been a new edition to the family; when my youngest granddaughter had been born recently in April. As yet I hadn't seen her and sadly I hadn't cuddled her either. I missed my parents and my brothers too. I missed my friends and sat feeling grateful for modern technology allowing us to keep in touch.

As I pondered my thoughts over a cup of refreshing jasmine tea, I realised how much this journey had changed me. I felt so very different from the person who had left the United Kingdom in January. I was certainly even more humble, even more grateful for everything I had after seeing so much poverty in India and the earthquake damage in Nepal. I was more appreciative of the very simple things in life; a smile, a hug, a private message from a friend, eye to eye contact, clean clothes, hot water, drinking water, a clean toilet and a suitable bathroom. It related to appreciation, respect and connection.

Seeing trees had become a luxury and my appreciation of Mother Earth had grown exponentially. I dearly missed listening to the sound of the wind blowing through the trees and standing under a tree in a rainstorm. I missed the smell of the trees; particularly pine trees. Pondering my thoughts, I recalled the very first time I had seen the river in Vrindavan, Uttar Pradesh. I remembered the tears of joy I cried that afternoon when I was relieved to finally see natural water flowing again. I loved feeling this intense gratitude more recently, when I was so honoured to see the ocean and paddle after many months.

Water has always been dear to me although now the appreciation was on a much more powerful level. It touched my soul in such a beautiful way. It was an honour to connect to the water and I reflected on the differences between seeing the unpolluted river in The Himalayas compared with the filthy Ganges. I knew the sad images I had in my mind of the beach in Mumbai would stay with me forever. The whole experience had deeply upset me. Surely there could not be an excuse for pollution in this century? Cause and effect were evident there on a world-wide basis. The phrase; 'We are all one,' came to my mind. Could this be resolved if we all worked together?

Obviously meeting Jay had been truly wonderful and I was so grateful for all that we had shared in our three blissful days. We connected instantly when we met and with such a rare and sacred intensity which demanded to be respected. Our subsequent emails had brought me much laughter, wisdom and more connection. There was that word again; connection. He had inspired me and I knew I had to follow my hearts passion to write. On rare occasions, the fear that I might never see him again had been crushing. I realised that in the simplest of ways, I was now more connected to myself; able to hold a higher trust in my future and in each moment. It would all reveal itself in due time.

Travelling alone made me realise that there were no hiding places from myself. If I was having a crap day, I was having a crap day. I simply had to push through it. There was no-one with me to share that day. There was no-one to blame; had their behaviour left me feeling sad, upset, or generally low. It simply was: whatever it was. I realised that the crap days would surely pass, as everything eventually does. I was even more grateful for the friends I could message to request a 'hug' through the ether. I allowed myself to feel and embrace these feelings of vulnerabilities. Although these crappy days were very few, they brought very powerful learnings for me and eventually a deep, abiding stillness.

Over these months I found my inner peace was deepening; regardless of whatever went on around me. I was learning to deal with disharmonious feelings very quickly through walking, exercise or meditation and by using the emotional freedom technique on occasions.

Sitting quietly with my tissues in hand, I realized that I had learnt so much about other cultures which had certainly taught me even more compassion, tolerance, humility and patience. I had learnt that I was safe and I always had been. I had perhaps more importantly learnt that there was so much more I had yet to learn.

Being in the moment had proved to be so important, each and every day. Waking to the birdsong, or listening to the occasional, very welcome rain. Listening to my intuition as to how I would shape each and every day was my priority. How did my body feel? Was I tired, or ready for a long walk? Maybe some T'ai Chi?

I realised I was ready to embrace something new each and every day. I set myself daily challenges such as exploring the village, or the town via a different route. I enjoyed seeking out new eating places and was happy to try different dishes.

Gratitude continued to fill my being as I thought of all the wonderful people I had met; Jay, Samuel, Niklas, my dear Indian family, Paige, Chetan, Ali, Anita, Deep and Knenpo the Tibetan monk. Putting my cup down on the table, I sent a quiet prayer of gratitude to each and every one of them. I had been truly honoured to have shared very precious moments with them. As I looked from the balcony over the rooftops, the surrounding trees and the huge, impressive palms, I was so grateful for the warmth of the sun. I had finally found the courage to make the decision to change my life through travel.

I trusted that I would find the breadcrumb trail that would lead me to wherever I was meant to go. I was still in unknown territory; regarding my present and my long- term future. Every now and again the feeling of fear gripped me tightly. Denying it was futile, so I honoured it, allowing it to pass in its own time. The words of my friend Brian often came to mind in these moments of uncertainty; "What you are seeking, is seeking you."

My destiny awaited me regardless of the fear. I knew that I could never miss whatever it was that lay ahead. Travelling had forced me to cope with so many changes. I took a quiet moment to appreciate the fact that I now allowed change into my life relatively easily and had adapted well in new situations.

I realised perhaps most of all that I had found a deeper peace within myself. Perhaps that realization was the most significant.

Looking at the time on my phone, it was now well past lunchtime. I was particularly hungry. Taking a last look at the precious photographs of my loved ones, I decided it was time to explore and embrace all that Ubud had to offer. It was certainly time to seek out a new favourite restaurant.

Chapter Forty Five

Ubud is an incredibly spiritual town; filled with spiritual shops, vegan restaurants and so much more. I loved it instantly. There were performances of the Balinese dancing every evening at Ubud Palace which was a five minute walk away. I instantly felt at home here and soon found several favourite restaurants.

When I returned I noticed that Wayan had left a brochure showing all the tourist trips that he offered to his guests. I had visited most of the sites already. The final listing mentioned cleansing of the chakras and the aura; a water purification ceremony would be included within the cost. I intuited that the healer was very powerful and I felt drawn to meet him for a private session.

Wayan explained that a holy man named Bape Mangku performed the healings. I knew I had to meet him at the earliest possible opportunity. Three days later Wayan picked me up from the homestay to take me to Bape Mangku's home. My whole being was shaking with excitement and I knew that this man was a very powerful healer. When we were introduced he looked straight into my eyes. He knew I was a psychic and a healer without the need for words. His assistant who was also called Wayan, explained the processes involved in the ceremony and the blessing. Bape did not speak English. As I looked from one man to the other, I could see how much respect they held for this man.

As the ceremony began I immediately felt so much lighter and was surrounded by bright white light. As holy water was poured over me I felt its power. Bape repeated various prayers and mantras. I could feel them working through each of my chakras and my aura. The whole experience was amazing, humbling and definitely felt as though it was life-changing. I was in awe of this man.

I was a little dizzy after the healing and he sat patiently while I came to again. After that the four of us prayed together; it was a sacred, most holy experience. As Bape placed flowers in my hair I cried. I had no doubt that this man was an enlightened Master. Being in his presence was a humbling honour.

A few days later we all met again and shared a meal. The energy that flowed between us was sacred and more powerful than anything I have ever experienced previously. As they chatted in Indonesian, I waited eagerly for it to be translated. I was grateful to be sharing these moments with people who were already becoming dear friends. They agreed that I should visit a sacred temple in the south of Bali and we made arrangements to meet up again on Sunday.

I was feeling very excited and was grateful that I only had two days to wait. Arriving at the remote temple I was amazed when I was greeted so warmly by the High Priests. I felt comfortable immediately as we were shown around the huge site. It took my breath away and I felt honoured when I was told that I was the first western woman ever to set foot on this sacred soil. The energy here was tangible and felt very much alive.

We were given refreshments while we were shown a short video of how the whole site had been created and designed; the gardens, pools, waterfalls, temples and so much more. It was incredible to see how one man's vision had become a reality within nine months. After the video we sat chatting and they requested that I walk around detailing exactly what I could 'see' and intuit esoterically.

Bape asked me at each of the eight points what I experienced. He and I were the only two who could 'see' the esoteric realms. I was delighted that eventually when we all gathered together again everything which I had intuited was confirmed. During the conversation the High Priest explained that there was another High Priest who wanted to meet me. He sent his apologies as he was unable to be present that particular evening. I tuned into his presence immediately and I knew I had known him in many other lives.

It was three thirty in the morning before we arrived back at the homestay. I had enjoyed a wonderful and totally inspiring evening. They requested I visit again soon and arrangements would be made for me to meet the other High Priest. As I drifted off to sleep I said a prayer of immense gratitude for all that I experienced in that mind-blowing evening. I dreamt of eagles and beautiful dragons.

The following day Wayan explained that the priests requested that I please visit again the following morning. I almost cried with delight. I would be spending my birthday amongst strangers who had already become friends in one of the most amazing, sacred places I have ever visited.

On the morning of my birthday, I was excited to meet the High Priest whom I had missed two days earlier. We both knew immediately when we were introduced that we had known one another in many other lives. It was such a wonderful acknowledgement that these people actually understood and accepted other lives with profound wisdom. They trusted both their intuition and their dreams. He said he had seen me in his morning prayers and meditations.

We chatted in private for quite some time about the responsibilities of being spiritual and I was honoured to be in his presence. After refreshments we attended all eight of the sacred areas; the High Priest requesting me to sit by his side throughout. As we prayed and meditated by the huge Lingham stone I was in tears as I received a personal message of thanks for all the earth healing work I have done throughout my life. I was so shocked by the power of the message that I asked for quiet time alone with the sacred stone. It was quite a while before I returned to the rest of the group; my eyes were still watery from the sacredness and profound intensity of my experiences.

Sharing lunch with approximately thirty other people added extra magic to my birthday. When one of the men placed a garland of marigold flowers around my neck to celebrate the day I was once again drawn to tears.

Wayan suggested we leave late afternoon before the rush hour traffic. The High Priest asked if he could accompany us as we were travelling in the same direction. When we arrived at his home, the celebrations continued. We were invited to celebrate further by sharing a meal with his family and he played traditional music too.

My birthday had truly been one of the most memorable and touching days that I have ever experienced. Sharing the day with over thirty holy, spiritual people was an honour beyond words. Meeting the High Priest was pure divinity.

On the Thursday evening before I was due to leave this magnificent island I was requested to visit a temple locally which was still under construction. Accompanied by Bape Mangku and both Wayans we drove eastwards. As we neared the temple I became quite dizzy and felt a tremendous surge of energy from the hillside to my left. It took me a while to shake off the dizziness. Once I felt settled again I realised the energy was very similar to that of the mountain where Jay and I had spent our last day together sitting near the sacred temple. Although I didn't have time to visit there that evening, I made a vow to myself that I would return one day and walk up this beautiful beacon of pure light.

It was another memorable evening. Once sunset fell the bats began to fly incredibly close to us and, as the stars began to light up the sky, it felt as though we were seeing glimpses of heaven. Meeting several of the villagers was memorable. Praying and meditating in this sacred place was touching. This experience like many of the others, was beyond religion – this was far more sacred and spiritual. One lady knew that we had also shared previous lives together as best friends. It was a little before two in the morning when we arrived back at the homestay. Sleep beckoned as I switched on the air conditioning and tucked myself into the lightweight blanket to enjoy another evening of peaceful dreams.

The following day was a simple one. I loved Ubud; the shops and the vibe of the town. I had by now explored much of the town centre though I wanted to venture further towards the outskirts. Late afternoon, when the heat of the day was easing, I wandered past Ubud palace. I walked at quite a fast pace until I came to a little stall were the owners were advertising various island tours. I noticed there was a 'spiritual tour'. I was intrigued. I wanted to know more out of curiosity. We chatted easily about religion, spirituality and the many different nationalities that visited the island. They asked me what my experiences of Bali had been so far. I explained that I loved the island dearly and was sad to be leaving in the coming days. The conversation changed as we discussed the other places I had visited; India and Nepal. I was desperate for the toilet. They were kind enough to allow me to use the one in their home. When I returned I noticed one of the tours included a walk in the nearby rice paddies. Within minutes the three of us set off chatting easily once more and discussing life in its simplicity.

It was quite a walk to the rice paddies at the very edge of the town. I heard the quacking of ducks and thought I was hearing things. When I turned, I was surprised to see several ducks gathered between the rice plants. I was truly astounded to see them here in Bali.

The guy stated that he had grown up in the local area and had loved it all dearly. His wife moved here when they married. I found it hard to believe that she had never walked these fields before. The three of us chatted and laughed as we all struggled walking between the various terraces. I was already muddy and the thought of landing directly in the rice fields had crossed my mind each time I stepped down another level. The laughter between us reinforced the friendship and we agreed that we felt we had known each other forever. We passed what looked like a snakeskin and I asked what it was. His wife agreed that it was indeed a snakeskin that had only recently been shed. She suggested that it had been within the last day, possibly only hours earlier. I thought of the many 'skins' I had shed since my journey had first begun.

The sun was beginning to set and the sky began to change into the most beautiful colours. Taking photographs as we walked, I loved listening to the stories about their lives and experiences. We passed a local farmer and they all chatted easily. It was his uncle and I loved listening to them speak in their native tongue. Somehow the simplicity of listening and watching them felt sacred. The loving connection between them was touching.

As we wandered further he explained that when they were children he had come down to the rice paddies to play with his siblings. In the evenings they would bring their lanterns and look for eels and frogs in the waterways. He said life was simple then. They explained that they had a teenage son who was only interested in his motorbike and his mobile phone. Their son had no interest in visiting the paddies and few of the youngsters now wanted to learn about farming their native land. We all nodded in agreement that the modern world lacked connection and real communication. I will always remember them with fondness for their loving kindness and the power of trusting strangers. What we shared that afternoon was simple, though incredibly precious.

My time in Bali was coming to a close. I was sad and yet filled with joy to be seeing my family at long last. I spent the last full day with Wayan, chatting and laughing while we drank dragonfruit juice. I knew I would miss him dearly. Once he left I ordered a taxi to take me to the beach where I could walk by the sea and watch the sunset. Paddling in the water as the sky changed colour, I watched as the coconut trees produced an amazing backdrop to the setting sun.

The following day I was incredibly sad as I packed my suitcase, especially my personal photographs. There was no turning back now. Wayan was waiting for me downstairs in the car. I had said my private prayers of thanks to Ubud. We were travelling with Bape Mangku to see the High Priest; Ida Rsi. Late afternoon, I would be dropped off at the airport. Arriving at Ida Rsi's home, we all knew these final hours were incredibly precious as we discussed healing the planet, helping people understand their souls and general philosophy. I felt truly honoured to know such wonderful people. We were all sad that I was leaving though I promised I would return within three months. Bape had promised to teach me more about healing and I knew my soul had longed for this moment for eternity

Duality played a huge part in the days leading up to me leaving Bali. So much had changed since I had met Bape Mangku. After the initial healing I had with him, I knew immediately that my life would change. I was so grateful that he and Wayan would be accompanying me to the airport that Sunday evening.

Bape looked as though he was about to cry as we hugged each other goodbye at the airport. Although I did shed some tears, I was relieved that I hadn't cried too much. Wayan too looked very sad, as I reassured them both that I would return in the coming months. I had a golden opportunity that I had to embrace. Learning more about healing from this humble Master would be a real honour. The whole point of my pilgrimage had been to feed my soul. I found it incredible that it had all come to fruition in the final fortnight. I was indeed grateful that I had allowed the purpose of this pilgrimage to unfold at its own pace, trusting each and every day that it would eventually become apparent within its own perfect timing.

Chapter Forty Six

The flight to New Zealand was relatively easy. When the fellow passengers and I caught sight of the mountain peaks a loud gasp went around the aircraft. There was a tangible sense of awe in the air. Everyone became silent admiring the incredible beauty of Mother Nature at her best.

I gasped again when I descended the stairs from the plane on to the tarmac runway. I was surrounded by the most amazing, truly remarkable mountains. The air was crisp and clean, the sun was shining brightly. I knew immediately why they loved being here. I fell in love with the island instantly.

Once inside the airport building, I was desperate to see my sons and found it hard not to push through the long biohazard queue. I struggled to hold back my tears as my heart pounded against the walls of my chest. Their beaming smiles awaited me on the other side. Hugging them as the tears fell, I was so grateful and proud to be their mother. It was an incredibly special moment. I felt overwhelmed as love and connection flowed between all three of us.

The journey from the airport was stunning. Mountains ran alongside the road to the right and the lake to the left. The air was so clean here, the trees so green and the water was a beautiful turquoise. I kept staring across at my son. I was finally here.

Matthew and I ventured into the town. It was so modern with stunning architecture, a far cry from the buildings I had seen in the last few months. Matthew asked if I was hungry and we decided to visit one of the local pubs. As I walked in I was shocked as it was so similar to an English pub. The wooden tables were so lovely and clean. Reading an English menu was surreal; English meals such as fish and chips, sausages and pies too. Even speaking and hearing the English language was odd. The bar staff were so friendly and we thoroughly enjoyed a hearty meal. It was rather like being in England which felt peculiar since I was at the opposite side of the world.

Phil joined us a few minutes later. I felt completely at home here. Everybody was incredibly friendly and they all had a welcoming smile, handshake, or a hug. The feeling of comfortability was almost overwhelming. I kept looking across at my sons to make sure they were really here with me at long last. Rachel was working; I would have to wait a few more hours before she finished to see her once more. I was so excited.

Walking down to the lake with my sons for the first time will remain with me forever. The sound of the tiny pebbles scrunching under my feet was wonderful together with the gentle sounds of the water lapping against the shoreline. The water was incredibly pure and clean. The lake was surrounded by mountains. They were much bigger than any I had seen previously. Everything had a certain magic to it here and a sense of awe enveloped me. This was a sacred place and full of majesty.

The peaceful ambience of the whole place touched me. Although there were many people nearby no-one was shouting, no children crying and the feelings of respect and peace seemed to be everywhere. I have never seen this in the modern, western world before. There was a genuine feeling of profound regard in this sacred valley. As we walked towards the rose gardens I vowed I would come here daily to soak up the beauty.

I loved everything about the town. Everything. The water was crystal clear as it was sourced directly from the glaciers. The mountains surrounded the whole valley and were simply magnificent in a perfect way. They were set against a beautiful blue sky with the sun shining brightly. Listening to the gentle waves touch the sides of the lake I was totally in awe of all that Queenstown had shared with me so far. The gardens were so neat and tidy, the paths clean and no litter could be seen anywhere. I thought of my mother and I knew she would love it here. I kept looking across at each of my sons and listened with such pleasure to the stories of how they had settled here and what they clearly loved about the town.

Arriving back at the house, Phil helped to carry my luggage, showing me around the house to ensure that I felt settled. It was a spacious three-bedroomed semi-detached with spectacular mountain views. It was clear that they were settled here and that they both had many friends. I relaxed more and more, knowing my time with them was precious and promised I would make the most of every day. It seemed strange to be staying in a house rather than alone in a hotel room. I was looking forward to many, lengthy conversations and spending quality time with them. I appreciated everything here as I was shown around the kitchen. I looked forward to cooking them all a meal as I put the kettle on to boil.

We agreed to share a pizza later and watch a movie together when Rachel arrived home. Her excitement was obvious when she burst into the room. There were many more hugs and I was so thrilled to see her. She immediately referred to me as 'Mo-Mo'. It felt very endearing and was such a welcome gesture from my son's partner. As we settled on the sofa snuggling up together, I felt privileged to share this special evening with people I loved dearly. After spending so much time alone these last few months; especially away from my English family I felt truly blessed. Ordering pizza from

‘Fat Badgers’ was fun as we all decided which toppings we would prefer. It was a perfect, memorable evening.

The following morning I was so cold. I had awoken several times in the night shivering. I even had a cold nose. The British weather is so changeable and I assumed I would adapt to the New Zealand climate very easily. Clearly I had been mistaken. I had been in temperatures of up to forty two degrees in the last few months. The New Zealand winters meant temperatures were down to eight degrees, or even less.

Shivering violently when Matthew called to collect me the following morning, we agreed I needed to shop for winter clothing; urgently. Despite wearing four; sometimes five layers of clothing, I still felt quite cold. I was glad the weather was sunny, though once out of the sun, the temperature dropped dramatically. It was winter here in the South Island and I prayed that my body would adjust. I was surprised that I felt so cold; despite heaters and wrapping myself with numerous blankets.

After clothes shopping, Matthew and I then walked in to the main town. He introduced me to the famous ‘Ferg's Bakery’. I had not enjoyed a delicious hot chocolate since January. Watching her pour the precious liquid into the cup made me realise how much I had missed it. It tasted like sweet nectar. Enjoying each and every mouthful; very slowly and with deep appreciation I realised how much I loved my favourite drink. I even licked the lid of the cup. I was instantly hooked. The bakery was amazing and certainly the busiest in town. It felt particularly weird being in a busy, western-style shop again. It was another almost surreal experience.

We walked by the lakeside once again and chatted whilst we drunk our hot chocolates. Catching up and sharing precious time together was lovely. I was grateful that he was off work; having recently suffered a back injury. We chatted easily about the rest of the family and how we had missed each other. He was obviously very settled here. I noticed how many friends he chatted with in the town. I was so proud when he introduced me to each of them. Life was so restful here and there was a tangible calm about Queenstown. He clearly loved it. Everyone I met seemed genuinely happy and it was a most welcome surprise to me that no-one seemed to be consumed by the material world. It seemed those that were here enjoyed being here and were grateful for the scenery, the lake and the whole island. It felt so refreshing in a modern town.

Lunchtime was fast approaching and he offered to take me to Arthurs Point. I have always loved exploring new places and it was absolutely breath-taking. The clear, blue water in the gorge ran under a huge bridge. The place was renowned for gold mining several decades earlier. Watching the jet boats glide gracefully across the water at full speed was awesome; though I made it clear that I had no interest in participating in the experience. Matthew thought it was highly amusing to know that his mother was still sensible; if not a little boring. Sitting by the river, listening to the history of the island and how the population had grown and prospered I was surprised by its relative youth. It was certainly now part of the modern world and had evidently developed at an amazingly fast pace.

As we journeyed through the mountains towards Arrowtown, I kept repeating the word 'Wow'. Matthew smiled as he drove his van; clearly delighted to see my love for this place. Sitting in the van, I was still wearing my thick, padded coat, hat, scarf and gloves too, while Matthew wore a simple light jacket.

This treasured land was mostly untouched. There were so few houses along the route and as the eagles flew alongside us, I was touched by its simple, natural and breath-taking stunning beauty. The mountains were so grand and seemed to touch the sky. Some were covered in snow and the ski-slopes looked inviting. There was a tangible peace here which radiated all around us. The landscape stretched out in front of us, the beauty of Mother Earth was everywhere to behold. Parts of the road had huge mountain drops and others led to natural pastures where the sheep grazed. It was so unspoilt and perfect.

Arrowtown was lovely. It was one of the original goldmining towns and looked so similar to the goldmining towns in the United States of America; with wooden buildings lining the main street. Finding a lovely restaurant was easy and I no longer had to question the standards of hygiene, or ask where the water was sourced. Sitting in the bar, listening to the modern pop music felt odd. I hadn't experienced the modern world since January. I found a space to sit near the log fire where I could keep warm. The food was delicious and I loved the salad, even the fresh orange juice tasted divine. I savoured every mouthful of the nectar. It was wonderful to share a meal with good conversation and spend time with my beloved son. Rachel and Phil both had work commitments though I looked forward to sharing time with them later.

Matthew was clearly in pain with his back and was struggling to walk. I was grateful he could at least manage a short walk by the river before we returned to the van. It was easy to imagine the original gold miners being here finding nuggets of gold in the clear mountain waters. I loved being in nature again and here it felt like the pinnacle of all that Mother Earth represented. I was truly blessed to be here.

As we drove back I could see the pain had tired him and agreed when he suggested he would drop me back at Phil and Rachel's house. He promised he would return later. The house was a lovely three-bedroomed semi-detached. Phil and Rachel had agreed that I could use their bedroom, as they were happy to sleep in the lounge. The other two bedrooms were occupied by their house-mates. The house was at the far edge of Queenstown, overlooking the lake and the town. The views were absolutely stunning from any one of its aspects. Each and every time I looked out across the valley it took my breath away.

The house was empty when I returned. Everyone was at work. I put the kettle on to boil, looking out of the huge patio windows, simply absorbing the love I had already received from the three of them and also the welcome from their house-mates. It felt strange as I found I was adjusting to being in their company quite easily. As I sipped my tea slowly, I knew the time would eventually come when I would need to explain to them that I would be returning to Bali for several months. I was dreading telling them. They all knew I had a sponsor here in Queenstown and could apply for a work visa immediately. In our conversations thus far, I encouraged them to talk about their lives here and I was happy to listen, rather than participate.

The peace and quiet of the house was most welcome. It was the first time I had been alone. As I listened to the nothingness I felt very much at home. I tuned into my body and how I was feeling. I had only awoken a little after nine in the morning; which was certainly quite a change from my usual six thirty; when I had been in much warmer climates.

As it was winter here the sunset early in the evening. They were stunning and so colourful here. As night fell; with very little artificial lighting, the stars were breath-taking to view. I was still feeling so cold, and as I stood on the veranda for a few minutes admiring them, I shivered violently. I was grateful for the warmth of the air-conditioning unit and snuggled under a blanket, waiting for them to return from work so we could all gather once again to watch a film together. As we shared crisps and chocolate; another very rare treat for me in the past few months, I felt very contented to be here.

The following day Phil managed to get some time off work. Rachel had already left for work and the three of us agreed to share lunch. I watched my sons engaging in conversation and laughing as brothers do. I was proud they were settled and obviously very contented here. I was also grateful that they had each other; as they were literally at the other end of the world from the rest of the family who were in England.

We agreed to visit Arrowtown again and I loved the healthy food and ambience of the restaurant they chose. I felt so at peace in their company and was pleased to listen once again to their many stories of how their lives had changed since they arrived here almost four years ago. Listening to stories of how they loved their work, how Phil and Rachel had met and how they had settled made me feel a deep sense of pride. They had clearly adjusted to the New Zealand way of life which was laid back and clearly more authentic than the British way of life. There was no competition between anyone I met; no comparisons of salary, how someone was dressed nor what car they drove. It seemed there was no judgement of a persons' means. It was so refreshing and most welcome. Here they were even more connected to nature than they had been in the United Kingdom. It was easy to see why from all that I had seen thus far. They shared stories of other beautiful locations as they were deciding which we should visit during my stay. I listened in awe and trusted their decisions.

My first weekend was so memorable. They were thrilled and excited to show me around the island. Glenorchy was our first destination. The drive alongside Lake Wakatipu was stunning with some of the most spectacular scenery I have ever seen. They mentioned that it was listed as one of the most scenic routes in the world. I could clearly see why.

Arriving in the small town felt strange. It was very different to Arrowtown and Queenstown. There were only a few buildings. Once again we were surrounded by beautiful mountains which held an ambience of peace. We sat together in a lovely restaurant with a huge open log fire. I was still struggling to adjust to the cold weather. When the waitress came to take our order, I thought her accent sounded familiar. I asked whereabouts she was from originally and she mentioned Preston in Lancashire, England. We were all surprised as it was our home town. She explained that when she first visited New Zealand, she had fallen in love with the place instantly and had never looked back. I had spoken to so many English people since I had arrived; they all said the same thing; they fell in love with New Zealand and knew they had to stay.

I was grateful to be able to sit by an open log fire again. We sat laughing, sharing stories and jokes. It really was a perfect meal in every sense; great food, great service and wonderful company. Wandering down to the lakeside to see the most clear, turquoise water once again, I found I was experiencing the absolute joy of being here. I felt so lucky to share each of those precious moments. We gathered some drift wood for Matthews log burner and enjoyed the camaraderie. The whole place was growing on me. I pondered what it must be like in the warmer months. Matthew had already mentioned that the autumn colours here that caressed the trees were absolutely stunning.

When we arrived home again we settled down to watch a film together once more while we decided what tomorrow would bring. Phil and Rachel had plans to ski though Matthew and I did not wish to partake; especially with his back pain. Dependent upon the weather we might visit Lake Wanaka. I was happy either way. I had company, my loved ones around me and loved the area so much that a simple walk to the lakeside brought me much joy. Being a small town, I soon memorised the layout and I found my way easily down to the beach by the lakeside; usually with a hot chocolate in hand.

Over the coming days we settled into an easy routine. Matthew and I went out together, or met up in the town most days. Phil and Rachel were both working full-time. I usually spent my time writing for a couple of hours in the morning. I was surprised to find that I was still feeling the cold and often sat with one blanket across my shoulders and another around my legs. Once inspiration faded, I would take a walk down to the precious lakeside. I was so happy to sit by the water's edge and watch the waves while admiring the surrounding scenery. Life was simple. Several hours later, I was contented to wander back home, especially if I began to feel too cold.

Collecting any shopping that we might need from the local supermarket was easy as it was on the main route home. I found it strange the first time we had entered the store. I hadn't seen so much food, or so many products for months. It was quite overwhelming. In India and Nepal I had shopped from small market stalls, or street vendors carts. Any shops I had visited were small and usually sold a limited variety of products. Adjusting to using another currency yet again was also strange. New Zealand prices were far more expensive than those I had been used to paying in the last few months.

I hadn't cooked for months and it was a simple pleasure to prepare a healthy dinner. I loved smelling the onions and the garlic as I fried them in fresh butter to make a curry. I felt connected to it all. To life, living, eating and breathing, to sharing and laughing at the simplest of things. I even enjoyed hoovering the house and cleaning the bathroom. Nothing was a chore. Everything I did, I did with love for them and for their home. I even enjoyed weeding the tiny patio at the front of the house and sweeping the stone steps. I found it all effortless.

In the evenings we would settle down and watch a movie together, catching up on the day's events and sharing a lovely evening meal. Occasionally we went to the local cinema, or sampled the local cuisine in the many restaurants. It was pleasurable and most memorable. Each and every day was blissful, yet simple.

Visiting Wanaka the following weekend was a real celebration. The drive through the gorge was magnificent with stunning scenery and deep snow in places. The glacier waters were a rich turquoise colour. Listening to the water rush down the valley from the mountains was incredibly noisy and brought such a beautiful restorative feeling. As the roads here were so windy, I was glad I wasn't driving as I trusted my son to navigate the numerous bends. Black ice was a real problem here despite the use of grit on the roads. I was looking forward to driving in due course, though for now I trusted their experience.

Arriving in Wanaka, Rachel suggested we visit the local bakery. The vast selection of pies, breads and cakes was exceptional. They had won numerous awards and I could clearly see why. I was salivating before I had chosen what I wanted.

As we walked by the lakeside and the surrounding beach area I pondered if I could ever leave this heavenly, unspoilt place. Rachel wove her arm around mine and reminded me of my daughter Emily in England and how much I missed her. Collecting pine cones for Matthew to burn on his log burner and wandering into the woods brought such laughter between the four of us; which got louder and louder when we began to throw the cones at one another. The lakeside was like nothing I had ever seen before; despite having visited many of the English Lakes and the Scottish Lochs. The sense and the presence of Mother Earth was more tangible here than anywhere else I have ever been. There was an abiding sense of peace and a harmony which was not unlike Bali and yet it was completely different.

On the journey home we celebrated with another wonderful meal in a nice hotel bar called 'The Cardrona'. It was so lovely with huge open fires, a beer garden with a chimney and a lovely ambience. The hotel rooms looked inviting as I wandered around to explore. I felt so very privileged to be here. Sharing time with them, watching how they interacted with one another, listening to their stories and their jokes was all part of the simplicity of our connection. There were no uncomfortable silences or misgivings, no misunderstandings nor unspoken words. I felt so grateful to be a part of their lives. I felt incredibly blessed to be their mother and to be welcomed with such warmth by Rachel.

We had visited the cinema earlier in the week and watched the film 'Yesterday'. Afterwards we decided to go to the local bar where we met up with some of their mutual friends. Once again I received a warm welcome from complete strangers. Seeing them all get on together was a lovely experience. As I was introduced to each of them in turn, they too called me 'Mo-Mo'. I was surprised, yet felt most honoured. As I sat with Jess; a beautiful lady from Essex, she mentioned that it was very rare that anyone's parents came to visit here from England; due to the distance and the cost. Whenever parents did visit, they were 'shared' between everyone in the community as the English 'Mo-Mo' (mum), or father. She explained that they were all travel orphans and valued each other's friendship greatly. Her honesty touched me and I was certainly beginning to understand what it was like to live without family close by. Jess and I chatted and laughed easily. She was yet another stranger who I came to love and trust.

Rachel and I shared so much when we were together. She always had a hug when she left for work and she always had a huge beaming smile on her face when she arrived home. It wasn't long before the boys and the house-mates called me 'Mo-Mo' too. It felt most endearing and held such affection. I was delighted when they mentioned we would be visiting Milford Sound together. Matthew and Phil had visited there previously and were keen for us to share a 'girlie' day. I was delighted.

It was an early morning start to Milford Sound as we boarded the tourist bus with a glass roof. The sun had not yet risen so we travelled in darkness for a couple of hours. We chatted easily as we enjoyed getting to know one another more. As the daylight began to filter through into the morning we passed another huge lake. The guide explained the legends of the lakes and many stories of how New Zealand had changed over the decades. It fascinated me and I loved listening to the 'Kiwi' accent.

Travelling past the mountain ranges and seeing the open plains of New Zealand were stunning. This was a sacred, mostly untouched land. Rachel explained that once we were through the gorge ahead the scenery would become even more breath-taking. As we neared the gorge the driver also suggested we look out of the windows as the view would change and become even more beautiful. The road seemed to hug the mountain and the scenery was indeed impressive and awe-inspiring. Sheer rock faces and waterfalls that dropped down at an angle of one hundred and eighty degrees. It was surreal. The whole valley had an eerie feeling. Avalanches were common here as were falling rocks, driving was done with the utmost care.

Arriving at Milford Sound itself was very memorable. It was incredible and such a place as I have never seen before. I felt like a genuine explorer here and gasped several times as I looked out towards the ocean.

Our boat was docked in the harbour and we would be boarding within the next few minutes. I was so excited. I love water and the thought of travelling to the open ocean with the possibility of seeing dolphins was beyond words. As we watched from the windows whilst we ate our lunch I expressed how grateful I was to Rachel; for taking time to come with me on this day; for making me welcome and for making Phil even more happy.

Several minutes later we walked out on deck. The cool air touched our skin and I was grateful for my hat, gloves and scarf. The other tourists were smiling, laughing and it was clear each of us loved the magic of the whole place. Once again the cliff edges were at one hundred and eighty degrees with the cliffs going straight down into the water. The Captain explained that we would be moving towards the massive waterfall to our left. I wanted to get to the front of the boat, despite knowing that I might get soaked with water. The boat slowed and was still moving rapidly up and down with the wave action. Nonetheless I steadied myself and carried on towards the front of the boat. The whole scene was amazing and unlike anything I have ever seen before in my life. I could see why it had been chosen as the location to film 'The Lord Of The Rings'.

Several minutes later we were heading to open coastal waters. As the valley opened out to the sea the waves became too powerful and we returned to the safety of the cove.

Everything about the whole trip that day was memorable. Although we didn't see dolphins it didn't detract in any way from the delight of the whole experience. The journey home was also stunning and being welcomed back into Queenstown by Matthew and Philip was a reminder of precious loving connections.

I kept in touch with both Wayan's and Bape Mangku most days. I missed them and often felt Bape around me; watching over me as if he was checking that I was okay. I hadn't yet decided when I would return but as the winter cold was still affecting me, I had a 'knowing' that it would be sooner, rather than later.

Matthew was in tears when he watched the video of my healing purification ceremony with Bape and Wayan. He was clearly touched and deeply moved. He said he could clearly see the light around Bape Mangku and felt his spiritual presence. He understood exactly why I had to return. I had his full blessing.

Rachel and Phil were equally supportive in my decision and I will be forever grateful for their endearing love and much valued support. I felt blessed. We still had a few weeks to share together and although I could not be sure when I would return to New Zealand, at least Bali would be close enough for them to visit me. They were planning a holiday in September and they were about to book their flights. Phil enquired while he was in the local travel agents about the price of the return airfare to Bali on my behalf.

I was amazed when he was quoted a price which was a quarter of the price I had paid to travel from Bali to Queenstown. He said the agent; Grace, said it was very rare that it would be so reasonably priced. She and Phil suggested I book the ticket.

Fate had stepped in and the date I would be leaving was to be the 23rd of July. It meant I would be returning to Bali within six weeks. I had a decision to make and intuitively knew that it was right for me; even though it meant leaving them much sooner than I had anticipated. There was incredible duality around that decision. I was dreading leaving them and all that Queenstown and New Zealand had already brought to me. I was also looking forward to seeing Bape and my friends again.

The time passed so quickly. Each and every day I treasured being in Queenstown. Opening the curtains in the morning was the start of another wonderful day. Looking out at the spectacular view of the mountains and the lake below touched my soul daily.

Matthew's back pain continued and he was unable to work. I was delighted as it meant we could spend more time together. We usually went out for lunch or met in Queenstown itself. The Bathhouse Café had become a favourite of mine, especially when I had seen Lady Grey tea on the menu. It was literally on the beach of Lake Wakatipu and I loved to watch the waves on the shoreline. It was warm enough to sit outside if the sun was overhead. We often met here and shared a meal or a drink; usually with cake. After that we would wander around the gardens and chat easily.

One afternoon Matthew asked me to meet him by the lakeside. He was accompanied by his dear friend whom he had wanted me to meet since my arrival. Rosco was such a delightful man and the three of us played Frisbee together. The Frisbee course was built into the forest by the lakeside. The aim was to get the Frisbee into the various baskets. Each basket was positioned differently and as the course progressed, it became more difficult to achieve the target. We were howling laughing. I failed to get the Frisbee in most of the baskets though we thoroughly enjoyed ourselves; even when it began to rain. Later we shared a pizza in the local pub and once again, amongst the locals, I felt so at ease as Matthew introduced me to his many friends.

Matthew had been working on a huge building site near Arrowtown when he had injured his back. He clearly missed his work and loved the houses he had already built. He loved showing me around several of them and introducing me to his work colleagues. They too missed him being on site. As he drove me around the locality, it seemed everywhere we went the scenery was stunning; especially when we drove above Queenstown and enjoyed the magnificent view below of the lake with the clear, turquoise waters, the snow-topped mountains and the beautiful houses. This was one of the most wonderful views I have ever looked out on.

Phil often travelled with his work and as a busy manager he had little spare time. He really has a wonderful sense of humour and between him and Rachel the laughter flowed in abundance. Whenever we did get the chance to share time during the day we loved it. I met many of the staff that worked with him; their respect was genuine and affectionate. I was most proud of them all.

Rachel worked in a local hotel and on occasions I would visit for a chat and a coffee. She was always so pleased to see me and she too happily introduced me to her work colleagues. The restaurant there soon became a firm favourite and I was grateful for all we shared.

As my last weekend approached we were all sad. With work commitments that Phil and Rachel had, it could potentially be the last time all four of us were together before my flight on Wednesday morning. A dear friend of theirs was celebrating his thirtieth birthday and I was also invited to the big party on the Saturday evening. It was in a beautiful hotel and the theme was Hollywood Glam. I was so excited and I knew it was going to be a great evening. I was honoured to be invited and was looking forward to meeting Vitor. They each spoke very highly of him. I needed an outfit and was thrilled when I managed to get a beautiful black and red stylish dress and a fur coat; honouring the theme of glamour. Rachel had promised to do my hair and make-up. It was certainly going to be memorable.

Vitor looked amazing when we arrived. He was dressed very smartly in a gorgeous velvet jacket. He hugged me tightly and welcomed me to his party. The other guests were equally as lovely as their host. As we poised for photos I was thrilled to meet even more of their friends and found socializing with them easy. There was no agenda here. No ego playing out. We were all dressed up to congratulate Vitor on his special birthday and to enjoy the evenings' celebrations.

As I walked home later that evening I reflected on my many experiences. Looking up at the starry night and feeling the chill in the air was refreshing and memorable. Queenstown is such a beautiful place and as I walked back up the hill, I pondered whether there was anything else that I wanted to do before I left this magical place.

'The Earnslaw'; an old steam powered boat had recently been repaired and was now back on the lake. The following morning, I was told that we were going into Queenstown to enjoy breakfast at one of the local restaurants. I was amazed when they showed me our tickets to journey on the old steamer. It was such a treat. She was magnificent and once on board we wandered down to the engine room. Watching the men load the coal while the pistons got faster and faster was amazing. She had been built around the time of The Titanic. The journey across the lake to Walters Farm was perfect. The water splashed at either side of the boat as she glided through the turquoise lake. With mountains to the left and the right it was truly spectacular. I loved the whole experience. Being there with my loved ones meant I felt so honoured to receive such a memorable gift from them all.

Lunch was included in the trip. I had spoken to the engineer during the journey and he stated the food was excellent. As the four of us lunched together; enjoying the most fabulous buffet that I have ever tasted, I found myself struggling to conceal my tears. Their kindness and their love were overwhelming, endearing and so much appreciated. I knew I would miss them dearly when I returned to Bali.

The following day with only two days before I was due to leave, Rachel, Matthew and I went to watch 'The

Lion King' at 'Dorothy Browns.' It was the local picture house in Arrowtown. It was amazing, with sofas and blankets too. Both homely and cosy we thoroughly enjoyed the film. I cherished every moment we shared that precious day.

On the drive home, I pondered on my experiences over the last six weeks. I had been blessed to walk by the shoreline under the pine trees and I had thoroughly enjoyed so many special moments; either alone or with my precious family. The day I visited Milford Sound with Rachel had been a truly magical experience. I loved the magnificent scenery. Seeing was believing as the landscape; cliffs, waterfalls and the majesty of it all combined to leave quite a powerful imprint on my heart and soul.

Meeting their friends; especially Vitor, was very special to me. I could clearly see that they were settled and respected in the town. There was no materialism here in the sacred bubble of Queenstown. People were happy and I found it was so refreshing compared to other places in this modern world. I had always received a warm welcome wherever I had ventured in this magical place. Watching the sunsets daily had been such a delight as the colours changed the mood of the mountains. The whole experience was touching and I will be forever grateful.

Inevitably my time came to return to Queenstown airport. Phil and Rachel had said their 'Goodbyes' that morning and there were many tears. Matthew and I stood and hugged for many, long, blissful moments before I finally entered the security gate. We didn't know when, or where we would see each other again; although we knew for sure that we would in due time. We promised to keep in touch as I watched him disappear from view through my tear-filled eyes.

Sat in the airport lounge looking at The Remarkables mountain range by the side of the airport runway, I felt so many emotions. I remembered a quote which we had found written on the wall in the museum in Arrowtown;

THE MAORI –

"There seemed to be no cares, griefs or troubles in the Maori villages. There were none of the many sources of irritation that civilisation has created to mar his lifetime.

There were no mortgages, disputed notes, no unreasonable shopkeepers insisting on being paid, no lecherous lawyers getting rich over other people's arguments, no destitute widows and children needing charities, no beggars, no debtor's prisons, or to sum it up in two words.....No money."

Johannes Anderson.

It touched me when I had first read it and it touched me now, as I waited for the final boarding call.

Admiring the snow on the mountains and thinking of the glacier water which was so incredibly clean and pure, I thought of my love of water and how I feel so deeply connected to it. Here the respect for the water was so apparent. I reflected on my journey since leaving the United Kingdom in January and I pondered a simple question. What if we cleaned up the water across the planet, especially the sacred water from the Himalayas? What would it be like if clean, beautiful, sacred water flowed internationally and we returned to a place of respect for this precious resource?

Chapter Forty Eight

Now, with only minutes before I was due to leave New Zealand, my beloved sons and beautiful daughter-in-law, I was so pleased that they understood why I needed to return to Bali to spend time with Bape Mangku. His most kind offer to teach me more about healing is an honour. It is far beyond any words that I can ever use to explain the level of respect and the love I feel for him. I am blessed and humbled that he is willing to share his extensive wisdom and knowledge.

Where will this journey take me? All I have is the trust in my soul that this is the right path for me at this time. I must learn as much as I can from him and allow the breadcrumb trail to show itself in due time.

Will I ever settle again in the United Kingdom?

Where will I settle?

Will I ever see Jay again?

Will I fulfil my destiny?

Will I write more books?

Will I inspire more people than I had done while I lived in England?

Will I ever see my loved ones back in England? Yes I certainly feel that I will visit them again in due time. I have allowed trust and intuition to guide me this far. Now I must trust that whatever awaits me in Bali will allow me to fulfil my destiny and complete my soul and its purpose.

My dear friend Peter Sanderson (The Preston Poet) channelled this for me at the beginning of May. It touched me deeply and brought tears to my eyes. He was inspired to write it whilst he sat on James Joyce's statue:

God's Portrait

As I stare into the mirror of truth,
A river of authenticity flows, through the church in my heart,
Hail the gold not the glitter,
Feel the breath not the air,
Hear the voice within you, not the echo of others,
Behold the lightness and perfection of your sailing soul,
Not the lumber of the body nor the labyrinth of the mind.
As I stare at a sky full of stars,
My ego shatters into a million miracles,
All the questions of the universe are
Answered in the view from Earth's mighty window,
My reflections in the sea of souls,
Casts my body as but a vessel for one
small exploration amid many epic voyages,
Think not of the stumbles of each Passing day,
Fear not the waterfall of death,
For this is everything but the final journey,
T'is the point where your river flows Into a new world,
The graduation of your soul to the
next magnificent university of life,
Another adventure in your becoming,
Your next great odyssey through the
Sweet music of the stars,

Where the eyes of your heart will see
New worlds, brighter colours, dance
More daring dances, taste nectars
Sweeter than you ever thought possible,
For this is the infinite masterpiece of God's perfect portrait
OF YOU.

A Personal Note

I had no idea when I started this journey what the destination would be. I had outgrown my old life and I needed to start a new one. It wasn't easy making the break and I hope I captured the magnitude of the fear that threatened to engulf me at times.

Fear is often the only way through to the other side of whatever it is that awaits us. It takes incredible courage and determination; I am so grateful to those who supported me through my many 'wobbles.'

However this book has inspired you, whatever you have experienced through my writing, I sincerely hope that you have enjoyed the read.

I have loved writing this book. It really has been a beautiful, most touching experience. My intention throughout is to inspire and enthuse the reader. I sincerely hope that you have felt my experiences through the written word.

My love to you all.

May you allow yourselves to be led by your soul, together with the whispers from your heart.

May all your travels be sacred.

Mary x

Testimonials

Mary's journey is an extraordinary tale of courage, trust and letting go. Her story is a monumental example of how, if we can all find it in ourselves to leap into our magnificence, we can not only fulfil our soul's mighty potential but also find deep joy 'en-route'. Mary left her cocoon and embraced her inner and outer butterflies, soaring to new spiritual heights and allowing the winds of destiny to take her to a new undiscovered world of sunshine, freedom, wisdom and Balinese gurus. A phenomenal book from an inspirational soul.

Thank you Mary!

Peter Sanderson: Shaman, Author and Creative Spirit

This book charts Mary's personal journey of self-discovery and her experiences when travelling in India, Bali and New Zealand. I found it interesting, gripping, emotional and inspiring!

I have known Mary for about ten years, so I understand what a special lady she is but I am in awe of her now! What comes across, apart from the vivid descriptions – no holds barred – of the ups and downs of her travels, is the amazing love she has for her family, friends and the people she met along the way. I really feel that there is another book in the pipe-line and I can't wait!

Esmee Grossman: Lifelong Learner and Spiritual Seeker

'Dance of the Mosquito' is likely going to be the best book I read for a long time. Having known Mary personally for a few years now, I can honestly say she is one of the most beautiful souls I have ever met. Her story of her travels is such a deep, humbling account of life on the other side of the globe and she describes it with such detail you actually feel like you are experiencing it yourself - I have never visited the places she has here but I can see them so vividly in my mind's eye.

For those of us so accustomed to modern Western life it is a real wake up call to what is the true value of life, not the value of our possessions. I don't often cry when reading, but I found myself in tears on several occasions; not just from sorrow, but also from joy and laughter.

I recognise myself sat in the same place mentally in some of the recollections in the earlier pages. I hope one day I have the same courage and spirit to grow as I have watched her do as I continued reading.

I would heartily recommend anyone to read this beautiful book, as I would any of Mary's books, and I cannot wait for the next one so we can learn more!"

Emma Hall: Healer and Teacher

Mary really is a special lady and an inspirational writer, who shares her story in a unique & beautiful way, so everyone can learn something from each and every one of her books and I am sure this latest book will be just as powerful. Highly recommend all of her books.

Sheila Steptoe: Spiritual Mentor and Author

What can I say? I'm a huge fan of all of Mary's books; her writing makes you feel like you're walking beside her on all her journeys; you learn some, cry some and laugh some. 'The Dance of the Mosquito', I have to say, swept me into its pages from the very first to last page, which is rare in a book; so well done Mary. I felt like I was with her; she described everything so beautifully, she was honest and true.

I admire her bravery at setting out on her spiritual journey; you could feel that it took a huge amount of courage to walk through the fear of the unknown and to leave behind her beloved family.

I have learnt so, so much from all of Mary's books, for which I will be forever grateful. I loved every page of ; 'The Dance of the Mosquito' and as I neared the end I felt sad, so Mary we need more!!!

What a talented lady, not only has she written a fantastic book that everyone should read, but she is humble and has a huge amount of love within her that she shares so graciously with us all. Mary please don't stop writing us your fantastic books. I am waiting with bated breath for where you take us next.

Jeanette Pollard: Healer and Teacher

The 'Dance of the Mosquito' is told through the eyes of Mary. A lady who sells, and gives away all her possessions and leaves her beloved family and friends to set off on a brave adventure to far flung places to expand her spirituality. We are given everything from the agonising to the glorious and every emotion in between. The writing is so vivid and magical that you imagine yourself stood at Mary's shoulder. You will laugh, cry and rejoice with her all the way .

Joanna Dobie: Spiritual Warrior, Healer and Goddess

Another amazingly beautiful book from a very special lady. I'm completely in awe of Mary's braveness throughout and to allow us, as readers, to be part of her spiritual journey feels sacred.

The rawness and truthfulness/honesty of Mary's thoughts and worries throughout her journey is completely soul baring. The courage Mary has shown in fulfilling her soul's needs is beautiful and I'm sure will inspire many on their own journeys to keep going and to believe in themselves... it does me!

Sian Collins: Spiritual Healer and Speaker

I have revisited your book over this last couple of weeks.

Poetic channelling ends the beginnings to deepen the rivers of the water flowing in our hearts.

The darkest moments reveal the lightest dreams to become a clear vision of an awakening which no calm waters settle.

Our purpose become omnipotent with a richer understanding of simplicity in everything .

Love, Laugh, Live each moment with a caring echo of the wind rustling in our being of enlightenment.

Be still All is Well

Enjoy all things with a burst of the first essay each visit with an inner knowing of if becoming comfortable like a blessed journey.

Julie Burns: Close Friend

Every now and then something special comes into our world to enhance it forever, and my dear friend Mary's book 'Dance of the Mosquito', which I have been privileged to read, is that special enhancement to our world. It is more than just the usual story of one woman's search for enlightenment; it is a study of courage, a celebration of life, and, in beautiful, easy to read prose, it takes the reader on a glorious adventure to a very special truth. Thank you Mary for embellishing my life as you share your voyage with me.

Stan Phillips: Poet

I have just finished reading your book which I found very interesting. It took me a while to get into the heart of it as the scenes in India I imagined in my mind and knew I didn't want to experience them, and very sad that I couldn't do anything about their poverty and suffering. I also feel people's pain very deeply.

Bali opened up a brave new world as I could see colour, feel the love of the people and even the breeze on my skin. You worked your magic there.

New Zealand was a personal experience for you as your beloved sons greeted you ----- I could feel the warmth on the pages.

Thank you for the opportunity to see into your world and wish you every success with this book

Grace Robinson: Philosophy Student and Domestic Goddess

My friend Mary has been on an amazing journey. I have been lucky enough to follow her via the internet and phone calls. Now you can also follow her in her new book. It will take you to another world, and make you think of other things; rather than the news channels. Much Love Mary, from your friend

Margaret Miller: Reiki Healer

Here is my review of your beautiful book. Very last minute, so apols for that. I absolutely LOVED it and genuinely couldn't put it down. I think it's your best yet. I can identify with so much in there, having travelled and lived in the Far East as a child. It brought it all back. Your book paints a very real picture.

Bravo Mary, my heart is with you and thank you for sharing your incredible journey.

Ros Coleman: Visionary Artist

Mary's gifts are bountiful, how fitting she has been sharing her insight and blessings through the written word. That's why I call her 'Magic Mary'.

John Thomson: Actor and Comedian

Mary is a dear friend, who I've known for years. We saw each other at gatherings from time to time and just always gravitated to each other and enjoyed giggles and chats. Anyway years later, I knew she did Reiki, meditation and angel cards I believe. So I wanted her to help guide me as I'd always been interested in spirituality etc etc.

Now after that meeting my interest in everything Mary was about upped 100%. The fact that she spoke about my husband's dreams that he'd only had that night and described them to a T, made me realise she was amazing. Got my husband to see Mary too. He has also been friends with her for years and again she blew his mind and said all sorts about him; his thought patterns; his dreams; his future dreams etc etc was just incredible.

So ever since then, Mary has helped us become more in tune, listen to our bodies, minds and intuition so much more and WOW!!! Is all I can say. Every single thing makes sense and happens! Surround yourself with negativity; whether a job, person, or thoughts and all you get is negative in return. Whereas put out positive and TADAH.......! The magic happens, happy self, happy home, happy friends, happy job, happy times? It's that simple.

So to round this off. Darren and I have Mary's books with us. We read them, we go back to them, we recommend them. We may not have Mary physically with us, but these books echo Mary's words and give you the tools to keep going if needed. They are a piece of Mary in a way.

I truly hope people have the sense and wanting to bring light into their lives and home, and one definite way is to start by reading your books Mary. Love you always and forever and thank you for being you and sharing a piece of you with me and my family.

Emma Eckton: Actress and Spiritual Seeker

I really enjoyed this book written by Mary. What a fantastic adventure she had. Mary writes with such description I felt as though I was with her on this journey of self discovery, visiting the temples, experiencing the highs and lows of India. I was taken on a rollercoaster of emotions reading each chapter, happiness and sadness. I felt myself sighing with contentment and feeling spiritually involved.

After reading this book Bali is definitely on my 'bucket list' to visit. A great insightful read and would definitely recommend. Thank you Mary. X

Wendy Bruce: Reiki Healer

Printed in Poland
by Amazon Fulfillment
Poland Sp. z o.o., Wrocław

63046247R00222